Praise for

The Red Skirt

"O'Donnell-Gibson is an adroit writer; her accounts of being terrified to turn her back on God and moved to rapture while singing psalms...will keep readers committed to her story..."

PUBLISHERS WEEKLY

"...her riveting narrative will not be forgotten. The pages could not turn fast enough. Her writing leaps off the pages with vivid and descriptive scenes for the readers' eyes."

SHARON BLUMBERG, BOOK REVIEWER FOR *OFF THE WATER*

"As a non-Catholic, I found the descriptions of a nun's life absolutely fascinating..."

BARBARA SIMPSON, MFA, SUNSET COAST WRITERS

"The Red Skirt *is a thoughtful and very much recommended read..."*

MIDWEST BOOK REVIEW

Awards:

Winner of the 2011 Global Ebook Award for Memoir

*Finalist in Memoir for the 2012
Next Generation Indie Book Awards*

*Winner First Place Gold Medal in eLit Memoir for the 2011
Independent Publisher Book Awards*

*First Place: Cover Design for Non-Fiction in 2012
Next Generation Indie Book Awards*

The Red Skirt

MEMOIRS OF AN EX NUN

Patricia O'Donnell-Gibson

SR

StuartRose Publishing, LLC

Watervliet, MI

The Red Skirt
MEMOIRS OF AN EX NUN

By Patricia O'Donnell-Gibson

SR

Stuart Rose Publishing, LLC

All rights reserved. No part of this book may be reproduced or transmitted in any form or by any means, electronic or mechanical, including photocopying, recording or by any information storage and retrieval system without written permission from the author, except for the inclusion of brief quotations in a review.

Copyright© 2011 by Patricia O'Donnell-Gibson
www.TheRedSkirt.com

Edition ISBNs
Softcover 978-0-9836112-0-2
e Edition 978-0-9836112-1-9
Library of Congress Control Number: 2011906878
Third Printing

PUBLISHER'S CATALOGING-IN-PUBLICATION DATA

O'Donnell-Gibson, Patricia.
The red skirt : memoirs of an ex-nun / Patricia O'Donnell-Gibson.
p. cm.
ISBN 978-0-9836112-0-2
1. O'Donnell-Gibson, Patricia. 2. Ex-nuns --United States --Biography. 3. Catholic Church--United States--Biography.
4. Women in the Catholic Church --Biography. 5. Teachers --United States --Biography. I. Title.

BX4668.3 .O46 2011
271/.9102 --dd22   2011906878

"Do Not Go Gentle Into That Good Night" By Dylan Thomas, from THE POEMS OF DYLAN THOMAS, copyright ©1952 by Dylan Thomas. Reprinted by permission of New Directions Publishing Corp.

Cover and Interior Design:
Peri Poloni-Gabriel, Knockout Design, www.knockoutbooks.com

Chapters

DEDICATION

For Jesse and Amanda—
who asked the questions.

ACKNOWLEDGMENTS

FIRST, I OWE A GREAT debt to Leslie Brancheau, my high school friend. Her letters, which she sent home while she was in the convent, were saved by her mother. These forty or more letters stimulated my memory, supplying wonderful details that I might not have remembered.

Pen Campbell, a fellow writer and teacher, was my first editor of Parts 1 and 2 of the book. Pen offered suggestions, which became the rubric for all my future writing and revising. Her expert advice may have saved me days of rewriting.

Ellen Gibson, my stepdaughter and friend, who edited the entire book with care and thoughtfulness. She caught the many "missing links" in my book and often urged me to concentrate on my feelings. I cannot thank her enough.

Char Wenham, my friend and former principal in St. Joseph, Michigan who read my edited book with such excitement and energy. Her enthusiasm gave me a much-needed boost to continue revising when I thought I couldn't face another sweep of changes.

Finally, I owe so much to my husband Lou, who listened to drafts of my book at any time of the day when I needed a responder. He was lavish in his praise as well as criticism, and

I came to trust his expert ear for the correct word and tone, and his eye for grammar and structure. He continues now to tackle the business aspects of my book and allows me to enjoy listening to him for a change.

PART 1

Growing Up Catholic

Margaret, Me, Maureen & Jimmy on the back porch of our house in Detroit.

CHAPTER 1

The Calling

"SO, WHY DID YOU ENTER the convent?" my friend asks me many years later when she finds out I had once been a nun.

I think for a while, stalling. "Oh, it's pretty easy, I guess. I thought I was called."

"Called?" She asks; a question that doesn't surprise me any more. "Who calls you? Like a priest? Wait...you mean...like, God calls you?"

"Well, yes, in my case, I did think God might be calling me, but it was a long time ago, and I was only nine."

"Wow." My friend looks hard at me, taking it in. "So, how did God tell you?"

It always gets complicated like this—so difficult for most people to understand. I try. "It wasn't really God who told me." Her eyes open wide here, and I continue. "A missionary came to my grade school, and he talked to us in the church. It was very surreal. And scary. I'll just tell you the story, ok?"

"Sure," she says. "I think this is pretty amazing. You know?"

"I think I know what you mean, but it all fit into place for

me because I was raised Catholic; seriously Catholic. And I
believed all of it."

She nods and waits for me to begin. I place myself in the pew
in church, sitting with my third grade classmates, gazing up at
the missionary standing before us, and I start to tell her.

The missionary had a whole week to impress us with his
stories and warnings about being good and all. But he saved his
most important message for that last day.

The entire week of the missionary's visit to my school, I began each day with Mass in the church and finished it back in the
church listening to his sermons. Just like my teachers in school,
he saved his biggest points, the real message he wanted me and
everyone else in the church to take out the door, for the end.

He was standing in front of the altar. I could feel it coming.
He paused between his sentences for whole minutes and stared
at us as if we were supposed to *do* something. I looked around,
wondering if he had forgotten his words, but no, he continued
on like he *wanted* to wait and watch us.

I was glad it was his last day of talking because I was beginning to feel real bad about myself. I was selfish and mean
sometimes, and I know I didn't think of Jesus enough, like he
said we should. The whole week of his talks had made me think
too much. Wasn't it time for him to bless us with Jesus's body—
the round host bigger than the one we got in Communion—by
lifting up the golden holder with sharp spikes fanning out like
sun rays?

No, it wasn't. He didn't walk back to the altar. Instead, he
came down the steps closer to where we sat in the pews, not
saying one word. He looked at us again, and moved his head like
a fan from one side to another, and then from back to front. All
the time, his eyes drilled into the center of us.

I flinched and backed into my seat, and I didn't want to hear
what he had to say at all. Did he know that sometimes when

he was talking, a few of us might have been thinking selfish thoughts of cookies after school or a trip to the local drugstore for the latest Lana Turner cutout dolls?

His eyes looked like they were squinting from the sunshine, and I felt he looked at me for the longest time before he began to talk. "Do you know that God calls all of us to do his work? You must pray every day, be kind to your neighbor, study hard in school, and follow the laws of the church. Each one of you must be Christians in your hearts."

My heart had started to pound. Why was he talking so loud all of a sudden, and why did he keep looking at us with his face all serious and maybe angry? I felt scared of this man and wished he would just let us go.

He didn't let us go. He gave us a long look. "A few of you— only a special few, sitting right here in this church—God will call for himself alone. Those who are chosen by him to be his own will devote their entire lives to his work. He will ask you to 'Come and follow me,' as he did with the first apostles."

I couldn't take my eyes off him now, and my stomach was all jumpy inside.

He lowered his voice, "At least ten of you sitting in this church will be called to be his chosen ones. Ten of you have his seal upon you; a mark that sets you as his own. Will you heed his call and do the work he has planned for you from all eternity? Or, will you deafen your ears and walk away from God's divine plan for you alone?"

We were all silent as he stood looking at us as if waiting for an answer. Then, he turned back to the altar. My head was making buzzing sounds, and I sat frozen looking ahead without seeing.

My classmates had knelt, and I scrambled to the kneeler. The missionary lifted the golden holder with the host inside it high into the air so Jesus could see all of us.

I looked around at the faces of my classmates. Did they feel as doomed as I did? How would I know I was called? And how would it happen? What if I just didn't understand God? It was horrible. I might be in big trouble if I didn't hear God calling me. What a terrible thing it would be. I looked around at the other kids. They were kneeling, slumped over the pew, their faces calm and tired but not worried.

I couldn't wait to get out of church and see what my older sisters, Maureen and Margaret, thought. Maybe we would all be called. It wouldn't be so bad then.

I had to run to catch up with them, and when I got close enough for them to hear me, I blurted, "Did you hear what he said about being called by God?" I was puffing a bit, not only from running, but also from my rising panic.

Margaret looked down at me. "Yeah. So what?"

"Well, maybe he'll call you. And how will you know?" Both of them laughed at this, and Maureen even rolled her eyes.

"He's not going to call me," Maureen said. "And why would you worry about it, Patty?"

"Because...well...I don't think I want to go. And if I don't, I'll be in lots of trouble." I hoped they wouldn't laugh at me again, but it was the truth.

"Oh, my god, Patty!" Margaret said. "He wasn't talking just to you. There were three hundred kids in that church."

My steps slowed a little taking this in. "I know. But we don't know which ten he was talking about."

At this, they looked back at me in wonderment and walked ahead to the house.

It wasn't fair. They strolled away free. The missionary's arrow hadn't even hit them. They'd have a snack, listen to the radio downstairs and dance, do their homework, and sleep untroubled. How did they fling off his darts so easily?

I, however, knew immediately that a thought like an arrow, had imbedded itself just behind my eyes. It nagged at me, making my tummy flutter and sink and turn somersaults. I felt like a mark had been set upon me—slashed upon me would be more like it. I knew I had to be quiet; not tell anyone else. Maybe it would go away then. Maybe, if I was good and worked hard to forget, it would go away. Maybe.

From this day, I wondered if I were called, and hoped with all my heart that I was not. But there is more to my story than just this one incident.

My vocation began the day I was born to Peter and Pauline O'Donnell in Detroit, Michigan. My life and that of my parents and sisters and brother revolved around a close circle of home and school and church. This was our world.

From the time I was four years old and understood as well as used words, I went to Holy Redeemer Church with my parents. I had to be quiet, listen to the priest, and try to say my prayers. When I was old enough, I went to kindergarten class at Holy Redeemer Catholic School where every teacher was a nun.

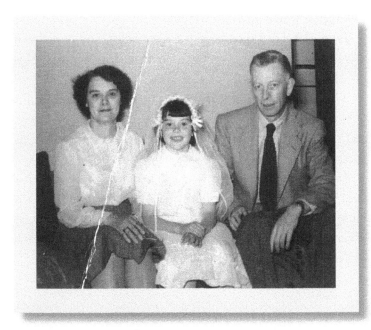

*Posing with my parents in my communion
outfit on the big day.*

CHAPTER 2

Immersion

M Y SISTERS AND I WERE in the alley behind our house and a group of girls I had not seen before walked toward us. It was unusual to see new people on our street since it was an old established neighborhood.

The girls smiled and waved timidly as they passed, clinging together as newcomers do. Instinctively, I moved my hand up to wave but was stopped sharply by my oldest sister's body stepping in front of me, her arm spread out like a crossing guard on a street, as if to defend me.

Margaret did not speak at all, and I felt the sudden shock of her warning prickling my skin. I followed them with my eyes as they continued on past us, their heads slackened now, their steps a bit hurried.

I was six years old. I attended kindergarten at Holy Redeemer Catholic School a few blocks away. I had no idea why we didn't like them; why we wouldn't say "hi," and I felt frightened. Were they bad girls?

When they had progressed a safe distance beyond us, Margaret—with the authority of a nine-year-old—said, "They're Protestants, and we don't play with them."

"Why? What's a Protestant?" I said.

Her voice rose with fervor and importance as she explained, "They're not Catholics. They don't go to our church."

Maureen and I, incredulous and confused, gazed at her. Margaret seemed to search around for more examples, finally blurting out in defiance, "And they got mad at our church, the church Jesus made! They stopped being Catholics!"

Her words were full of dark meaning, but not clear to either of us. Our questions piggybacked with each other in the air, hanging desperately like fading echoes. But, Margaret was through with explaining.

When she turned to leave the alley, we scrambled after her, our encounter with the girls having raised the jitters in each of us.

Within that year, Maureen and I would come to know a few particulars of this great divide. We heard from our parents that the Protestants broke away from the Catholic church, and started new religions.

I did not know why they did this, but I was made to understand that they would not go to heaven. They had turned their back on God. It didn't take long before the word "Protestant" would automatically stir in my stomach the tumblings of the kind that the word "boogey man" did, that ghostly creature my Irish father kidded me about.

The word "Protestant" haunted me like a nightmare. A Protestant was someone on the other side and not like me at all; a foreigner, maybe not as frightening as the "boogey man," but every bit as different and therefore unknown and potentially dangerous.

It was 1951 when I had that encounter with the Protestant girls. In just one year my family would leave our tree-lined Detroit street, with its older frame or brick homes sprawling back from porches with swings; homes with ample yards and wooden fences laden with rose bushes that bloomed all summer and windows without screens opened to the air.

Our street, called "Infantry," had a milk man who delivered our milk in glass bottles secured in a wire cage caddy, and had an ice man, whose large, jaw-shaped pick grabbed huge blocks of ice for our "ice boxes," and who always had time to pick off a few chunks for the trail of kids who waited by his truck on hot steamy days.

Infantry Street was a short walk away from Holy Redeemer School and Church. On the way, we could go to the potato chip factory, where we bought a small brown bag of hot, just-fried chips for five cents.

I was six years old and my street was a cradle that rocked my senses. I saw apple pies bubbling on the windowsill at Mrs. Wellman's, where I smelled the mix of sweet and tart Mcintoshes and the toasty whiff of browned crust.

I hid behind trees in the field next to our house while playing tag or Cowboys and Indians with the neighbors.

I sat on the grass in our backyard while my mother struggled to comb out the snarls of my long, reddish-brown ringlets. While sitting between her legs, I would try to get my mind off the pain of her constant yanking and pulling by focusing my eyes on my favorite bushes, the ones full of tiny pink roses that clung to the fence. I sat as still as I could and waited until a breeze would bring their lovely scent to my freckled nose.

By the early 50's, our little section of Detroit, which I remember so fondly, had begun to change. A group of boys on an adjacent street grabbed and held Maureen, only seven years old at the time, and terrorized her.

I saw my normally calm and steady father choke with anger. I had never seen him so palpably steaming, so ready for blood. He was a quiet man who valued good manners and taught us to respect everyone.

My mom and dad whispered about it, and we were warned

never to walk beyond our street, never to go anywhere alone. Eventually, my parents looked to an area of brand new homes west of Detroit. My father's fear for our safety had driven him from his childhood home and into the suburbs, a fairly new phenomenon back then.

My parents found much to like in Dearborn Heights, brand-new, white and unspoiled concrete streets and sidewalks, a baseball field kitty-corner from our house, a Catholic grade school and church a block away. They felt they had moved up in the world and didn't mind the lack of anything resembling a mature tree, the cookie-cutter pattern of most of the bungalows, and the eventual surge of construction on our block.

We were one of the first families to move in. We watched as other homes popped up near us; the mud, the dust, and the racket, a blemish on the shiny newness.

Naturally, my parents appeared at the school office at Our Lady of Grace Elementary School the day after we moved our belongings to Riverview Avenue. All four of us would be registered; Margaret in fifth grade, Maureen in third, me in second, and Jimmy in kindergarten. Imagine: we could see the school from our porch and each of us could walk home for lunch.

When my parents returned from the office, we noticed at once the dark cast of my father's face, so different from his smile and brisk walk to the school an hour earlier. Sister Columbine, the principal, had informed my father that the second grade was full right then. Three of his children would be able to attend, but one would have to wait. In the mean time, Sister Columbine would do whatever she could to get me, the remaining child, a place.

I cried and carried on until the entire household got sick of my antics. "I want to go to school with Maureen," I sobbed, and because my sister felt badly for me (what if she was the one without a place at the school), she sat next to me and tried to tell me it would be all right.

"Sister Columbine says it will only be for a short time, maybe a week." It was my mother who tried to soften the sentence I was given, and in the way that children always seem able to sniff out, I sensed that she wasn't fond of sending me like an orphan or an only child to the public school.

Would she help me out as she usually did? Yet she had said it might be a week before I could go with my sisters and brother. A *week*? I was waiflike in despair, imagining myself sitting in a desk at a public school so far from my home.

"Then I can stay ho-o-o-o-me until they get a spot for me."

"Patty, we can't keep you home from school. You can stand a few days there. It'll be over before you know it." My mother's sympathy seemed to be growing, but when I looked at my father, his face was turned from me.

"I don't want to go there with the Protestants. They're not our friends."

I had worked myself up into such a state that I didn't sleep well at night. My stomach was gripped in a solid ball of nerves, and I couldn't eat. Going to and from school without my older sisters, on a bus, which I had never experienced before, sitting alone at lunch, and walking the halls without my protectors somewhere nearby dropped me into a white abyss of anxiety.

Finally, my father had had enough. He raised his voice and looked at me; his blue eyes the color of steel, and pronounced, "I'll drive you there. You'll go to school. End of discussion."

I have saved, all these years, that picture of me standing near the school wall at recess, my body curled into the bricks. I kept to myself; ate at the end of a table at lunch and rarely raised my hand in class. I was serving a sentence and only waited for the day I could join my sisters and brother at the Catholic school.

A few kids tried to talk with me, but what could they do when my frightened mumbles were barely recognizable? How pitiful I must have looked; even worse, how amazing that I was actually scared of them.

Yet, being separated from my siblings was the real cause of my fear. Without them, especially Maureen who shared a room with me and stepped in when kids became mean, I was a little boat adrift on the huge sea.

In less than a week, however, I was relieved of my sentence and joined my family as Sister Columbine had predicted, gliding through the "safer" halls of Our Lady of Grace.

Like my sisters and brother, I ran home for lunch and played on the swings and slides next to the school at recess. I was no longer on the outside looking in when they talked excitedly at dinner about their teachers and classmates. I walked to the brick elementary school with them in the morning and, during the day I would see them in the halls. After a few weeks, I was placed in the top reading group, and my confidence, which was sorely in need of a boost, soared.

The most memorable part of that second year of school for me at Our Lady of Grace was not just being placed in the top reading group or getting good grades on my report card. Sitting in a row of desks, my hands folded properly, I heard over and over that my most important job in second grade was to prepare to receive Jesus in Holy Communion.

Even though the actual event would not occur until the end of the school year, I knew that I was in for a lot of attention because, to my dad, my First Communion would indicate that I had risen to a new level. He would no longer consider me to be a child; I would become a young person who had reached the age of reason, and this was important for him.

It was also important for me because I knew that if I behaved in a reasonable way, my father would take me seriously. I wanted desperately for him to like me, to brag about me to the neighbors. I wanted him to look up from his paper and see me, maybe say "How's school going? Are you doing all

your homework?" When I was playing outside, and he and my
mom were sitting on the porch, I wanted his quiet gaze to latch
onto me, follow me while I rode my bike. Every one of us kids
wanted his approval. He was the one to please.

Yet, there was another, not altogether religious or reasonable
side to my excitement about First Communion. It had little to
do with Jesus, and little to do with becoming a rational person;
it had much more to do with the longings of a little girl. I knew
that I would finally have a dress that my mom bought just for
me to wear. No third hand-me-down with thinned cotton and
rips and faded colors. My white, ruffled, flouncy dress would
be brand new. My white shoes would be shiny, the opposite of
the Buster Browns which I, and every other girl in second grade,
wore then. And my veil, well, that would be like a bride's, with
net hanging down and flowers on the headband.

A black-and-white photo with a crease across it remains from
the litter of pictures my family took on important occasions. In
the photo I am sitting between both of my parents on our couch.
My hair frames my face in square angles and my dress is white
with ruffles just like I wanted, but it is my face that glows through
the black-and-white print. My eyes are popping with excitement,
dark and sparkly, and my smile is one only a camera could catch,
that moment of an almost giggle. As a family, we didn't often sit
down and pose for pictures, so I knew this was a big event, not
just for me but also for my entire family. In this photo, I am the
center of attention—not one of four kids but *the* kid.

First Communion was a national holiday in my family, a day
in which just about everything was about you. It was bigger
and better than a birthday because those came every year. First
Communion, as a rite of passage in the Catholic church, was
a much more serious occasion than a birthday for Catholics.
It was a big deal because there was only one more step to full
membership in the church, and that was confirmation.

My little second-grade body was joined literally to the body of Jesus in the form of a round, white, flat piece of bread called a host, and I was on the road to heaven; to a morally upright life with help from the grace of God. It was all pretty heady stuff for an eight year old, but I did believe—right down to my shiny white shoes—that Jesus—the same one who looked out from the picture of the Sacred Heart—was coming into me; into my body and also into my soul.

Whereas the sacrament of Communion and later, the sacrament of Confirmation—a commitment to the work of the church for young adults—were the highlights of the Catholic experience, the every day activities kept me vigilant and truly immersed in the blood vein of the Catholic experience.

It was in this way that I was molded and shaped, my sense of myself as a person cleaved to my religious beliefs. For sure, some young Catholics wore the robe-of-religion as if a long cape, shielding them from the evils of the world, while others let the robe fall more loosely, maybe even trailing a bit behind them, but I felt the pressure of being a good Catholic from both school and home. My robe-of-religion fit like a second skin.

Every morning my sisters and I marched our half-asleep bodies down the street, not just to school as other children did but also to church for daily Mass. I sat with my class, with my second grade teacher behind us so she could watch us.

I know that I fidgeted in my seat because I really wanted to be in school and see my friends. I couldn't see the priest, and didn't feel the devotion I did with my father beside me like on Sundays, and I just wanted to get to the wonderful everyday hum and flow of reading, math and science.

Mass every morning before school was not like Sunday Mass where my family walked the block to the church and sat next to each other taking up one-half of a pew. That was the important Mass; the Mass the church said we *had* to attend. Everyday Mass was going way beyond what the church required, and because of it, we had to get up earlier each day.

And since Mass was really the beginning of the school day, coming late or trying to file in with your class at the end of Mass brought about such a ladder of questions and comments about "laziness" or "weakness of character" that I and everyone else learned to avoid the experience of being late. When circumstances prevented me from being on time, I approached my teacher, waving a note from my mom, so as to escape a scolding.

When I finally came to the school part of my school day, I had at least a half hour of religion class five times a week. With very little homework, some kids recognized this half-hour class as an easy "A" on our report cards. I know that I did. The Bible stories were always full of drama, and our tests on the sacraments were very easy. Who couldn't memorize the Baltimore Catechism, that book of questions and answers on the church creed or beliefs, the church commandments and the church sacraments and prayer? In this book, the church theologians gathered in a simple format the whole of Catholic doctrine.

Now books have been written on just one question and answer, but we had only a surface knowledge, a very simple understanding of these theological questions and answers. We also had to memorize a myriad of prayers for which we were tested. This too was rote memory, not real understanding.

I skipped through the Baltimore Catechism and the prayers as if I were jumping rope. Yet, as it turned out, many kids couldn't seem to recite the Act of Contrition without freezing up or rearranging the prayer, and as for tackling the hundred or so questions in the Catechism, some students never passed the test.

I still remember the questions as if I were sitting there in class: "Why did God make us?" Or, the first and easiest one, "Who made us?" The answers had a perfect, rhythmic, rote form, like multiplication problems that we memorized out loud.

"What is five times five?"

"Five times five is twenty-five."

"Who is God?"

"God is the Supreme Being, infinitely perfect, who made all things and keeps them in existence."

And another question: "What must we do to gain the happiness of heaven?"

The answer in perfect grammatical symmetry begins each part with a verb: "To gain the happiness of heaven we must know, love, and serve God in this world."

Since there were usually two or three parts to most answers, the patterns of language became like drums in my ears. No wonder I feel compelled to use three adjectives when two are sometimes cleaner, or why I seem to insist on three parts for a parallel grammatical structure instead of a more balanced twosome.

All of these patterns have been sunk into my unconscious from that early memorization; from saying these catechism questions over and over until I had mastered each one. I owe part of my skill and ear for the rhythms of language to the mighty Baltimore Catechism.

When the doors of Our Lady of Grace School were opened wide to usher us out, we walked the short distance past the playground and the ball field to our Catholic home, where the focus of our living room decor was a picture of the Sacred Heart of Jesus.

He had beautiful, long, wavy hair and the saddest eyes but his chest was opened up, and his heart hung out. A vine of thorns circled his heart, pinching in the sides, so that big drops of red blood spilled down on his gown.

On another wall was a crucifix, more than a foot in length, lifelike, with Jesus's body hanging, nails piercing his feet and hands, his face bathed in blood and slung to the side.

In the dining room was a somewhat brighter sight. Mary

stood on a kind of grotto made of plaster. The wall of the grotto resembled a fan, or the kind of seashell I used to see on some gas station signs. At the bottom of the shell was a ledge upon which Mary reigned in her blue, (always blue,) cape and white gown. My mother seemed to favor this bit of religious sentiment above all her other statues and pictures, and I have to admit it was prettier than the others, but at the same time I railed against it because, literally, it brought me to my knees.

In the summer months when I was free of the bonds of homework, my father insisted that the entire family kneel down facing Mary's grotto in the dining room and recite the rosary. This occurred after dinner, in other words, during prime play time, in that glorious space in the early evening before dark crept up and shadowed our balls and bats or jump ropes and bicycles.

The rosary ritual usually went something like this: my sisters, brother and I knelt on the floor, our rosaries in hand, while my parents knelt near a chair upon which they leaned for support. We waited until my father announced who would be saying the mysteries for each of the five decades. Each decade began with one of the mysteries, an Our Father, and then ten Hail Marys. There were three different kinds of mysteries to correspond with the life of Jesus and Mary: The Joyful Mysteries, The Sorrowful Mysteries, and The Glorious Mysteries, and each group of mysteries were assigned a special day of the week by the church.

Kneeling there, I hoped to be chosen, actually relishing the opportunity to savor every word of declaring, "The first Sorrowful Mystery: The Agony in the Garden," holding the A of agony to get the full effect and dropping down on the word "garden."

If I were the announcer for that evening, which happened to be a Monday, a Joyful Mystery day, I would say, "The First Joyful Mystery: The Annunciation," before we recited one Our Father and then the Hail Mary ten times. I knew my father would be listening for clear pronunciation of each syllable and projection of my voice so I stretched out every part of *Annunciation* and cut the air with my words, like Michael the Archangel must have done.

I knew it wasn't unusual to hear my father's booming voice ring out after one of us mumbled her way through a mystery, "I didn't hear that. Repeat the mystery so we can hear you."

After the third decade, our recitation of the Hail Mary (there were fifty in all) slowed down to a quiet rumbling drone, yet my father was ever vigilant; he'd have each of us jump, our hands almost spilling our beads, when he thundered, "Do we need to go back and recite this decade again?"

I tried not to wiggle too much, and I dared not lean all the way back on my legs to rest, but I couldn't avoid hearing the youthful banter coming from the street; the shouts and cries of my friends who were free to play and run around without me. Their fun became my torture. What was I missing tonight? Would it be too late to join in the game? And why didn't *they* have to say The Rosary?

Yes, very often growing up Catholic translated to a type of "delayed gratification." The sisters at school called it sacrifice. My parents called it unselfishness. Eventually I even understood the various meanings of *prudence*, my father's word of choice when discussing my behavior.

On Christmas morning, I jumped out of bed and ran down the hall. I'd stand back from the tree to take in all the presents. I didn't want to see which packages were mine though, because I knew I would have to wait till after Christmas Mass to open anything.

When Easter came around in the spring, I didn't dare try to look for my basket full of candy until after Easter service. Then, only when my parents gave me the sign, did I begin looking. I even had to delay breakfast on Sunday morning because after I made my First Communion, I had to fast like everyone else before taking the host into my mouth.

Waiting to eat was not easy for my sisters and I, or my parents. One Sunday at Mass, Margaret fainted first. She just slumped to the kneeler like she had been shot in the back. My father picked her up, and carried her under his arm through the side door to the outside.

Meanwhile, Maureen, who had been sitting back a little on the pew with her head down (a sure sign of being almost ready to faint), fell over toward the pew and would have fallen to the floor if the people behind us had not pulled her up and laid her on the seat. My mom helped her out the door and came back where I was the only one left in our row except my brother.

By now my dad had two girls outside getting air. But then, I felt my head get all dizzy and my body get hot and prickly in waves flowing right through me. My mom told me later that I crumpled to the floor like a rag doll. Our friends who sat near us merely smiled when they noticed an O'Donnell girl slump to the floor, but all three at one Mass was rather memorable.

We grumbled about all of these rules that made us wait until our religious needs were met before the superficial things in life were allowed. Yet, I never let my complaining go too far. I was a Catholic, and this is what we did.

But that's not all. I really listened to the words at Mass on Sunday. I wouldn't think of walking up to the Communion rail without my hands together in a perfect upward arch. I wanted to be a good Catholic. My father said our faith was more important than anything, and I believed him.

CHAPTER 3

The Beginning
of Words

B Y THE END OF FIRST GRADE, I had mastered all of
the *Dick and Jane* primers, those books with endless bright
blue skies and shafts of sun coloring the trees, the grass, and the
children themselves.

Inside these books were stories of mishaps or situations that
brought smiles and laughter to the entire family: of parents who
rescued Sally's teddy bear, Tim, from the jaws of a front-end
loader; of a father who fixed broken toys; and a mother who
sewed an extraordinarily lovely blue dress for Sally. I devoured
these books—over and over—constantly on the lookout for
more sunny stories of happy families with siblings who never
fought and parents who never yelled.

Back in the '50s, I could only progress as far as my reading
group in school, so getting my hands on more reading material
was difficult. Home, however, was a different matter.

At home, while Maureen was out playing, I could sneak
away her second-grade reader and consume more adventures
with *Dick and Jane*. Those humble books were a watershed for

me because they initiated my lifelong love of books and reading.

By the time my family moved to Dearborn Heights, I could forage the library for even more material than the simple offerings of second grade. Very soon, I found that I could follow right along in the church prayer books, or Missals, as the priest read the day's Epistle and Gospel.

Maureen and I had noticed with great longing and sighs that other girls our age had their *own* Missals, small hand-sized books with black leather covers, gold-edged pages, and, believe it or not, a real red ribbon to hang down over a favorite spot and come out at the bottom. We absolutely had to have our own little prayer books to hold and fuss with during Mass.

Here's the great part: When it came to shelling out money, my father never blinked an eye as long as the dollars he gave fostered our Catholic education. Not that we didn't have to beg a little, do extra house cleaning and lawn work, but eventually Maureen and I took our victory walk up Riverview Avenue to St. Bernard's Seminary Store on Ann Arbor Trail Road.

How I remember that journey; our feet jumping and skipping all the way up the four blocks of Riverview, anticipation shining like halos from our heads. Our mother had made us promise to look both ways, hold hands, and cross Ann Arbor Trail safely. We did exactly that; faces serious with this grown-up responsibility.

Before us, the Seminary loomed in the distance like a mansion, barely visible through the old, weathered trees and expanse of lawn. The central structure of the main building rose into the sky at least thirty feet above the lower sections, which spread out from the towering edifice, each wing resembling a school of classrooms with rows of windows symmetrically positioned on all three floors. The inner section of the central structure was carved out like an old-fashioned round oak door in which three large bells, one on top of the other, hung in the open air.

We knew the sound of those bells because every evening at six they chimed the *Angelus*, and their ringing floated on the wind all the way down Riverview Avenue to where we lived.

On the lengthy path toward the front door, our feet settled down and we approached our destination somewhat like Dorothy on the brick road to Oz; hesitant, our eyes and mouths opened in awe. I wonder now if we were still holding hands as we pulled on the large door in the middle of the right wing to enter.

The religious goods store was just off the main hallway. Here we encountered Jesus, his mother, the apostles, the saints, and every type of statue, cross, rosary, picture for framing, holy card, medal, and Missal imaginable. It was overwhelming, but luckily Maureen and I had a focus: Missals. We wanted the small ones with thin, crinkly pages, shiny gold edges, black leather covers with a gold cross etched on the front, and, most of all, that red ribbon streaming down through the middle.

After fondling each one of the smaller Missals, we had some figuring to do. We set aside the very nicest ones with colored pictures and extra ribbons, not without a touch of disappointment. Our plastic change purses had only a few dollars, and rubbing the money together in our pockets would not increase the amount. The Missal we wanted had to match our money, and eventually we counted out each dollar and dime and quarter into the kindly hands of the Brother in the store.

Arriving home, Maureen and I rushed to the bedroom we shared at the end of the hall and checked out our Missals. We found the Epistle and Gospel for next Sunday's Mass and slipped that red ribbon down between the books of Saint Paul and Saint Mark. Our hands carefully turned the sliver-sized pages, which crackled just like we wanted them to do. And, finally, we smelled the whole of our Missals—that part-wood, part-cottony, part-laundry-drying-in-the-sun-smell that might have been better than apple pie baking in the oven. We even remembered to put our names in the front.

Eventually, Maureen tired of Missal fussing and, hearing the sounds of play from our street, laid her brand new Missal aside.

I couldn't believe she was finished looking through it and fondling it. For me, my brand new "all my own" Missal was like a new book of cut-outs that might give me endless hours of choosing new dresses for the women and pretending they were moms or secretaries or teachers. I had so much to discover in my Missal, and my fascination carried me to unusual lengths. For me, it was an entire new book to read, and I began with that next Sunday's Epistle and Gospel.

Already I loved the sound of words, of words put together in a musical, lilting way, and every Sunday I heard aloud the beauty of Isaiah, of Ecclesiastics, of David. The Bible was my first introduction to the language of poetry, and how my fidgety body would stop, my heart holding its breath, when the readings began in church.

Before long it was not enough to just read these lovely words silently; I had to own them with my own voice, hear them rise on the air in front of me with all the fervor my nine-year-old lungs could muster. My very own Missal gave me that possibility.

For weeks I'd slip away to my bedroom when everyone was out playing and read aloud the Liturgy. I tried to read like our Irish priest at church, emphasizing each lovely phrase, letting the words flow like a river through my mouth, like swelling waves. I especially liked Isaiah and his offerings, like in chapter 60:1–5:

"Arise, shine, Jerusalem, for your light has come; and over you the glory of the Lord has dawned. Though darkness covers the earth and dark night the nations, on you the Lord shines and over you his glory will appear; nations will journey towards your light and kings to your radiance."

His words of hope and love were embedded into my

consciousness and became part of the palette upon which my emotions would feed. Soon I found other favorites like Ecclesiastics 24:13–15:

> *"There I grew like a cedar of Lebanon, like a cypress on the slopes of Hermon, like a date-palm at En-gedi, like roses at Jericho. I grew like a fair olive tree in the vale, or like a plane tree planted beside the water."*

I was this crazy "voice crying out of the wilderness" and quite soon I attracted unwanted attention. One of my sisters or my brother would open the door without warning, stand there with the most disgusting stare and demand to know what I was doing.

"I'm reading my Missal. Why did you barge in on me? Leave me alone."

And I would hear back, "This is so weird. I can hear you all the way in the living room. Why would you sit here reading your Missal?"

Of course, I'd feel like a total idiot. I was caught reading aloud so often; it became a major test because I loved hearing the words, and I couldn't help myself. I know that most kids see that they are different from other kids they know, but at this time in my life, I became aware of differences in me that went beyond superficial. Retreating to my room to read my Missal was one of them.

"What were you doing, Patty? We needed another person for Red Rover." I'd hear this when I finally walked out in the sunshine.

"Nothing."

Snickers. "Yeah. You were reading your Missal. Did you say Mass?"

"Leave me alone. You're just jealous 'cause you don't have a Missal."

Real laughter. It followed me all the way back into the house.

I wouldn't cry, but when the bookmobile came to our neighbor-hood in the summer, I'd be sure to have a bag full of books to read whenever I needed to get away.

I loved most the series about the Moffat family. I'd pretend I lived in their neighborhood with all the crazy kids who made me laugh and who were never mean, not even to the weird kid who tagged along wherever they went.

CHAPTER 4

Children of God

WHEN I WAS IN FOURTH GRADE another missionary came to my school from Africa, and he brought the
pagan babies with him. Not literally, of course, but after I heard
the sad, pitiful stories of the babies from the priest who had
come to us from so far away, the babies and children he talked
about occupied the stage with the missionary as if in real bodies. I saw them and heard them and longed with all of my being
to save them.

But then, the missionary said that without baptism, in which
each person becomes a child of God, each of these tiny babies or
bone-thin youngsters would not be able to go to heaven.

His words shocked everyone into making audible gasps. Still
the missionary went on as if he hadn't noticed and told us that
instead of landing in the fires of hell after dying, the church fathers created a place called *Limbo* for these unfortunate young
children. He explained that limbo was not heaven, and it was
definitely not hell.

After hearing his description of Limbo, I thought of it all
the time, trying to fix it for the children so I could forget it and

know they were safe. My imagination was pretty active so very soon I had my picture of it. I saw it as a place for the babies to get bigger so that they could see and really understand God. I created a kind of holding station in the sky where these poor, un-baptized babies floated around, like plumy feathers, all beautiful and clean and well-fed, waiting for the doors of heaven to open when they were big enough. At that time, a wonderful thing would happen. A beautiful, white-garbed angel would gently clasp them against her breast and into the kingdom of heaven.

When, after much ado about how fortunate my fellow class-mates and I were—living every day in our warm homes, sleeping in our snugly beds, and eating from our bountiful tables full of food—the missionary informed us that each of us could, in our small way, help one of these children. We were a ready army of wide-eyed, willing subjects. I wanted my baby right then. I felt the sting of disappointment immediately when I was told that I could begin this work of God the next day in my religion class.

The missionary was true to his word, but instead of handing out a picture of a special child that I would be helping, as I had spent the entire evening visualizing; my teacher placed a flat-tened piece of cardboard on my desk. I was instructed to fold the cardboard carefully into a small box.

My finished product resembled the pint-sized cream cartons of today; the ones in the grocery store without the waxy outer coating. Each box had on it a picture of a child whose huge eyes looked out with a mixture of sadness and longing.

I thought my child was a girl, even though the face that looked out at me could have been either girl or boy. She had straggly, dark hair, and her cheeks bore smudges that my mother would never allow. Even though everyone in class had the same child on their boxes, we claimed our box with our child as our own. His or her life became a story we added to and embel-lished as we helped our baby.

The top of the box folded into a peak much like a house, and on one side of the peak, there was a slot into which I could plunk my coins through. The words "Pagan Baby Drive" or "Save a Pagan Baby" graced the top of my box and identified my mission.

Where would I get the money? From my piggy bank? My father's linty pockets? The answer, according to the sister who taught religion class, was through sacrifice. To save my baby, I must work for my pennies, tapping every means possible to fill my box to the top by the date the sister wrote on the board.

"Would our little box go right to our baby?" someone asked. Sister had to smile at this one, and then in a most serious manner tell us that the missionary would get the money. He would use the money to travel to places without roads or stores or homes all grouped together like ours. He would take food for the hungry children, clothes to cover their skin from the sun, and most of all, he would carry the message of Jesus, of love and salvation for all eternity.

Wow! My small box of pennies, nickels, and very few quarters would help to do all of this? After school that day, I marched home with my sisters like the little soldiers we were, our precious boxes held tightly in our hands, ready for God's work.

In the end, my parents bore most of the burden of filling the cartons, even though we actually did sweep the porch or take out the garbage or clean our side of the bedroom for the coins. I was so proud to have my box on my desk each day, and I jiggled it incessantly. Whose box was the heaviest? The most full? Even at that age, all of us knew that heaviest meant more quarters and most full could be a bunch of pennies.

My siblings and I took our duties toward the pagan babies very seriously. Whenever Maureen heard an airplane overhead, she put up her arms and scanned the sky for a pagan baby to drop down right into her open hands! Since the missionary had said that pagan babies were heaven's gift to us, and since heaven is somewhere in the sky, the babies must be dropped from airplanes, she thought. This was a logical solution for Maureen, and a way to transform her pagan baby whom she dreamed about into someone real and alive.

One day during the missionary's visit, and without any warning, Maureen declared to me that she had decided to become a missionary. She wanted to go to Africa, too. We were outside skipping rope on our concrete driveway. My arms dropped like rocks when she slipped this news into our happy rhythmic jumping. What did she say? A missionary? Africa? I couldn't believe her, yet she sounded calm and definite, with a far-off look in her eyes.

"But...but...that's a long way away...far from Mom and Dad. You won't even know anyone." I was so stung by her matter-of-fact announcement. Didn't she realize she was leaving *me* as well?

She brushed off my protest with that older sister smile at my naiveté. "Of course I won't know anyone, Patty; it's a different country. And Mom and Dad know we aren't going to stay with them forever." She hadn't even stopped skipping rope at this point, as if this was just our usual everyday conversation.

"Well, you'll probably change your mind when you grow up. Besides, you said you wanted to be a secretary," I challenged, but my voice was rising like the child I really was and who couldn't believe she would consider deserting me and separating our family.

"I'm not going to change my mind. I want to help those children. Anyone can be a secretary." She looked straight at me now, her rope hanging from her long, thin arms.

"I don't want to be away from Mom and Dad," I said. "Who would help us if we got in trouble? Please don't go there, Maureen...I don't want to go! Can't we stay here and help the children?" I felt literally pulled in two. What would it be: leave my parents or allow Maureen to leave me behind?

"Patty, you don't have to go just because I am." She turned away, her jump rope trailing behind her and headed toward the house.

So I stood there in the fullness of the spring air remembering that Maureen and I had vowed to stay together all our lives. She listened to my sad tales at night before we slept, and quietly demanded that I be allowed to tag along with the other girls in spite of my whiney ways. Well, I had to go even if it was as far away as Africa. I really had to be with my sister; she was all I knew about day-to-day security, about comfort and real acceptance. She was my first real friend.

Did I realize that missionaries were usually wrapped in the robes of priests, brothers, or nuns? It never occurred to me. My romantic vision of a missionary never included religious life. It was a fuzzy dream of walking into a place where the poor children sat hungry and dirty, looking at me with their huge eyes and wanting me to be their mother so someone would love them. And, for sure, I would love them.

Tripping over my rope, I dashed into the house to tell her the news, "I'm coming with you, Maureen! I'll be a missionary, too!" I shouted at the walls.

She was downstairs, and when I saw her, I said, "Did you hear me? I'm coming with you!"

Always the steady, unruffled one, she looked up briefly and said, "OK, Patty."

"Well...all right then. I guess I'll go back and jump rope."

Would she ever know what a relief it was for me to get the Africa Situation settled? I was beginning to resent this man who came into my town and tried to take sister away from sister. Just because he wanted to go far away didn't mean any of us had to.

The missionary had a status that neither my parents nor my

teachers could match. He really knew what was happening because he lived with the poor and the orphaned children.

When my mom complained about the food I left on my plate and asked me if I knew how much a starving child in China would love to eat my scraps, it landed on deaf ears.

Not so with the missionary. When he said that we had to sacrifice more, and think about the thousands of children who had little to eat or drink or children who had no home or parents, it was real to us because we had heard his stories. He was there. He lived with them.

For that week of his visit, I thought about these children often, and I promised to give to the poor. I tried not to grumble when I couldn't have what I wanted.

Of course, my good intentions did not last. Still, my awareness of others was heightened, and our teachers in religion class constantly urged us to think of others before ourselves, which in practice was very difficult to do.

Yet, the message kept coming. We had so much more than other children. How could we complain? From our homes, our school and our church, we heard the same chant, and in this way we were molded and shaped into good children—Catholic children.

CHAPTER 5

The Decision

BY THE TIME I WAS in fifth grade, Maureen looked to Margaret more when she wanted something to do. They had similar interests, one of which was boys. Maureen was an almost teenager, and, as she saw it, I certainly was not. Because of my new lowered status, I had to venture beyond our street to play with friends I liked from school. Some of the girls lived a half-mile away from our house, but extending my world beyond Riverview was eye-opening for me. I entered homes that were completely chaotic compared to mine, with upwards of nine children running wild, screaming and fighting as though their life depended on it. Once when I stayed for dinner at Therese's house, the kids pounced on the food so quickly and with such shoving, I retreated back into my chair and got nothing to eat. Her mom ordered a few of them to hand me the extras on their plate.

Therese was so much fun, and she had few inhibitions. I loved to go to her house because there was always something happening, some wild adventure or crazy game that one of the kids made up.

By seventh and eighth grades I had an even wider circle of friends. My mom allowed me to walk over a mile to visit their homes, and I began to feel the headiness of freedom. I fell in love for the first time to a great looking guy who did not fancy me in the same way. I've never forgotten what he said when my friends told him that I liked him. "Well, she's got a lot of freckles." Just that. As if it could sum up the whole of me.

The missionary's words had faded somewhat during these years. I went to dances, longed for another guy, then another, and the circle continued. I got in trouble at school, but found out I should never tell my mother because she always sided with the nuns. I became more secretive.

When my friends were thinking about where they would go to high school, whether the public school near us or a private school, I had already made up my mind. I began early to tell my parents that I wanted to go to Divine Child, a Catholic school near us. My dad said, "It's not a choice, Patty. You're going to Rosary like your sisters."

Rosary. An all girl school. Ugly uniforms. No guys. I became pretty rebellious. In the end, I did go there, and after a couple of months, I found a way to get along – even like it. My parents would say that I thrived there. Perhaps I did, but the rigid rules and heavy emphasis on being a good Catholic brought me back to my dilemma, and my thoughts centered more on the idea of a vocation.

One afternoon I sat in the back seat of my sister Maureen's red and white Oldsmobile Cutlass. We were heading for home at the end of our school day at Rosary High, and to my chagrin, Maureen had a car full of her silly friends packed into the front and back seats. I grabbed a window seat and hugged the door; perhaps that is why I was so vulnerable. My British literature book was in my lap and I was rereading "To A Skylark" by Shelley. I had learned not to read aloud by now, but each word was lifted off the page into my seventeen year old teenage heart—romantic to the point of nausea, as I see it now, but, nonetheless, beating the wild song of the young and free. Even today I can feel the words:

Hail to thee, blithe spirit!
Bird thou never wert.
That from heaven or near it,
Pourest thy full heart
In profuse strains of unpremeditated art.

In between verses, I'd look out the window and savor the words, looking up like a besotted child at the sun. Maureen's friends were chatting endlessly about this guy or that one, about dates for the weekend, or about other girls and the dramas played out because this one said that and then she said this and on and on. The cars on Joy Road were lined up like a funeral procession and the opposite lane never let up; but I was lost in the sun and the way the rays seemed to come down like they do in holy cards, all forked and kind of hazy. That's when it happened. A moment only, a thought like a meteor hit me without warning.

Where did it come from? I shook my head at the window, willed the thought to go away. The thought didn't even have words. No one spoke. I just knew or felt this bolt hit me. God was choosing me. Right then. Really calling me. It was crazy and scary and awful.

Maureen drove on. My book had slipped through my knees. I sat stunned and shaking. I wanted to go to sleep. Sleep for a long time. Maybe wake up to a fresh sun without omens and auspicious messages riding its fingers.

The girls chatted on. The sun kept shining. Maureen's car still moved forward past the trees and houses and stores. But I was stopped in time; frozen, as if a movie screen jammed. Did I breathe in air in the ten or so minutes it took to pull up in front of our house? I must have, but I was swaddled in a white fear that held my arms and legs in rigid stillness, my mind in a foggy blur without words or even thoughts.

I don't remember what happened when we got home. Maybe I walked to my bedroom and tried to sleep. I remember feeling very tired.

And then life rolled on with me in it, but the idea did indeed latch onto me. It was different than the missionary's words; now it was a certainty that haunted me. I wasn't just one of a few who *might* be called.

It followed me like the "Hound of Heaven" all through the rest of my junior year and into my senior year. I was older now, yet the third grader sitting in church with the missionary was still around, and both of us had questions. How do I know for sure? Why me? Shouldn't I have been sitting in church when this happened? How did I get into this mess when I didn't want it? And the worst one—what would happen if I was supposed to go and didn't?

I knew the answer to that one. I would be turning my back on God, and I would lose him because I would be saying "no" to God, "no" to my faith, and "no" to heaven.

And what if I chose something else? Would another choice ever feel right?

My dad always said he hoped one of us would enter religious life. Well, if I was called, didn't it look like God had answered his prayers? No one else seemed ready to jump into the convent or the seminary.

Finally, in the early spring of my senior year, I couldn't bear any more of the turmoil. Anything was better than what I was feeling. It all came down to what I would lose. If I walked away from this God who was calling me, what other god would I go to?

There was no other God. How could I go to church with my family again when inside I'd feel like a traitor? I could see myself staying away from them, making excuses for Easter services (reliving Jesus's death for me and my sins); it would be too difficult. I wouldn't feel right around them, and so I would lose them, too.

I would go. I would go. It was the only way out. I was a senior now, and I had to choose. I would tell my drama teacher, Sister Regina, and see what she thought. I would do it soon.

CHAPTER 6

The Rosary Girl

FOR ALL OF MY FOUR years at Rosary High School, I had tried to avoid Sister Mary Paul, my principal.

I first met her in the auditorium where the student body had been gathered to hear a lecture on proper behavior or the importance of our education or some issue concerning school policy. Freshmen like me had to take their places at the back of the auditorium, while the seniors sat near the front.

Once, a group of girls in the row behind me started whispering back and forth to each other, leaning over someone to be heard. I didn't think a thing about it until Sister Mary Paul's booming voice, which had been reminding us of the school's rules and regulations, was clipped off mid-sentence. In the silence that followed, she pounded down the main aisle, her face red and her eyes boring into the bunch of us sitting near the last row.

My amazement followed just behind my fear that she could be, just could be, coming for me. It certainly looked that way. It seemed to take her forever to make it to the back of the auditorium, but when she did, much to my relief, she passed my row. I turned my head slightly and watched as she looked at the poor miscreants with disgust and said, "Is your willy-nilly conversation important enough to interrupt me?"

The poor girls, three of them, shook their heads fiercely at her.

"I didn't hear you!" she boomed. I felt the girls next to me flinch and watched the ones in front of me jump as well.

Almost in unison the culprits seemed to bleat like sheep, "No, sister. No, no, it isn't. I am sorry."

For the remainder of Sister Mary Paul's talk, I sat frozen to my seat and looked neither to the left nor right, only ahead. Sister made her point, and I now understood a new kind of fear worse than anything my parents had ever managed, a fear of shame and silliness and stupidity. Oh, how I wanted to be out of her line of vision.

Because of this first impression of Sister Mary Paul in 1959 when I was a freshman, I went out of my way to avoid her rigid frame watching the parade of students getting to classes.

At times I took the steps up to the second floor so that I would not have to walk past her, even though my class was on the first floor. I noticed other girls look up at her and smile as they walked past and a few who actually waved at her. I didn't understand how they might have come to such an easy rapport with her. What was wrong with me?

Enjoying Rosary High took a bit of time because it was the one school I didn't want to attend. Most of my good friends from grade school were going to a coed Catholic high school, a short ride from my home.

I stopped eating those first few weeks of walking the halls of Rosary High because my parents would not enroll me at Divine Child where I knew I would have more fun. I sat at the table, but I never let a bite into my mouth when they were around. Of course I ate in secret, or I might not have made it, and I actually thought my little protest would work, that I would wear them down. I used every rational argument I could think of, drumming my mother and father with questions. Why did I have to do just what my sisters did? It wasn't fair, and besides, neither Maureen nor Margaret ever liked Rosary. How could Rosary be better than the Catholic school a few miles away from our house? Besides, my friends from Our Lady of Grace were all Catholic, and their parents thought it was good enough for them.

My father ignored my arguments and fasting, and my mother worried and pleaded with me to come to the table. Finally, I just got tired of my little tantrum and decided I'd have to put up with this all-girl high school where I knew practically no one.

As she always did before, my mother put up with my insecurities. I could always go to her during times of anxiety, and I seemed to have a few more than anyone else in our family.

In fourth grade, during one of the nights I had trouble getting to sleep, I lay in bed listening to my breath going in and out of my chest. When I stopped listening enough for my body to relax and get off to dreams, I'd jerk awake. It was unnerving, but I'd go right back to listening to my breathing, until eventually, I had the idea in my head that if I didn't keep listening to my breath, I might stop taking in air! For days I walked around fuzzyheaded and weepy; the smallest noise jerked me into involuntary shouts, and I longed for someone to knock me out. My eyes drooped, and inside, my nerves seemed like they might poke through my skin. My mom noticed. She kept me home, and fixed up the couch with sheets and a blanket so she could watch me.

When my dad found out I had stayed home from school, he fumed. "Pauline, you can't give in to this nonsense. What she really needs is to rein in her overworked imagination and quit all the drama."

But my mother, the parent I barely noticed until I was in trouble, looked at him calmly and said, "Well, it was just for one day, and she hasn't slept for two nights. Let her rest." She rarely ignored his wishes, and I waited for his reply, but there was none. I turned my face to the wall and felt the sting of his disappointment; the comfort of her hand on my head and soothing words all day were lost with his chastisement.

Before I became interested in the stage and public speaking while at Rosary, I tried other outlets for my energy. In my freshman year, I had a crazy notion in my head that I could play basketball. A few friends had joined the team and begged me to come along (a mistake.) I was not especially athletic, even though tall for a girl back then. I huffed at practices, ached all over when I came home and after a few weeks wondered how I could get out of it.

Our first game seemed a cakewalk. Later, our coach told us we weren't "hungry" enough and would we please quit "acting like we were at charm school." She was right.

My mouth dropped into an "oh no" of shock when I saw our next team hustle onto the floor. They were big, they weren't smiling one bit, and they grabbed the ball and edged each other out during warm-ups.

After five minutes on the floor, I had been shoved, jabbed, called names I had never heard but knew were very bad, and got my face wiped with a sweaty armpit. I quit the next day.

Most Catholic schools required uniforms. We wore them whether the style was downright awful or almost acceptable. Our gabardine jackets and skirts were the worst possible color—a drab, flat blue-gray. The jackets, with shoulder pads that gave us a bit of bulk, hung down to our hips. And the skirts sported halfway sewn pleats, which flared out to the hem. Not too bad really, except the hems continued past our knees.

I'd usually get caught offending the skirt rule before school started because I just couldn't ride the Detroit city bus without rolling my skirt at the waist so that it fell *above* my knees. I strolled into the main door near Sister Mary Paul's office, gabbing with my friends, until I looked up and saw her examining me. She wagged her finger toward me while my friends hurried away down the hall. One-half of my heart stopped, but I moved my legs forward.

"Patricia, I don't think your skirt will touch the floor. Kneel down so I can check it." Girls passing our little scene smiled like grown-ups do when they see a kid get in trouble; the do-gooders loved to be seen being good.

So, I got down on my knees in front of her, and sure enough, my skirt didn't even come close to the floor. I waited. She asked me to unroll it. I stood up, and as I fumbled with the tight rolls, I could feel the gabardine fabric hit my calves.

"We do not want a Rosary girl representing her school with a skirt halfway to her thighs, Patricia. A Rosary student is modest and chaste at all times. You do understand where your skirt should fall?"

"Yes, sister."

She sent me off with a few demerits, but I would break the skirt rule a few more times until I figured out that I could roll my skirt down on the walk from the bus to school and roll it right back up on the way home to the bus. It shouldn't have taken so long to master this deceit, but I had so much on my mind— like boys riding the bus, schoolwork that had to be rewritten and friends I met on the walk to school.

The skirt rule was not enough to transform most girls into a *Rosary* girl though. We needed another big one; big enough to make our life perfectly miserable, and have the public school kids look at us in wonder as if to ask, are these girls really teenagers?

How could I avoid the "flat hair rule" when every teenage girl in the United States wanted to look like Justine from American Bandstand and the other girls whose hair fanned at least five inches from their faces? I had lots of hair, and I back-combed, or "ratted" it as we used to say, until it stood out from my head in a perfect flip.

Now, because Rosary had this rule forbidding me to back-comb my hair, was I supposed to let it hang limp around my face? I couldn't. And I didn't. The punishment was awful too. Sister Mary Paul made me go into the girls' bathroom and not only comb out the tangles, but wet it down like a helmet! She was ever vigilant, and even my sister Maureen was sent to the washroom to calm down her mane. I, however, fanned the flames of my stubbornness until Sister Mary Paul threatened to call my parents, and I learned to relax my mass of hair enough to pass her inspection.

How the other sisters at school stayed true to this rule since so many girls violated it was interesting. I thought we might break them down. So I figured that Sister Mary Paul was watching the nuns as well as the students.

Fortunately, I grew up a bit in my junior and senior years, and I found out what I loved, and that was anything that involved dramatic speaking or acting.

When I was asked to come to the office to pick up some medal or trophy that I had won in a speaking or dramatic reading competition, Sister Mary Paul would hand the award to me.

After one particularly successful competition, she handed me my medals, and then, facing me squarely, said, "You know, your ability to speak well does not come from you. It comes from God. Be sure you keep that in mind."

I wondered if she had seen pride in my behavior or a pretended humility. Perhaps I was looking for attention when I worked so hard to move my audiences, see their eyes fill with tears or know they hung on my every word. I really didn't know, nor did I know how to change the passion in me for speaking.

Yet all of these activities - acting in plays, taking part in speech contests, a few short seasons in basketball and baseball, my English classes – none of these could stop the little arrow of a thought that might cross my brain when I least expected it. The words "maybe I am called" would flash without warning, and I was hit again and again with this little reminder of the missionary's frightening words.

I couldn't pretend anymore that I had all the time in the world to figure out what I wanted to do. I was a senior now. Time was running out. My friends were talking about different colleges. What was I going to do after graduation? Stay at home with my parents?

It wasn't difficult for me to seek out Sister Regina. I had put it off for a month or two after the day in Maureen's car, and I lived in a state of nervous panic. I ate little, slept little and finally, I knew I had to go to her. She was more than a teacher to me, and she would listen, help me if she could. Sister Regina knew me better than any teacher at Rosary because we spent hours together practicing my speeches or readings, as well as plays that we produced at Rosary High. She watched over me too, because at times I could behave in a witless manner, and she quietly tried to run interference for me. She listened to all my tales of woe, and was a cheerleader during my frequent lapses in confidence.

When I sat across from her large oak desk and gave her the news that I was thinking of entering the convent, her face lit up, and she rushed over to hug me. I knew that she may have seen my vocation as a way to continue her wonderful work in drama, but I also knew that she loved me and felt I was doing the right thing. She told me I had much to give and was happy I had decided to enter the Adrian Dominicans, the Order of the sisters who taught at Rosary. I told her I was scared, that I wasn't sure, that I wondered if I would ever feel "sure."

"Not all of us who entered did feel sure at first. Yet after we came to Adrian, we had the time to test our vocation and see if it was right for us." She smiled. "We couldn't know for sure until we were here."

"Well, maybe that's what I'll have to do." I said. "Try it. I think it's what I want. I could leave if I changed my mind?"

"Of course you can. Take a few weeks. Think hard about it and let me know. I'll support you no matter what your choice."

I left her room, relief flooding me. My decision didn't have to be as closed as I thought. Everyone had doubts about choices. I could too. It was all right. It was amazing how much better I felt.

I did what Sister said. I imagined myself as a sister. Some parts of it felt fine, yet others like living away from my family forever, made me very sad and anxious. I tried to remember that I would be growing as a person, just like anyone who leaves home does. I might get used to it. And if I didn't, if other things bothered me too much, well, then, I could leave, knowing I gave convent life a real chance

When I walked into her room a week later, Sister Regina could tell from my face that I had made a decision. But she had a surprise for me. I needed to speak with Sister Mary Paul as soon as possible.

What? Why was this, I asked? She explained that since Sister Mary Paul was my high school principal, she was the one who would accept (or reject, I suppose) my application and send it on to the Motherhouse in Adrian. I had to talk with her and give her my news.

I found Sister Mary Paul in the hall right by the office one day after school. She was alone and didn't seem to be agitated or scowling. I walked over to her and without a preamble or any type of introduction, I declared my intention. "Sister," I said. "I've thought about this all year and I want to become an Adrian Dominican."

She looked at me as if fully bewildered. "Well..." she said, as if at a loss for words. Then, after what seemed like an entire minute, she mused aloud, "I always thought your sister Margaret would be the one to enter our Order."

Margaret? My sister? She wanted her to enter? Now what do I do? I had to say something while she stood there lost in thought, staring straight ahead with no thought of me right next to her.

I offered a pretty weak, "Oh... well, I wanted you to know." I wasn't sure if she even heard me, but I knew one thing. I didn't want to stand one more second in front of her face. The blood rushed up my neck, and all I wanted right then was to twirl on my heels and leave her with a "So, thanks, I'll see you later."

Instead, because that would have looked childish and would have broken my father's warnings against imprudent behavior, I waited right there while she came out of her reverie. She recovered enough to give me a short talk about the seriousness of a vocation. It was not something to be decided lightly. I should pray to God to help me get in a proper frame of mind to serve Him. She fixed her blue eyes, icy and distant, upon me as she spoke. I could have been the custodian receiving a lecture about dusting her office more thoroughly.

Even though I was shocked and hurt by her dismissal, I rather understood why she might have wanted a girl like my sister to enter the Adrian Dominican Order. Margaret walked the halls of Rosary High quietly, attracting little attention and fuss, whereas I seemed to be drawn to the energy in the school, whether positive or negative. She kept under the radar, engaging in just a few activities, and in class she let other girls raise their hands to answer. Her teachers probably thought her shy and perhaps she was then.

I plastered every emotion on my face— happy, sad, and disgusted; I was never much good at hiding what I felt. In many ways this helped me, especially in drama and speaking, but at other times, my expressive face and body singled me out in a crowd, when I might have wanted to be unnoticed.

My decision, which I told Sister Mary Paul I had thought about for a long time, was really an idea that nagged at me, popping up without warning somewhere behind my eyes. The idea was always the same: the missionary's woeful words "God has put His mark on a few of you to be His own." I used to wonder, am I supposed to be listening to this voice that penetrates into my consciousness and never stops following me? The words came even though my life was full of all the important details a young girl mulls over, day after day.

I had kept busy and was rarely home in the evening. I acted in plays, which brought me to Father Schurman at Salesian High School. He would become a mentor and a friend. Salesian also brought me into a circle of young men, a situation I never, ever, encountered at our all-girl school. I read constantly, devouring Thomas Hardy, the Bronte sisters, Dickens, Jane Austen, and many more. I lived on an emotional high through the pages of British poets, novelists, and playwrights.

So, what was I to think when a message from a long time ago, a message about being called by God to serve him, did not go away? How could this message, so determined to rear up at any time not be from God? Why did it come for nine years? When I told Sister Regina and then Sister Mary Paul I had decided to enter, I was accepting that it might be God bringing the message back to me over and over. My "choice" was a half-choice. It was not a choice of what might be the best one for me, but what might not be the worst one for me. In other words, a dilemma. Such "choices" only seem to lengthen the quandary. Perhaps that was all I could do at the time.

Linda and I with a beer at my "going into the convent" party.

CHAPTER 7

Conversation: Convent Material

"MOM, I'VE GOT TO TALK with you." We're in her bedroom. She's just finished smoothing the spread down with quick swipes of her hands.

"Mmmm...?" Her eye notices a spot near the corner where the comforter must be pulled to drape evenly.

"Mom," my voice rises, "I don't think I want to go. It's not me. I'm just not like them. They're so judgmental."

I pace in the small space between the bed and the wall and turn from her. When I come back around and meet her eyes, I see her head and body raised in concern.

For once she comprehends immediately. She sits on the bed and looks at me, her eyes surprisingly decisive. "Well, then, I'll call them now. You don't have to go. It's not too late." She looks hard at me, brown eyes clear and untroubled.

I didn't expect this and drop myself to the bed next to her. She shifts her body toward the door, and I extend my arm out in front of her waist. "Wait. Not yet."

Her simple gaze and determined head, raised for some kind of battle, worry me. "We've got to think about this. I mean, how can I not go...all those...undershirts we've bought, and the black tie-up shoes...the towels, that huge, expensive trunk for my stuff you and dad paid for. Mom, they're expecting me in three weeks."

"They can just not expect you. You can still change your mind."

I wonder where her bold sureness comes from.

"I'm upset, that's all," I say softly. And, now, in some strange reversal of my own feelings, I must convince her that I overreacted because she has this idea so locked in her new picture of things.

"Remember when Sister Mary Paul wanted to see me at the high school this summer?" A nod. "Well, Anita's parents called the school about the party we had at their house after graduation. They told everything. How we drank champagne, threw up, spent the night. As if it was our idea, as if Anita's arm was twisted, I suppose. As if she didn't get the stuff herself. So Sister questioned my vocation. She asked if I thought I was 'convent material,' if I was ready to 'humble myself and leave the world behind.' I couldn't believe it, Mom. How could one night of fun make me unworthy?"

"Rosary girls always represent their school with honor," sister said to me. And not a word about how perfect Anita planned the whole thing, knowing her parents would be gone."

All the while, my mother's face is wide-eyed, unbelieving, and finally set in squinty anger. "She has her nerve!" my mom says. "You're not a Rosary High student anymore! She has no right to interfere in your life."

My mom stands and I fear for a brief moment that she's going for the phone. "Mom! Mom! Listen, it's OK. I'll go. What do I have to lose?"

A quick turn of her body and a flat look freezes me.

Nonetheless, I proceed weakly, "I mean, I can go and see what it's like. I can leave if I hate it. They told us that. Mom, really, if I don't try, I'll always wonder. I couldn't stand that."

I can see my mom relenting as she studies my face and sits again beside me. I want to hold this rare moment of collusion, with both of us on the same team, but then her eyes cloud over. She looks down at her hands and back up at me. "All right, if you're sure that's what you want to do."

I smile, shaking my head with a conviction I do not feel. She breathes out a small sigh as she stands, laying a hand on my shoulder, and walks to the door slowly, even heavily. My mind wanders somewhere in these moments, so it surprises me when she turns at the door, her brown eyes earnest and direct, and says, "You'll let me know if you need to talk again?"

I look up at her and nod, "Yes...yes, I will. Thanks, mom. Don't worry."

Then, a final word before she leaves the room, "It's not a sin to change your mind, you know."

PART 2

Postulant

Linda and I transformed into our postulant outfits.

CHAPTER 8

Handing Me Over

HOW CAN A DAY START too early? Days just do what they do—begin with the sunrise and end with its setting. Yet for me on that August morning, the bright light flooded the walls and floors of my bedroom hours before it should have. I had slept very little, in fits and starts, lingering most of that long night on the edge of awake and asleep. It was a fuzzy place where dreams become bizarre movies with dialogue that never ends.

I tried to face my family with some semblance of joy or eagerness, but the tingling fear creeping up from my toes left me muttering. It was easiest to keep my eyes averted and try to look serious, as if I were pondering the commitment I was about to make later that day.

I couldn't even pretend to look pleasant or serene. The long, hot summer had only nurtured the bubble of doubt inside me to a bulbous hot air balloon, pushing for release. How could I tell my family now, the day of reckoning, that the fear of *not* going was much greater than this gnawing clutch I felt whenever I pictured myself changing into the postulant outfit and leaving them?

I was to be given that morning to the sisters of St. Dominic of Adrian, Michigan. As fate would have it, no one in my family wanted to grab me by the shoulders and beg me to reconsider before we assembled in the Ford.

And why would they? I had presented to them a girl trying to pack an entire year of fun into one summer, which left little time for them to talk with me. I even had a going away party a week before the big day. My high school friend, Linda, who was also entering the convent, posed with me in some of the pictures, the two of us pretending to slug down a last beer.

I did not look at my family at our breakfast of bacon and eggs. I ate very little and wished mostly that my stomach would stop clenching and releasing its fist of muscle.

My sisters, Maureen and Margaret, smiled encouragingly whenever our gaze found each other, all of us uncomfortable as our silverware clinked and scraped our plates. But they couldn't ask the obvious: Are you sure you want to do this?

Why would they want to stop me when we were already beginning the journey? It was simply too late for questions. My intense summer of fun had ruled out any chance of real dialogue.

Years later, I questioned my sisters about my decision to become a nun. How did they really feel when I insisted that I had a vocation?

Margaret, almost three years older than I, thought it such a waste of a perfectly good person. She had never really embraced our all-girl Catholic education at Rosary High School, and had developed a serious mistrust of nuns from her long history with them. In high school, she thought that the "smart" girls, the debaters and honor students, got the attention. Girls like her, who did not swallow the Rosary girl image completely, were overlooked. She was totally befuddled by my desire to give up men, marriage, children, and our family for the pleasure of spending my life with dried-up, prudish women.

Maureen, who was a year older almost to the day, and who

shared a room with me for most of our growing up, saw different problems. She couldn't understand how I could give up make-up and beautiful hair, clothes, parties, and guys.

In contrast to my sisters, my brother Jim, the youngest sibling who was sixteen when I entered the convent, told me he did not remember much of that August afternoon. In pictures of that day at the Motherhouse, he looks glazed-over and merely present, not participating. I wouldn't have blamed him if he spent the time dreaming of his next basketball game or his current girlfriend to transcend the flutter of women in habits and those in summer dresses who clucked about like hens at every opportunity.

Yet, on that day in August, even though both of my sisters had internally questioned my choice, they would never have taken me aside and said, "You can still get out of this, Patty."

Only my dad spoke during the two-hour drive to the Motherhouse in Adrian. In Saline he mentioned that the German restaurant would be a good place to stop and get a bite when they came to see me.

Of course, this put me in a more intense state of panic because "me" would not be with "them." I would not see the inside of the restaurant, would not walk with my family to the table or enjoy a rare dining-out experience with them. Luckily, my mind was too fuzzy to think in enormous bites. It was a hot August day with air so thick it seemed too heavy to breathe. The six of us were stuffed like limp dolls in the Fairlane.

I had been to the Motherhouse, the home base for the Adrian Dominicans, once that summer with a group of girls from Rosary High who were entering with me. It was an orientation of some sort, a tour of the campus at Siena Heights, but especially, the buildings where the sisters lived, one of which would be our new home come August.

A young professed sister, who must have been warned and prepared for us, took us on the tour (she wore the black veil and had made her vows).

We had driven from Detroit as any other eighteen-year-old girls might have—laughing, smoking, talking about our boyfriends or the latest party and who broke up with whom, and so on.

When our guide took us into the recreation room and explained that this was where we would have an hour or more of fun time to be with the other postulants every night, we looked around at the array of clunky wooden furniture and end tables. Behind her back, we poked each other and mouthed, "Where are the ashtrays?" Finally, Linda asked the question with the rest of us giggling behind her.

Our sister guide, who seemed to have handed over her sense of humor with her civilian clothes, whipped around and pronounced in a "nunny" tone we all knew quite well, "There is no smoking in the convent."

It took a while for her words to sink in. "We can't just quit gradually? Why hadn't we been told this?"

Our sister became irritated; she informed us that we had chosen to enter religious life, not some college campus where we were free to do whatever we wanted. Her words seemed a revelation to all of us; we continued the tour quietly, each of us stunned into sober thoughts and alarmed by the "rules" we had never thought to consider or question.

Our drive back to Detroit that day of our summer visit exploded with one exclamation after another. "That was pretty scary!" and "Will we become like her?" careened off the windows and roof of the car. Our fear escalated until our voices cracked in shrill notes, "Will we ever have fun again?" and "Maybe we better find out the other big rules we will have to follow."

One of the older gals entering with us tried to calm our wild speculations with some sense, but I knew instinctively after our tour with the dour sister that my rosy perception of life in the convent didn't come close to the real thing.

The long, hot journey to Adrian on that August morning did not find any of my family bursting forth with conversation; we seemed to simmer inside instead. I would have welcomed some kind of exchange, even if only teasing—we were all experts at that—but each of us sat quietly, uncharacteristically mute.

My father parked the car, and we walked to the convent grounds where my parents and I approached a table situated right in front of the reddish-brown building. Sure enough, "Patricia O'Donnell" was printed there in black and white on the official roster. The sister placed a check next to my name.

We were informed by a cheerful nun standing next to her (as they all seemed to me that day, so endless were their smiles and rows of shining teeth) that my "guardian angel" was Sister Justin.

"She will help you with everything and take care of you just like a guardian angel," she said.

When Sister Justin appeared, she shook my hand, bouncing around me as if I were a long lost relative, and whisked me off to a room in the Motherhouse to help me put on my new clothes.

She talked the entire way to the changing room. "Wasn't I excited? Did I even sleep last night? Did I ever think this day would come?" and on and on. It got worse. She was a very active guardian angel; buttoning my black blouse, holding my black skirt, arranging my black veil.

She jumped around me like a coach, exclaiming after each addition, "Now we're getting it. Here we go. Can you wait for them to see you? Oh, look at you. Beautiful. You look perfect. Let's go out and introduce them to Sister Pat."

She never let up on the perkiness, the overly large smile, and the smothering. I let her take me outside, let her gush and cheer over my new look and did my best to lose her when we found my family and friends.

Someone in my family took several rolls of pictures. In some of the photos, my newly donned veil seems about ready to fall forward down my nose. Many sisters from Rosary High School came, but the one I was happiest to see was Sister Regina, my drama teacher.

I was also relieved to see Father Schurman, the priest who had directed me in plays at Salesian High School in Detroit. Having him sit there with my family, while chatting easily and smoking cigarettes with my dad, (who seemed positively intrigued with him,) was the most special thing that day. It was the first of Father Schurman's many visits to the Motherhouse. He would be there for each of my transitions—from postulant to novice and from novice to professed sister.

My dad stood out from everyone else in my family with his unabashed delight with my decision. Now he had a coupon straight from God. I was it. He'd brag to anyone we met, "Giving my daughter to the convent is my ticket to heaven."

It used to make me cringe, but I understood. My dad was the one who drilled the Catholic faith into us, who demanded that we go to Mass on Sunday no matter where we had gone or what we had done the night before, and who ultimately took the credit when we valued our faith.

I went beyond practicing my faith, however; the way he saw it, I had become a part of it. He embarrassed my siblings often when he bragged about us, but they must have wanted to cover their ears when he went on and on about me.

My mother took it all in, happy to see my dad beaming with pride, but I had shared my doubts only with her, and she held this secret quietly. When I found her gazing at me with concern, I wished I had kept my last minute "chills" to myself so she would not worry.

My friends, who had made the trek to the Motherhouse from Detroit, refrained from giggling at the outfit I was now model-ing with my guardian angel, all-aglow, beside me. My skinny table legs stuck out from the extra long skirt, and the very shoes I had mocked at my going-away party, clomping around with them on my feet amid gales of laughter from my friends, were now my actual shoes, spreading out like monstrous things from my ultra-thin ankles.

They smoked their cigarettes in a kind of nervous happiness for me, observing the scene on the Motherhouse lawn. I watched as they dropped their arms down to hide their cigarettes whenever a nun from our high school came over to visit and join in the festivities. I remember that they were unusually quiet, sitting among the legions of priests and sisters who walked in and out of our gathering.

And yet, they supported me from this milestone of entering the convent all the way to my day of profession. Each ceremony brought them together to sit again on the Motherhouse lawn, and even though our access to each other was all but over, they didn't lose interest in me. I was still their friend.

My family radiated their encouragement, as stoic in their support of me as I had been all summer in my armor of fear and doubt. How could they know what I felt when I couldn't begin to tell them? I smiled till my mouth was stretched and sore, but I wished they would go because I had caused them to endure this difficult charade. Yet, when I looked over at their easy, familiar faces, I dreaded the moment they would leave.

The previous night of half-sleep, with my overworked mind playing scenes of horrible confusion had been simply the prelude. This was the real thing. I had to walk this one alone now and enter the looming building they called the Motherhouse—as if it were my new home—and perhaps if I were lucky enough, I would find a mother somewhere to soothe my uneasy heart.

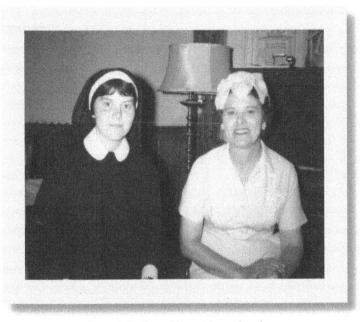

One of the first visits with my family.
I am in the recreation room with my mom.

CHAPTER 9

Walking Through
the Oak Doors

O N THE DAY I ENTERED, when our visiting time was over, a young novice, dressed all in white, stood on the steps of the Motherhouse; the same steps I had walked up to change into the clothes that would identify me as a postulant.

She swung a large bell in wide arcs with such fervor, it could have been a call to arms instead of a call to my first experience of Vespers and prayer in my new community. It was a call to leave my parents, to hug that last friend good bye, to turn and wave one more time to my sisters and brother and join that sea of black up the wide steps and through the large double oak doors of my new home.

I was not being left at a college in Lansing or Ann Arbor; I was truly handed over, like those who chose the military, to a place that would now claim me as a member. I had changed my dress as a symbol of my new purpose, and I gave up my family and my family's rights to see me for a different "family."

Many of the girls were crying, but I shored myself up for my parents. My mother was dabbing her eyes with a tissue, and my father was standing very tall as I gave them all a last look over my shoulder.

Not until I turned away did my mouth tremble. My body felt numb when I walked to the chapel of the Sacred Heart, my head down to my chest to cover my fear. I filed into the pews in back of the sisters dressed all in white; a whole group of them who looked just like my newly appointed guardian angel.

Kneeling there gave my body and my face a place to rest and hide, as if folding myself into the pew would alleviate the strange sensation of being out of my body, as if it could bring me back to myself.

Out of this daze of paralyzing fear, I raised my head in wonder when voices spilled with song into the small chapel. I watched as these women, strangers to me, stood facing each other in the pews, chanting the Psalms back and forth in voices that rode the air like butterflies.

When I dared to look around, I saw a black still life of stupefied grief. Beside me and before me stood the hunched over bodies of other postulants like me, staring blindly ahead during the chants of Vespers, only awakening slightly to mumble the rosary that followed the chanting.

On that first day we moved everywhere as one group, as if we were a large black herd of some sort, and I was blessedly unable to think about myself, to process what was going on.

After Vespers, the two sisters who had shuffled us into the chapel led us down a set of winding stairs into a dining room for dinner. We proceeded into the refectory, and I was able to sit near Linda and other friends from my high school. We were able to talk with each other this first day, but the comments from some of the girls seemed so close to hysteria that I wanted to cry. I didn't have much to say.

Bowls and platters of food appeared at either end of the long tables, and we passed them to each other like we would at home. I was a pretty fussy eater, and realized with some alarm that my mother had a rather small cache of vegetables and very little exotic fare in her daily dinners.

After what seemed like hours of moving my food around my plate, those same two sisters who had herded us before—each of whom had taken chairs at the head of one of our long tables—stood up from their seats and rapped the table with their rings.

Again, we moved our black ensemble to a very large room upstairs toward the back of the Motherhouse. I recognized at once with just a tinge of a smile that it was the very same room with clunky furniture and no ashtrays that my friends and I had seen with the snippy nun when we visited the Motherhouse.

We were instructed to find a seat on a chair or the floor, and I noticed a distinct change in tone from the softer voices the two sisters used as they directed us to the chapel and to our seats in the refectory. Either because of the more brisk exchange or because of our nervousness, most of the postulants dropped to a chair or the floor. I watched, like a runner waiting for the gun to go off, to see what the sisters would do.

The shorter sister addressed us, and I just knew she would be fine. She smiled and seemed to be thrilled to see us while she scanned the whole breadth of us sitting there. She was our postulant mistress.

The other sister, the taller one, was our assistant mistress, and from the time we assembled to go into the chapel, she had captured my attention. Her dark eyes watched us, and even though her lips faintly curved in a smile, she walked ahead of us in a stiff, rigidly upright gait.

So when the postulant mistress delivered our instructions with what I came to know as her smaller, curled-lip smile, the rules seemed more palatable for me, even though her voice still had a definitive clip to it. She told us that a sister would walk through the Motherhouse ringing the large bell I noticed earlier that day, and we would not say a word after that evening bell. We would wake at 5:10 in the morning by the same bell, and continue to keep perfect silence. Someone would lead us to chapel and our first full day as a postulant would begin.

And this was simply the introduction—the practices and rules of religious life would be expanded every week, little by little, until my shoulders tightened with their weight. It was not a life for the faint of heart or spirit. Each of us was given just one week to adjust, to cry in our beds at night, or walk with the forlorn look of the lost, because the next day and the next month, whenever we sported a gloomy or disinterested face, we were advised, "If you want a red skirt, go get a red skirt."

This challenge by our mistresses soon became the catch phrase for that "other" life (wild, silly, and superficial) from which we had turned away and became a familiar refrain in our boot camp training for religious life. The Red Skirt choice was often waved before us during those first few months when we entered.

Just as our postulant mistress told us, a bell clanged through the halls of the dormitory at 5:10 that first morning we awoke as postulants. A few girls were startled and yelled out in fear or alarm and others bolted up from their pillows, looking around at the room in wide-eyed confusion as the rest of us scurried to our clothes. Some of them never seemed to get over the fire-engine ring interrupting their sleep with such surprise. I figured that their mothers must have softly laid a hand on their shoulder, shook them, and then whispered the bad news to them for all their years of growing up. Since my mother always woke us up by hitting a wooden pole on the ceiling of the downstairs, I was used to immediate awakenings.

I entered the chapel and found a seat, but watched as my friends from high school and others came in with puffy faces and morning scowls. Most seemed to be rushing to the seats, worried looks in their eyes.

I can't remember if we tried to chant with the novices when they rose to sing Matins & Lauds on that morning, but right from that first day, I listened to every word of their chanting. Back and forth they sang Gregorian Chant, the same kind of singing I heard the day before.

It wasn't long before I learned to chant in the key of *A*, at times changing the key or pitch as I was instructed. It was more beautiful than Mass to me and at that time, more spiritual.

The second half-hour was devoted to meditation so it was easy to sit with my head down and my eyelids closed.

Mass followed our half-hour of meditation with all its parts of offering gifts to the altar, consecrating the Host, and taking Communion. By the time we stood up to leave the chapel, we had been up for almost two hours!

Fortunately, I was served breakfast before the first class of the day because by the time I heard that last "Dominus Vobiscum" and final blessing at Mass, I stumbled down the steps to the refectory, lightheaded from lack of food, my stomach grumbling in symphonic growls with the postulants near me.

Breakfast was a quiet meal, which, although a surprise, wasn't a terrible hardship since many of us were still staring at the world like sleepwalkers. It was barely seven a.m.

When we were released to go to our classrooms for daily instruction, I found that I was to have as my instructor the postulant mistress who preferred getting her point across with humor, the wry smiling one whose name was Sister Therese.

The other mistress, the taller one who was the assistant and whose name was Sister Louis Edmond, also directed a morning class of religious instruction in a different room with the other half of our hundred or so postulants. She seemed to have a more severe look, and in my growing paranoia, her dark eyes appeared to be looking directly at me when she studied us at recreation, at chapel, in the halls, or in classes.

My postulant mistress could have been a straight woman for a comic. She had impeccable timing, a Jack Benny in a habit. Even when she'd try to assume a serious face, her mouth would not turn down, and her permanent rosy cheeks beamed out at us.

One morning, she began with a little recap of our supper hour the night before. She reviewed the menu of sausage, sauerkraut, green beans; an innocuous start but we knew better. Her next remark, "I thought I was eating at the local butcher shop," got our attention. The punch line was coming. She drawled it out, "I saw several postulants chopping up their sausage all at once like they were splitting up a side of ham." She'd wait a moment or two before giving a raised eyebrow smile, which translated to "Do you know what I mean?"

Relieved that this was all we'd be scolded for that day, we'd laugh heartily, some of us covering our faces because we had chopped up all of our sausage before taking a bite instead of cutting just one piece at a time, and class would continue to more serious topics.

Yet, our knowledge of table manners as well as other types of social etiquette would be important some day. Sister Therese suggested that if we were not sure how to approach our food or which utensil to use during our meals, we might watch our mistresses to see what they did.

One of our more no-nonsense subjects had to do with keeping "profound silence"; the silence our postulant mistress had only touched upon when she instructed us to keep quiet until morning. The adjective "profound" gave me a big clue. It hit a mark somewhere between my eyebrows with its hint of the cloister and the canyons of stillness I imagined those nuns lived within. I had known the silence of an angry friend or parent, the silence of church and funerals, the silence of an audience at a theater, and the silence of a walk on the beach or in the woods.

But this silence was different—it was *profound*, as in "absolute and unqualified," not as in "deep or thought provoking." The serious treatment it received in our education reminded me of mortal sin, the kind of sin which was so grievous that one went straight to hell with no possibility of forgiveness or mercy.

Profound Silence began immediately following our evening chant of Compline and continued until the morning bell, which woke us at 5:10 in the morning. We were prohibited from uttering a word during this time. I had a habit of talking in my sleep at night and worried many nights wondering if I would break my silence without even knowing it.

While I undressed for bed, brushed my teeth, and tried to get to sleep, I was supposed to examine my conscience, searching for faults, ways I had fallen short in my adjustment to a life which asked me to leave behind worldly pursuits and self interest.

I gave up this suggestion after a few sleepless nights (the list of faults was way too long and my commitment was too shaky for such cross examination) and promised to examine my behavior during meditation if I could stay awake.

Although I literally scowled at the sound of the bell in the morning, I did enjoy the silence of meditation in the chapel. My enduring desire to greet the morning before the first signs of smoky light and enjoy the silence with a few lit candles might come from my days in the chapel at five thirty in the morning.

But back then, at eighteen years of age, I was a miserable failure at meditation. I tried in vain to think holy thoughts or re-create stories from the Bible or talk to God without asking for something. We were told that the best way we could pray was to listen to his voice so that we would know his plan for us, not our plan for him. I felt ashamed that I never heard his voice or had a rush of illuminating ideas descend upon me. It worried me. What kind of nun, I wondered, can't talk with God and have some type of two-way conversation? We were given little help with our enormous task. Most of us simply struggled to keep our heads from drooping or falling to our chests, or worse yet, jerking up with an audible grunt.

We each had a box in a second-floor room of the Motherhouse, something like a mailbox or messenger box that informed us of packages and, of course, mail from home or from our friends. Every letter was slashed open, and at times, words, even sentences, would be blackened out. It was spooky to think that someone else's eyes had foraged through my personal letters. The blackened-out words were another matter entirely. I'd call a few friends over, and we'd get in a huddle to try to figure out the crossed-out words by context, or by trying to see the handwriting lines beneath the black marker. I wanted to know *what* my mistress had crossed out, even though I knew I might never know *why*. After all, those blackened out words were written by someone in my family, and they wanted me to see and read them. When one brave postulant asked why our letters were read this way, our mistress replied simply, "This is to protect you. Your friends and family do not understand completely the life you have chosen."

Every Sunday, without fail, I had to write a weekly letter home, which I submitted for mailing, unsealed. It was a tricky business at first because several times I found my envelopes returned in my mailbox. Sentences or paragraphs would be highlighted accompanied by a comment in the margin about the suitability of such "news."

In our morning instruction class we had a session devoted to the topic of writing letters home. Why would our parents want to hear that we were lonely? Why would we tell them that we had to kneel to ask for things like Kotex or toothpaste and, when these items were granted, reply "Blessed be God and His gifts?" How could we expect them to understand the life of humility we had chosen—to honor God before ourselves? And what good did it do to complain about the meals in the refectory or the 5:10 bell? How did that further God's work? Or better yet, how did that help to comfort our parents who truly missed us and might be worried about us?

My usual wide array of topics shortened considerably. I'd sit at the library tables curling a piece of hair or tapping my pencil or staring into the void to find something to say.

Our families loved to send us packages filled with all types of goodies from home. It always felt like Christmas to get a package—that is, if you were allowed to keep the contents.

I remember once when one of my friends, Linda, was notified via her mailbox that she had a package. Linda rushed to the postulant mistresses' office to claim her package. She had to kneel down before the mistress and with head bowed, ask if she could please have the box. At this point the mistress, shaking her head in mock dismay, showed Linda the censored items: cookies, candy, and other favorite Polish recipes put together with her mother's hands. Linda could have none of the items her mother sent to her. She responded with the line we were instructed to say after asking for something from our mistresses, whether it was granted or not, "May God reward you, sister." Even today, Linda remembers with a slight laugh that forbidden box of treasures, her mother's contraband gift.

I felt forced into a secrecy about my life, withholding certain stories and feelings from my family. On visiting Sundays, I'd sit in a circle with my sisters, brother, and parents in the big recreation room. How I struggled to look happy, avoiding my mother's pointed questions, "Are you eating enough? You look thin. Have you been homesick? There're dark circles under your eyes. Are you sleeping at night? Is everything OK?" I did not dare to tell the truth. I put on a happy face and discussed safe topics: my college classes, recreation time, and various activities like singing folk songs with Gwen's guitar, or silly mishaps like taking an afternoon nap at the library and missing Vespers. It was dreadfully dull stuff and rather difficult as well, since both my family and I were playing a part in this drama.

I can see it in the pictures, which I still have: my brother's blank stare into nothing, my postulant friend and I sitting on either side of my father with dull, almost sad looks. How awful, I think now. Why aren't we looking a bit happy to have a family with us? And in another photo, we are all sitting poised and ready toward the edge of the bulky wooden furniture, as if we can't wait to get away. It's no wonder; we felt compelled to keep up a relentless stream of words for more than two hours. We worked very hard at it, all of us.

Visiting days were such a dilemma for me. I felt so much like a stranger to my family and found so little to say that sounded like me—the dreamy, absentminded kid they used to know. The silences left us floundering and tense, and I watched the clock, waiting for the escape to Vespers and peace.

It didn't help to raise my declining comfort level when I saw a sister crumple her body to the floor, lay on her tummy with legs stretched out behind her and kiss the floor in the chapel. I had no idea why she did such a thing. I thought she was perhaps a kind of strange zealot. It struck me as an ancient ritual with pagan overtones and a red flag went up in my head because this was going too far; it unsettled and frightened me. My chest froze inside and my eyes darted in panic. What had I gotten myself into? Did they just put up with this weird behavior from a few sisters, which seemed to me to be very showy and bizarre?

At the time, I didn't realize that all the sisters performed this act of submission as part of their evening ritual before going to bed. Furthermore, before walking up the steps to my dorm room, I, too, would eventually visit the chapel for my own evening prayers and lay flat on the floor in the venia. I would examine my activities that day, consider the purity of my actions, and then when leaving, kneel to the floor and, with respect, lower my body in humility to God.

Unlike chanting the Psalms four times a day and the quiet of meditation, this practice of laying myself prostrate on the ground never felt quite right to me. I was told to perform this; I was never told to love the poetic language of the Psalms and the silence of early morning. Those inclinations came naturally to me.

As a very young girl, I sat in the pew with my family and followed every word of David or Isaiah in the readings of the Mass; even saying them aloud in my head as I listened to the lilting flow, the lovely poetry, and the great longing of the sentiments.

I knew, too, that silence could be magical. I was the only one of my siblings who would pull my droopy body, heavy with sleep, out of bed at five in the morning to sit in the rowboat under the early morning spell of dawn with my father, the light barely breaking through the dark gray sky. We said not a word as we gathered the minnows, the poles, the tackle box, the cushions, and the gas can to the shore. It was always cold, the kind of misty mornings that come from up north. We fished for hours, and I never thought of talking—it was enough to watch my bobber in the water, smell and feel the air around me and just sit.

Dealing with all of the new directives concerning the proper conduct for a religious applicant had an interesting effect on our group of postulants. Some of us skipped along easily, it seemed to me, sorting out those items they accepted and those they did not. They followed the rules of conduct but never lost the ability to discriminate and judge what was asked of them, and most of all, they did not seem too bothered by the disparity inherent in this division of how they appeared outside and how they felt inside. They sat through instruction with a raised eyebrow, a hint of a smile, or a chin jutting up in vague defiance and thought.

Others seemed to buy the dogma whole and complete, like swallowing an oyster. They were easy to spot; they were the first ones to walk with their heads down and their hands under their short capes, the only ones to actually stay awake during meditation, the ones who stayed in the chapel later at night, the few who scolded us with a look, a *shush!*, or a word of warning when we broke a rule. They appeared to want this confinement and structure; in fact, they could have been waiting all of their eighteen or so years for such a life.

Finally, there were the rest of us fractured souls who lived in inner and outer turmoil. We wanted so much to accept everything we were told, to be successful at our calling, to make everything fit. Alas, we were already formed in the seriousness of our idealistic nature, our brutal and naive honesty, our youthful, unchallenged sense of truth and goodness, and we couldn't dissemble without consequences. The tension was apparent within the first half-year of postulancy. Some of my friends developed ticks or acne, others, like me, had stomach troubles and lost weight.

I remember Sharon, who transformed before my eyes from a bubbly, very funny person into a shaky, somber shadow of herself. Already thin, she lost weight until her clothes hung down from her stick frame, and her beautifully tanned skin burst into red, flaming pimples. She seemed to drag herself from one place to another. Finally, her asthma took over, and after suffering a severe attack on an outing where hay was piled up around a field, she was whisked away in an ambulance. After the incident, she was encouraged to leave, and within a week, she was gone.

I observed this frightening change in myself as well as in many other postulants. While I became melancholy and withdrawn at times, I had to watch as others manifested their pain outwardly with shrill laughs and loud, overly enthusiastic attemps to appear happy at our recreation time.

It never occurred to me that many of my friends who had not entered the convent might be suffering similarly, as they adjusted to life away from home at a college or, if not college, a new experience at a job where responsibilities heaped up around them. That realization might have helped me.

Perhaps I wasn't the only one who was expected to have a positive attitude. If I had gone to college, would I have commiserated with my roommates about how much I missed my parents? Would I have walked around with a long face hanging down to the ground? Probably not.

We have to grow up no matter where we are. Yet, and I still feel this is a substantial difference, I was enclosed in silence, in a stream of constant self-examination, of intense rules and restrictions and the steady narrowing of my world. Was I asked to shave off too much of what I knew to be me? Or what I liked about me? Now, it feels as if I was asked to change too fast; as if I had always been painted in green and now had to think of myself as yellow. Externally, I looked the part and changed my outward colors, but what about the inside? Doesn't it always lag behind? Perhaps that is why I felt out-of-step, struggling to make the two halves of me come together, like my hands in prayer, like a wren's song so in sync with every part of him.

CHAPTER 10

Black Tie-Up Shoes

EACH DAY DURING THAT FIRST month of our initiation to religious life, new responsibilities were added to our schedule. By late August we had begun our classes and all the preparation that entailed. We chanted four times a day: in the morning, at noon before lunch, in the late afternoon before supper, and after recreation before bed. In addition, operating a Motherhouse as large as ours demanded a reliable cleaning crew to keep it tidy and organized, and we postulants were that housekeeping and serving crew.

One morning during our instruction hour, Sister Therese announced that at the end of class, each of us was to check the list she had posted to see our special job. Looking a bit sideways at us, she quipped, "This work that you will be doing is called your *obedience*. It is not a task but a small part of what you have offered to do in your service to our community. You do this in obedience to God." We would begin our work the next weekend and, for a few of us, our jobs would demand attention each day.

I was in line waiting to see my special task on the sheet, and all around me I heard groans, and sighs, and mutterings like,

"I can't believe this." One of my friends wasn't so lucky, we thought, because she had our bathrooms to clean. Like a wildfire passing over fields, we heard in a matter of minutes what many of these tasks were. A few postulants' duties were rather innocuous, like cleaning the recreation room or our dorms or some sister's bedroom. Others, who did not seem so fortunate, had a kind of manual labor job in the kitchen before one of our meals. These postulants peeled potatoes, scraped mounds of carrots, or snapped the ends of hundreds of green beans. And, as if that was not enough, they had to clean the kitchen as well.

Only a select few were assigned the special jobs. Those postulants were usually older, more mature and quietly confident. One of our very-together postulants sat at a desk in our mother general's office and performed secretarial work.

"Aren't you scared to death to be working for Mother Mary Jean?" I asked. I wondered if I could get my mouth to speak or my fingers to hit the right keys had I been chosen to be her personal secretary. Of course, she loved the job and found the leader of our entire order to be very kind to her.

But for me, the job I yearned to have was the switchboard. Answering phones, plugging cords into pegs, looking so awfully official and professional, it was my secret wish to be in the center of things, talking and making all those important connections.

Our switchboard center was right in front of the back door with a counter enclosing it, and just about everyone had to walk past the postulant operators at some time during the day. When the lines were not ringing, a group of sisters or other postulants would gather around to visit. I must say, their job looked like fun until I watched these efficient women; when a deluge of calls came all at once, not one of them raised her voice or jumbled up the phone plugs.

After seeing this, I figured the mistresses knew what they were doing when they handed out the jobs. Except for my job. As far as I was concerned, it was terribly ill-suited for me.

Our Motherhouse had a white marble staircase made for the likes of southern plantation-era parties. I used to imagine that women in lush, many-layered skirts might swish their way down each step with satin slippers or delicate pumps amid the admiring gazes of the local gentlemen. It seemed to me that such a dramatic staircase needed different people walking down its steps; not sisters in black or white who were never going to shimmy down in silk dresses, as they eyed the adoring faces below them. Fanning out in stony, white splendor, a visitor opening the heavy carved oak doors that faced the stairs might stop, mid-step, hand still on the knob, at the impressive sight.

I learned to know very well the dimensions of these marble steps, all twenty or so of them, each about sixteen-feet wide. My obedience was to clean them every Saturday morning. It certainly helped that two postulants were assigned this duty. Despising it as we did, we felt grateful for the extra set of scrubbing hands. My feet dragging, I'd take myself to the closet full of cleaning pails, mops, vacuums, and Murphy's Oil Soap, an orange, gelatin substance in a round container like shoe polish.

The sisters loved Murphy's. I never figured out why. It didn't make any foamy, white suds, which was a sure sign of cleaning power. The smell of this cleaner was not filled with rose or lavender hues or laden with fresh hints of citrus. It assaulted my nostrils with sharp and deadly whiffs of marigolds or wet grass, and I'd gag as I mixed it in my pail and lugged it to the steps.

My partner and I filled our pails and armed ourselves with cloths and scrub brushes like soldiers preparing for battle. Our enemy was huge, littering the steps in vast numbers: skid marks. Black jabs on the stairs, scuffed there by the rubber soles of our all-purpose, black, tie-up nun shoes.

Standing at the bottom of the stairs with my pail sloshing in my hands and my head raised, I would assess the task before me, and feel as forlorn and abused as a nineteenth-century servant. The assignment seemed insurmountable, and the waxy black marks had as much charm as red marks on one of my compositions. They glared in the light as if daring me to wipe them off. I truly despised them.

One of us would begin the slaughter of the marks at the top of the steps, the other at the middle. We'd do only half the steps at a time; this way the sisters could still use the other side and mark it up while we worked. Many sisters found it necessary to comment as they climbed or descended past us. Some sisters lifted their skirts daintily and tiptoed past us. I usually turned my head upward to acknowledge their passing. These were the nurturing sisters who promised not to add one more mark as they went down. A few of them patted our heads and offered a "poor dears" to our kneeling bodies. Other sisters swooped past us briskly, their skirts brushing our bowed heads, as if our backs bent to the marble with our brushes swishing over a stubborn spot were nothing unusual. One of the sisters actually stopped midway to remind us that this job would build character. I dared not make a response, but kept my head close to the brush until she had walked away. My partner and I stopped our scrubbing to raise our eyebrows and offer up a sigh of complicity. Most of the sisters said nothing as they whisked past us, and that was all right with me.

The enemy we faced every Saturday was tenacious, and it took every bit of underdeveloped muscle I had to rub it out. My long and lean body was not built for this kind of work, I thought. And yet, I felt the disappointment of such weakness. Why was I trembling and feeling light-headed after only a half hour of scouring? I wanted a more substantial frame like my partner, who finished her work before me and seemed to have staying power, something my mother called "stamina." Halfway through my part of the job, I had to work my fingers out of their cramps, shake my arms into feeling again, and raise my lower back very slowly and carefully to stand. Even then, I stood stooped like an old charwoman.

Our intense involvement with the marble steps took two hours or more. I'd feel sweaty and dirty, but most of all, I wished I could take a shower to get the Murphy smell off me. The suds had seeped onto my skirt and shirtsleeves like a cheap perfume. I was grateful, however, that on Sunday I would get a clean-smelling, pressed outfit for the week ahead.

My partner and I would shuffle back to the cleaning closet and hope that our work would meet inspection. If not, we would be seen the next day back on our hands and knees. After a few weeks of intense involvement with the beautiful, wide marble stairs, one of us asked the question: Why don't the sisters wear shoes with different soles? We'd look at each other and wonder, hasn't anyone thought of this?

Eventually, but in my estimation, not quickly enough, I was assigned a new obedience. It was a delight after the stairs because all I had to do (again with a partner) was wash and buff the recreation room floor and dust the dull wooden furniture. Perhaps the best part of this job was that I could stand upright, and even though the hulking buffer machine was larger than I, my mood was cheery and friendly as groups of sisters walked through the room. I loved to stop and share a laugh or just a smile with anyone who passed by. After a few months at the job, I knew which sisters would be striding through, and awaited their arrival, even wondering sometimes if they hadn't showed up. For sure, this job was a step up from the staircase.

Yet, at night when I slipped into a pew in the chapel to say some prayers before bed, I couldn't help notice one of the novices, her white habit all aglow, skimming across the sacristy, changing the candles or placing new linen on the altar. The sacristy novices never raised their eyes to look at the sisters in the chapel, never hurried through the work of preparing God's sanctuary, and always reminded me of pictures of women saints, lovely in their pure piety. This was the obedience I longed for, the one I thought I was meant to perform. I could only hope that next year—if there were going to be a next year for me—I would be the novice moving like an angel before the kneeling sisters at the end of the day. I wanted to be the one offering a final image of saintliness to take them to their beds. My self-promoting dream of virtue, however, may have been precisely why I was never offered the work of a sacristy sister. Back then I wouldn't have seen the irony in my intentions. Today, I can only smile at my secret dramas, starring me as the perfectly put-together nun.

CHAPTER 11

Lessons for Bedtime

VERY EARLY IN OUR POSTULANT training we were
instructed in the fine art of taking our "under things" off
and donning our long, white, billowy nightgowns. For eighteen
years we had managed this procedure quite easily, so it came
as a bit of a shock that there might be some type of skill to the
process. The unmentioned implications of this simple instruction were not lost on us: we would not be showing our body to
anyone from now on.

We postulants stood by our small bed and dresser in the half-
light of night in our large, drafty dormitory. One bed followed in
line after the next, stretching down the worn planks of flooring
to the windows, wide open to the fall evening air. Once dismissed from evening prayer to bed, we commenced our Houdini
sleight of hand all together, each of us taking our position by our
Spartan space in the dorm room.

First we took off our short veils, and then our black blouses
and skirts. This left us standing in our white slips and undershirts, ready for the undergarment disappearing act. At this
point we were told to put our nightgowns over our heads,

keeping our arms under the gown. Our arms were then free under the voluminous folds of the gown to pull the slip from our waists, and shimmy it down like a puddle at our feet. Next, we slipped off our white shirts and unhooked our bras.

I always thought it such a magical moment. I'd look up and see row upon row of girls in white completing this transformation. In the beginning, almost all of us struggled to free our clothing from our bodies, our elbows and hands bulging through the cotton like cats in a gunnysack. I'd peer up from my own tangle of arms and catch another gal equally tied up, and we'd roll our eyes and heave a sigh at this nonsense. At times I'd hear frustrated grunts coming from a bed near me, turn to where the guttural outbursts were coming, and see a postulant whose wild movements and angry gestures (all underneath a gown) looked a bit like violent assault. It was equally humorous when our silent maneuvers were sliced by a voice hissing, "damn it" or "shit" in the dark around us, and then a short hum of half-restrained laughter rumbled across the room.

After a few weeks though, we were able to undress with almost seamless grace, our nightgowns barely ruffled by the activity underneath them, and when our arms, fanning out like dancers, pushed through the sleeves, we resembled a group of night moths taking flight.

I was always curious to see what was going on in the room around me, and with the beds so close, it was difficult to pretend privacy. Yet, it amazed me how a few girls never, ever looked up from their undressing. In fact, they even closed their eyes and seemed to be offering this ritual up to God, as if it needed to be a prayer. I wondered if they felt that watching someone else, and imagining the struggles underneath the gown, would be a violation of the vow of chastity. Of course, we hadn't even taken a single vow, but perhaps they had taken the "being pure and chaste in mind and body" lectures seriously. After all, wasn't our new way of undressing supposed to be chaster?

Even though Profound Silence began with our dismissal from the chapel at night, it did not forbid glances and acknowledgments. These dedicated girls, who kept their eyes down or closed to the rest of us, carried the chapel with them into the bedroom. They never even looked at another person while they dressed or undressed, lay in bed or woke up and washed for the day.

Their extreme piety appeared to be over the top. They both annoyed and intrigued me. I wondered how they could surrender so much so quickly. How could a normal young woman be so ready to turn off her senses and her feelings and jump into this spiritual bath? Weren't we still highly social beings dependent upon normal, healthy contact with our fellow humans? It distressed me and I did not trust the self-righteous display of their sanctimony. I have always been inspired by a quiet, inner-spirituality, which usually finds expression in joy and love, not asceticism. I became rather critical of some of them, which was not exactly holiness in action, but their personal "holiness" branched out to include us.

A few self-appointed "police" couldn't resist calling our behavior to task. One of them closed her eyes, put her finger to her mouth, and shushed us. It was difficult to keep a straight face when her pouty, hurt look was meant to chastise us. Another postulant cleared her throat to get our attention, and when we turned her way, she shook her head back and forth like one of our teachers in school might have done. All of this fussing was meant to help us see the error of our laughing or silliness during meditation or some other silent time.

I shared a room with my sister Maureen most of my life before entering the convent. It was the 60's, and our bungalow house was small. Yet, eventually, we became used to our cramped quarters, and even though the imaginary "do-not-cross" line in the middle of the bed kept us on our own sides, we giggled and sometimes laughed our way to sleep.

As kids, we played "footsie," a game in which we lay on the bed feet to feet, our knees in the air, the bottom of our soles trying to force each other's feet across an imaginary centerline. We could carry on this way for ten minutes or so, laughing as the power switched from one of us to the other. Invariably though, our legs would slip and jab into a thigh, which prompted either howls of true pain or screams of anger. But before this point, we would enjoy our bedtime wrestling match, which served a larger purpose—letting off the steam and frustration of being a child.

As we got older, our activities changed to quiet discussions about the betrayal of a friend, or strategies to get the guy we fancied to look our way, or the best way to convince our parents about a party or outing we "had" to attend.

It was not easy for me to give up this camaraderie. In the dorm at the Motherhouse, our beds were no more than five feet away from each other. I would lay awake at night and listen to the steady drone of sounds, some of which came from beds very close to me, and others, much louder sounds, rumbling in the air from a few rows away. I heard noises like clicking lips and snorting and whistling puffs of air that I had never heard before. For quite a while sleep escaped me, and in the beginning as I lay there alone and awake, I felt so desolate in this sea of a bedroom where my bed sat like a lost boat in the water.

CHAPTER 12

Getting in the Habit

IT TOOK PERHAPS TWO WEEKS for Janet to give into temptation. Already we had heard about the prioress's underwear, which Janet described as huge, billowy pantaloons that would reach down to her knees and bra cups big enough to cover her head. The prioress of the Adrian Dominican Motherhouse, who managed the building in which we lived when we were postulants, was a big woman—not tall big, but wide big. She had a square-shaped body, a solid muscular woman who favored a permanent scowl. Janet's obedience every Saturday was to clean the prioress's bedroom, situated on the second floor, right at the head of the stairs. While my postulant partner and I were scrubbing away on the marble steps, Janet was dusting Mother Prioress's furniture, changing her sheets, vacuuming, and eventually, rummaging through her drawers and personal effects.

Janet had no fear. She told me that she had buried a bottle of whiskey in the field behind the infirmary. I didn't believe her at first, but other friends had seen it. I never saw the bottle with my own eyes, but I knew she had the spunk to do such a thing.

She often caused a disturbance, slight but ever so noticeable by many of us, during morning meditation. I confess to watching her when I couldn't get quiet and prayerful. Sometimes she batted her eyes at me if she found me watching her. I looked down and tried not to react, but there were times when it was really difficult. Turning her face to me, eyes down so reverently, she'd flash me a look, for just a second, of a pouty, angry child. The surprise of it, of this bizarre breach into the calm of the chapel, was too much. I'd bend toward my lap to hide in the folds of my veil.

Her face seemed to be set permanently on the edge of a giggle, and her eyes actively searched for the next bit of mischief. While I marveled at her courage, her total lack of reserve, I knew that I would never have her boldness. In my naïveté, I accepted almost every rule: don't talk after lights out; stay with the group at recreation; do your obedience with great care; take some of every type of food at table, even turnips; and never wander from the main area to the wild fields beyond the Motherhouse.

I quivered at the thought of one of our postulant mistresses asking me to report to her office. I heard the details. You knelt before her, she bore into you with her eyes squinted in disapproval, and demanded to hear everything about your misconduct. She might offer, "You broke Profound Silence last evening. Please tell me about it," as if the conversation was going to be about the weather. It was the stuff of my nightmares.

Janet, of course, was called a few times to our postulant mistress. Some of us would wait near the office to give her our support because we hated to see her get into trouble. But when she emerged from our mistress's office, her head lowered to the floor, we were dumbfounded when we saw her pixie nose in a scrunch and her eyes crinkled in gleeful triumph. After we had walked some distance, she rolled her eyes and repeated the postulant mistress's warning as if it was supposed to be our laugh of the day, "'Sister Janet, you might seriously reconsider why you decided to join the Lord's service. Childish pranks are not the activities we expect to see from our postulants.'" Not one word of her scolding seemed to ruffle her steel-plated shield of sassiness.

Later, in a huddle during recreation hour, we listened in shock to her strategy, "I keep my head down and never look up at her." Then, as if it were a tried and true formula, she would add, "Then I say how sorry I am and promise to try harder to be good." She'd wink her impish eyes at us and shrug. And we, her audience of careful, fearful postulants, would stare in wide-eyed, open-mouthed awe followed by discomfort. Her penance of praying with her arms out wide from her body during night prayers did not faze her. "It's just for a few days," she'd remark.

One Saturday my partner and I were encouraged to come to the top of the steps by Janet's petite frame waving at us, her arms outlined by the bright sun of the landing's tall windows. We were so engrossed or dulled by our steady scrubbing that we might have thought there was an emergency; however, Janet's voice beamed down a "Come on, come on" to us that bubbled with fun. She pulled us forward down the hall, whispering rather loudly that she'd found the Mother Prioress's headgear – the white fabric and plastic forehead piece that covered all but the very front of a sister's face, and upon which, her veil was draped. "We can all try it on!" she giggled.

I stepped back from her then, my eyes wide and unbelieving. "Oh my gosh, no! We can't do that!" My voice was a hoarse hiss of wonder and shock. I warned her that this was big trouble and we'd be killed if someone found out.

"Don't worry," she crooned, her eyes smiling in innocence, "no one will find out. We'll have a lookout at the door and it's so much fun. Wait till you see me!"

At this point, her best friend and partner in crime, Mary Ann, joined us, and the two of us were shuffled into the room. When Janet pushed her round angelic face through the opening in the headgear, we fell back on the prioress's bed in helpless laughter. She tried on all kinds of "nun" looks from solemn and prayerful with her beautiful blue eyes downcast—and she did, of course, look angelic—to the angry nun of our school days with her eyebrows arched, her lovely, round mouth screwed into a curly snarl and her arms pointing, waving to each of us crumpled on the bed in muffled squeals. Her very best imitation was the wild and harried nun, eyes darting around the room, shiny and wide-open as if she were a madwoman, her sweet face twisted beyond recognition like a gnarly tree root. We remembered this kind of sister because we'd all pushed her to the limits in grade school just to watch the way she would wind herself up to a sizzling frenzy.

Mary Ann was stationed at the door, cracking it ever so carefully and risking a look around the hall. She'd flap her right hand up and down as she closed the slit in the door, and each of us took our turn with the contraption, but none of us put on a show like Janet. I remember how fat and bulging my face looked, pinched into the white material and plastic forehead piece—it was a true harbinger of things to come. Only Janet looked really lovely when she batted her large eyes in a pious pose.

At times our lookout would hush us as someone came up the steps or walked down the hall. We knew we had more to fear from one postulant than any regular Sister; in fact, it was the postulant who worked down the hall from the prioress's room that we worried about most of all.

She was younger than us by a year or two, most of our group of a hundred were eighteen years old, so we figured that she might have been promoted somewhere down the long hall of school classes. Her face wore the pudgy pout of someone who'd been made fun of all through school, defensive and ready. We avoided her for many reasons, not the least of which was that she often had the nerve to correct us about the proper way to make our bed or some other insignificant matter. She amazed us with her "nun" look; her perfected steely stare. She aimed this scolding face at us if we laughed during meditation at another postulant's gurgling and yawning stomach or some poor tired sister's head drooping down and jerking up while fighting sleep.

On this particular day, the day of our headgear naughtiness, she had probably heard our laughter and investigated. She was waiting not four feet from the door as we emerged into the hall, our eyes in tears from the wonderful exhaustion of constant giggling.

She told. All of us were called to our postulant mistress and confronted with this horrible deed we had done. Kneeling before our mistress and hearing the disappointment she felt in my actions was a stunning moment for me. My "good girl" image of myself slithered away, and I felt bereft, quite lost and shaken. I'd never known such shame, such notoriety. For a week afterward, my stomach churned as I moped along the corridors of school and dormitory, refectory and chapel. I couldn't look at anyone without thinking that now they might see me as immature.

My punishment was to spend several weekends working in the laundry, pulling clean habits through the ringers, feeding scapulars to the giant arm of the presser, and folding every type of underwear imaginable. The steamy, heavy air was almost unbearable, and my body seeped moisture everywhere, so that my black blouse and skirt clung to my skin. It was a perfect chastisement. Even though I was mildly successful in making our sisters' habits look new and fresh, I could not remove the nasty sweat and stench of my actions so easily—I had to spend the rest of the day wearing my soiled garments.

Janet was too fun and too much of a friend for any of us to blame her for getting us in trouble; besides, we knew that each of us let Janet pull us into the bedroom. We simply wouldn't have thought of judging her or discussing her "incidents" with each other except to have a laugh, but I, for one, wished her cavalier attitude would rub off on me. I suspected that she did not lay awake at night alone in her skimpy bed with the quiet hanging over her head like a funeral shroud, ruminating about her sins and shortcomings. She probably slept with an angelic smile on her face; her lips curled just enough to show that peace reigned inside that lovely head.

And she was lovely. Brown-gold curls hugging her face. Skin smooth with a hint of amber tones. And, most prominent, wide blue eyes fringed with dense, dark fern lashes. You couldn't ignore them, as she knew very well the power of her gaze. They were eyes meant to shake some guy down to his toes from across a filmy bar, burn into the heart of a thoughtless lover or husband, or hang limp with love into the face of a lucky man. When she left the convent for a life in the larger world outside, I knew it was a blessed event; at least for some young man who would cross her path.

CHAPTER 13

Ring Rapping

PROFESSED SISTERS WEAR A RING on their right hand, a simple band that declares to the world their devotion to Christ as their bridegroom and master. I found the ring declared other things as well. Our sisters at Our Lady of Grace Elementary School used them to get the attention of our distracted and highly mischievous seventh-grade class. When a sister hit the ring on her desk at full throttle, the rap would whip each and every head back to front and center. We'd wait with slitted eyes to see who would be singled out for chastisement. "Mary Ellen, keep your nosy eyes on your reader. You'd think God gave you an owl's neck the way you twist and turn, distracting the class."

Mary Ellen would roll her eyes, but lower them to her textbook because we never won at the "sister did, sister said" game with our parents. If I was foolish enough to complain to my mom about how some sister ridiculed me, she would ask so many questions about what I did to deserve the ridicule, I gave up and told her to forget it. Even then she would not stop, and I found myself getting a warning: behave in school or suffer the consequences.

Ring rapping was serious business, much more heavy-duty

than just plain scolding, and to ignore or ridicule the warning would be foolhardy, maybe even disastrous if a sister called home. We faked compliance and bowed to the sister in charge to avoid any unsavory discussions with our parents. Later, in high school, the sisters might rap their rings to get the attention of the class, but rarely to admonish a student. It became a benign signal, which called us to order or dismissed us from our room.

There was no change to the ring rapping when I became a postulant. Our mistresses called us to order (we were a large and often quite lively group) by knocking their rings on the desk or lectern to begin our classes on scripture or religious life. In fact, the practice seemed to thrive, and I liked the clean efficiency of it. A call to order was literally at the end of one's fingers; however, not all rapping was utilitarian. In the refectory, while we ate dinner, the ring rappers' bullet-like drumming would send shivers of worry through each of us at table.

We had all of our meals in the bowels of the Motherhouse in a room resembling a long, dark hall. Eight institutional-type tables filled the space of the dining hall—four tables in perfect alignment were situated down one wall, while the other four stood adjacent to them along the opposite wall. On each side six hard wooden chairs were pushed in under the tables so that only the high backs could be seen, like soldiers facing each other at attention. This somber ambiance was emphasized further by the custom of devotional reading during our luncheon meal. It was not the dining room of our growing up; the place of our warm Thanksgiving meals and memories.

Each postulant was assigned to prepare a chapter or two of our current book of study for noon dinner reading. You knew that you would be perched above the group on a tall stool in the middle of the tables, that your voice would ring out unnaturally like laughter at a funeral, and that, like the guy on the seat above the dunking pool, you should be prepared for a thorough "washing and dousing" if you forgot to prepare your chapters for the day. We were informed that our thoughtful attention to these words of inspiration was vitally important because the ideas reaching our ears at about the same time the chicken and rice found our mouths were the equivalent of soul food. The lesson: neither man nor sister live by bread alone.

It all made for dreadfully dull eating. The relentless drone of the postulant's voice was accompanied by the lonely, yet persistent clink and clatter of fork and knife hitting a plate. It was a kind of strange symphony that could have driven me mad if I had actually listened to it. Instead, my mind would be oceans away thinking about the novel I was reading in literature class at the college, or the reading assignment I hadn't finished for biology, or the sweet smell of my sheets back home where I could nuzzle myself into the mattress and actually sleep, when the sharp bark of sister's ring would hit the thick oak of the table. My fork aiming for my slack and slightly opened mouth would jab my cheek, or my knife would peal across the plate, and if I had just raised my glass in midair, I would invariably send smooth waves of milk onto my plate or worse, my blouse.

The reader's silence would seem unnatural, like the moment after a movie reel has jammed. Each table around me showed stunned postulants hardened like statues with forks and knives and glasses poised, their faces dreading the ordeal to come—the postulant who had been reading had mispronounced a word.

The unfortunate reader would be asked to repeat the sentence, and we sat in great distress knowing she would have no choice but to mangle it a second time. Of course, she repeated the word quietly, partly because she knew she would make the mistake again and because her heart would be beating madly and her eyes steaming up with tears. She knew she would feel a perfect fool when sister was finished with the "lesson" on pronunciation.

The oral reading talents varied amongst our very large and

diverse group of postulants. For many of my friends it was as dreaded as speaking in public. They would spend an hour or more bent over the chapters with a dictionary, and if truly frightened into a panic, seek the help of an English major.

Many of us stumbled disastrously on the likes of *demagogue*, *propitiate*, or *evanescence* even though we had looked up the pronunciation. And yet, some "invented" pronunciations of rather common words would jar the sensibilities of even the comatose diner. Although none of us had rings to rap, another postulant might arch an eyebrow at me or catch a piece of meat in her throat at unusual renditions such as, "the *soolace* (solace) of his arms," or "sinking into a *reeveerie* (reverie) of pleasant thoughts," or "taking heart by thinking of his kind *viisag* (visage)." After hearing an unusually preposterous jumble of syllables hit the air, my head would involuntarily shoot up in amazement, but I would just as quickly lower my head down to my chest to quietly hide that amazement away.

So it was with a bit of enthusiasm that I approached my turn at the lectern. Public speaking or reading was not an alien art to me. I had performed in numerous plays while in high school, had prepared several interpretive readings for contests, and had won the state forensic championship in declamation. Perhaps that is why I merely glanced over the selection I needed to prepare; I trusted my instincts at figuring out unusual words. Plus, I was very busy with my classes—papers to write and reading assignments that I barely completed by the designated time. How difficult could ten pages of some devotional book be?

The ring rapped while I was well into my reading, just as I was beginning to feel this job was a breeze. The book jerked up in my hands and with effort I managed to keep it from dropping to the floor, which would have been a long fall. Sister's voice stung the moist, warm air and our ears, "Please read that last sentence again, Patricia."

Frantically my eyes scanned the cumbersome sentence for the culprit; there it sat toward the end of a most unremarkable compound/complex construction. I had no idea how to pronounce it differently, so like many of my postulant friends before me, I was forced to repeat the screaming error a second time. By now, my hands were shaking. Yet, I repeated the passage quietly and with a great deal of dread, "...and we must *akweeses* ever to the will of God in these matters."

I waited for the sharp sound of sister's voice, wishing much too late that I had spent more time scouring my selection.

"Patricia, the word is not pronounced *akweeses*. Did you prepare this reading and use the dictionary for unfamiliar words?"

Of course, I lied. "Yes, sister."

"Well, the word is not *akweeses*, Patricia. Do you know what this word means?"

It seemed mean to push my stupidity to such extremes. Wasn't it obvious that if I did not know how to pronounce a word, I might not know the meaning of it as well? "No, sister."

"In the future, Patricia, prepare your readings carefully for your sisters. The word is pronounced *ac qui esce*. It means to comply or consent. Please repeat the word and continue your reading."

I've never forgotten acquiesce. It was a perfect lesson. My pride took a nosedive, and I think I regained a bit of perspective. Yet, my memory of this word does not carry with it the horror of my public scolding because, once I learned how to pronounce it, I came to love hearing the word spoken aloud.

It is such an unusual word; it reminds me of something thick and sticky, like quicksand or dark, silty mud at the bottom of a lake. It squishes delightfully in the mouth, especially at the end when the *s* slithers off my tongue and through my teeth. The word comes from the Latin, *acquiescere*, to rest.

So, finally I put to rest this error of my past and admit that this word did not deserve to be mutilated by me. A lovely sound-ing word such as acquiesce deserved to be lifted onto the air for my fellow diners so that its lilting rhythm might be enjoyed—if only by a few word lovers like myself.

CHAPTER 14

Father Schurman

I WAS ONE OF VERY FEW postulants in the convent to have a gentleman caller. Well, priest caller, actually. Yet, it was easily one of the more sublime moments I can recall of that year in Adrian. It was an unusual event since we never had company except on the designated family-visit Sundays, which were held once a month with few or no exceptions. Nonetheless, in the middle of the day during the week, I was summoned. The message stunned me: *You have a visitor. Meet him in the front parlor of the Motherhouse.*

As I wove my way through the winding halls to the rather large parlor where we laid out our dead, or, as the case might be, greeted our visitors, I couldn't imagine who might have been granted access to me. The words "meet him" lingered there in perfect understatement. A man? My mind raced as I followed the halls to the front parlor. Was it my Uncle Johnny whose sad eyes watched me with resignation when he came to visit? Johnny, who, after he saw me wave goodbye and take my place in the pew, left the chapel in tears? Had he created a scene so that now they had to send for me? I had just seen my father and

my brother, and the sisters would never make an exception for
a boyfriend (unless he might be dying).

It was with complete and utter shock that I found Father
Schurman, framed by the tall window. The heavy drapes were
pulled; the bright light from outdoors outlined his figure as he
stood with his back to me, his head leaning to the right as I
always remembered. He turned toward me, a slow smile unfold-
ing on his face. My exclamation of "Oh, Father Schurman!"
had not ruffled him in the least. He simply came up to me and
quietly took my hands in his. I blubbered something about how
surprised I was to see him and how nice it was of him to make
the trip all the way to Adrian.

When I looked around the parlor for a place to sit, he asked
if I wanted to walk outside while we visited. My eyes widened
in surprise—we would not be politely chatting in the straight-
backed chairs of this enormous, stuffy room. Instead, I would
be walking on the paths around campus with a man! My stomach did a few leaps as we headed for the giant oak doors and
slipped into the still-wintry March weather and the freedom of
that crisp, sunny day.

He was not the first priest I became enamored with. In high
school we had a young, handsome priest come to our all-girl
Catholic High School to teach religion class. Each class only
had him once a week and he was so much better to look at than
the assigned nun. He would sit on the desk while he talked with
us (which our nuns never did) and he made up nicknames for
some of the prettier girls. If he had liked me and my looks, he
might have labeled me "freckles" or "Irish." But I was not one
of the chosen ones.

Basically, he was the only man we saw walk down those
halls, except maybe a maintenance worker or one of our fathers
looking for the school office. We all loved him. We all tried to
get his attention. And I think we did, since he clearly liked to be

around us, attending some of our after-school events and such. He didn't last, though. One day he stopped showing up and was not replaced. We were never told the real reason, but we suspected that he just liked the girls too much.

Father Schurman was a quieter handsome. I met him while I was at Rosary High School. Our drama teacher announced one day during my junior year that the drama director of Salesian High School, an all-boy academy in downtown Detroit, needed a few girls to help out with parts in the school's next play. Father Schurman knew we had a strong drama department, so he called our school. A group of us tried out and I earned a part in a production of *Charley's Aunt*.

I remember how excited I felt to be working with guys my age, to get to know them and hang out during rehearsals. The female halls of Rosary, so dull during the day, would be spiced up by my journeys to the all-male auditorium at Salesian in the evenings. It was the chance I had waited for. The guys were fun, a bit crazy, but great company for me, and I went out with one of them.

Yet, amazingly, with all these young and virile guys around, it was Father Schurman who had us girls whispering in the women's room at Salesian. We thought he was mysteriously interesting, which in our teenage language usually translated to "very sexy." His face was open, peaceful and relaxed; his smile, somewhat boyish, had a most genuinely happy look that reached all the way to his eyebrows. He had fine brown hair combed back off his forehead like a movie star, and soft brown eyes.

I always thought him too elegant and graceful for the rambunctious teenagers he worked with. Yes, he might have wreaked havoc in an all-girl school like Rosary if he had been assigned there. And yet, not because he would try to be anything but a priest—he was just wonderful to look at as well as kind. Besides, as every girl since Eve knows, forbidden fruit can be the most appealing of all.

He had the gentlest touch with everyone. Even the most annoying guy in our cast, the one who made up lines of dialogue that confused the other actors or forgot his blocking and bumped into actors, making our rehearsals a joke, was treated with patience while some of us looked on with frustration. Father Schurman was so much more laid back than any of the nuns at Rosary. He let the guys be goofy, let them learn their parts at their own pace, only pulling in the reins when opening night loomed closer. I had never met a teacher like him, and at times, I wanted to get in and help him control the pandemonium that seemed to me like total disorder.

Sometimes, he would come up to the stage and put a hand on my shoulder to show me where and how he wanted me to move. His touch was automatic and instructive, but my teenage heart fluttered. I loved to look out at him in the auditorium and find his eyes on me. And, after working with him on three plays in my junior and senior years, I discovered that I had never been this close with a priest before, close enough to laugh with him, talk about my daily nonsense, and work for hours on a creative endeavor that we both seemed to love. He had become a special person to me before I knew it.

When I had finally made my decision to enter the convent, I wanted to tell him. I approached him during that last play of senior year and stumbled around with my news. I remember taking forever to get the idea out of my mouth.

"Well, I just thought I'd tell you about something I think I will do."

"Oh? What is that?" He waited, looking at me the entire time.

"Ah... well...I've been thinking about it for a long time." More patient waiting. "I'm still not real sure, I don't know if this is the... life for me. But I guess I will give it a try." He nodded as I carried on, and then, I threw out the words in a big rush, "I'm going into the convent."

At the time, I was still unsure, struggling with this "vision" of what I was supposed to do. The thought that I might have a vocation consumed me; my insides were still curling around in little knots every time I dared to look at the decision I had to make, which, in the end, I did out of desperation and exhaustion.

He listened calmly, his warm eyes showing mild surprise. "Well, whatever happens, I'm pleased you told me." He was not a man to speak quickly, and he smiled slightly as he continued. "I'm honored."

I looked up at him then, and knew he really meant it. But the idea of "honored" to be a part of my life was very difficult to take in. I was just a teenage girl, and he was a priest, someone who stood taller and higher than a mere person like me. I would think about those words for weeks, and each time I played them over in my mind, I'd shiver inside, my amazement turning to sheer happiness that this could happen to me.

Then, as if that were not enough, he said, "I'll be happy to help you through your decision if you need me." I was unprepared for his next observation. Did he really say he was not that surprised because he had noticed my spiritual bent and wondered where it might lead me? I knew I had been preoccupied, maybe rather serious at times, carrying the weight of my decision around all those months, but I never thought I might appear to be a spiritual person to anyone. Wow. Is this who I am?

He wasn't ready to let me go until he had assured me of his help, "Will you let me know what you decide? And, remember, I'll be happy to help you if you need someone to talk with."

I thanked him and slipped away, but I have never forgotten the happiness I felt at his concern for me and his true desire to be a part of my life even after the curtain came down on our last performance of the play.

On the day that Father Schurman came to visit me in the

convent, we walked around the campus like a forbidden couple in this world of women only. At least that was my sense of it, and I relished every step, every turn in our path. He asked me all about what I was doing, about my college classes and my new life as a postulant. I had to think about what to discuss because I did not want to burden him with my problems, my failure to jump into this new life with every part of me.

By the time he visited, I had put together a few programs for visiting dignitaries. He was interested in the process. How do you put together a program with no script? He seemed impressed, and I would have loved to show him one of our programs, but I knew I couldn't go back into the building and leave him.

Even when I was acting in his plays, he wanted to know how my classes were going. What was I reading? Which authors did I favor? It was the same during his visit to Adrian. We fell into the literary discussion quite easily, and he enjoyed my enthusiasm for Jane Austen and *Pride and Prejudice*, which I was reading at that time in one of my courses.

I kept little secrets from him though, like the panic that would rise up in me while lying in bed at night, or the buckets of loneliness that would descend upon me at our recreation times while I was surrounded by my fellow sisters laughing and engaged in "fun." I'd never mention the fear I had that I couldn't meditate; that my mind couldn't focus; and that I never heard a word God might be trying to say to me. I wouldn't tell him how bereft I felt when a good friend would be gone—just like that. I'd come up to my dorm after chanting Compline and her bed would be empty. She would have gone home, deciding that she wasn't cut out for convent life. I'd wonder for nights why she didn't say goodbye, why she didn't tell me she was going, why she left as if she were doing something bad that we couldn't watch or understand.

When other sisters, postulants, or students at the college walked past Father Schurman and me as we strolled the walkways on that frosty day, they took note: an arched eyebrow, a stolen glance, a lingering look our way. My diminishing confidence in my identity soared. I was walking with the genuine article, a man—true, a man who happened to be a priest, but a young and handsome one, nonetheless.

I was feeling so special and lightheaded that it's little wonder I can't remember if I had the presence of mind to ask him about his activities or news. I wonder if my giddy, romantic feelings were as transparent to him then as they appear to me today.

I saw Father Schurman again when I took the veil as a novice, and then later when I took the black veil and made profession. That was the last time. I wonder if he felt that after my profession, because I was no longer a sister in training who might need encouragement, he should back off. Besides, he knew I would be leaving the Motherhouse to another city or state to teach school after I made profession.

I never had the slightest feeling that he was attracted to me in the same way I was so taken with him. He was always a perfect gentleman, and he never acted as if he wanted anything more than to be a mentor and a support to me. I guess it was the mystique of knowing a priest, one who wanted to see me, wanted to be there for my convent journey that impressed me; the mystique that left me lying in bed at night, imagining us as "friends" who got together when I became a professed nun. I wondered if I'd be allowed to go to the theater with a priest? Or have lunch with him? Who knows what might have happened then?

I didn't have a chance to explore these possibilities. I left the convent about four years after this visit; and I lost him, like we lose many people in life, yet nonetheless, never forget.

CHAPTER 15

The Real Deal

F OR WEEKS IN THE SPRING of our postulant year, we
worked in the sewing room, cutting a creamy muslin cloth
into various shapes to make our habit, the outfit we would wear
as an almost "real" sister when we became novices. We were
told that making this gown and taking special care to make it
beautiful was a sign of our love for our bridegroom. We would
wear this new habit for the ceremony in August, which would
signify us as brides of Christ. For this reason, our work had
to be perfect. How could we give less than our best when our
beloved was God himself?

I hated this job. Back in 1964 our sewing room was equipped
with antique sewing machines, something akin to a player piano
where the person has to pump the pedals to get the roll to turn
and play the song. This type of machine required a rhythmic
movement, a balancing of feet working the pedals near the floor
in sync with fingers holding and pushing fabric through the
needle for a successful line of stitches. No electricity, just dancing
feet, steady hands, and a good pair of eyes.

It seemed like an easy task, and I had the required parts to perform the job. Or so I thought. My feet either pumped too quickly for my frantic hands to feed the fabric or too slowly for any progress. My runaway machine would send the fabric off the table, a trail of white thread oozing from the needle and the bobbin. I couldn't curse, and I dared not strike the machine but I was thinking words that weren't exactly bride of Christ material.

We had to complete a sort of pre-sewing test—sewing straight lines over and over on a piece of remnant fabric. I'm not sure how I passed the test, or if I passed with an emergency clause. I do know that when we were working on our real habits, our seams had to be inspected by the sister in charge, the "Rip-it-Out-Sister."

Every seam I sewed was subject to her approval, and it took forever for one of my seams to be judged straight enough. I ripped till my hands shook. Even the easiest stitches, the ones I had to run down the length of our long, very straight scapular, were challenges for me. The tunic with its rounded collar and large sleeves, which had to be fitted into a circular opening in the tunic, gave me a feeling of such dread; I could barely go back in the sewing room. It was no help that I watched other serene seamstresses hang up their neatly ironed work, like trophies, and walk out of the sewing room with smiles of joy and satisfaction. I hated to see them go and leave me behind, frustrated and panicky as my week in the sewing room was quickly coming to an end.

Before the last of the acceptable seamstresses left, I decided I would have to ask—no, beg—one of them to help me. It wasn't necessary. Evelyn, who had been quietly working on her habit a few tables away, noticed my rising urgency and stopped at my machine on her way out the door.

Moments before, I had seen her carry her finished handiwork, all pressed and lovely, up to the front.

She had a lithe, ropelike body that fell easily into itself. Many times as she sat crescent shaped at her machine, her head curled to the fabric, I approached her with my latest challenge, which would be a wavy line of sewing or a seam that wouldn't stay together. Always calm and gently chiding as a mother might, she would take my rough muslin in her hands and with little clucks of "Let's see here" and "No, no, no, not such a big problem" and "Mmm...OK...all right...." would lift her head up to me, her Irish eyes squinting in a smile, and announce that all would be well. And it was. Just like that. Evelyn would charm the wild beast and the muslin would purr through her machine.

I wonder today if she had always planned on finishing my habit, because that is what she did. The miracle was that I walked away with a completely finished habit, and she made it look like I had done it myself. She was one of the older postulants who did not enter our order right out of high school, but the mere two years she had on us did not explain her sweet, unruffled, kind way with everyone. I figured that Evelyn was just one of the truly good people, and I was fortunate enough to find her.

Evelyn and I knew each other in another, less frustrating way. She and I worked on programs together for visiting cardinals and bishops or for any event that needed a presentation, the same programs I spoke with Father Schurman about. I enjoyed working with Evelyn. When we were asked to tackle one of these presentations, we had to do our research in bits and pieces during our recreation, after our studies were finished, and on weekends. After securing a huge pile of books with promising material from the library, we sat on the floor of the recreation hall, drooped over a book, tearing little pieces of paper to mark the spot for a possible selection.

We loved reading the parts aloud that we thought would work, and each of us found that we both delighted in the sound of words. After perusing many, many works, we would pluck a theme out of the air of words and sentences and piece together a program, writing our own transitions and fitting all the parts into a whole. The entire process engaged every fiber of our beings. We were lost in the hunt, in the finding, in the organizing, in the creating.

After our work had gone through some inspection, Evelyn and I directed the postulants in performing our mini-masterpiece. Throughout our working together, Evelyn, even though she was more intelligent than I, never pushed her own agenda. She always listened to me, always stopped to consider and really think about my suggestions. I came to know the meaning of her clucks and taps of her pencil, her nods of the head, and her anticipated gaze toward me for my idea. What a team we were! I have this clear impression of two heads, two bodies side by side, connected and in sync with a singular purpose.

In addition to sewing the habit we would wear at our reception, we had other critical preparations to complete. One of the most important was a serious study of the vows we would be taking during our reception ceremony in which we took the habit, the very one we sewed with the trundle machines. Our postulant mistresses began this study many months before we were asked to take our vows. There was a hierarchy in our vows, and according to our mistresses, we began with the least important of them, poverty. I wondered how never having money of my own and giving up the right to purchase and keep personal property could be minor, but I listened.

We were told that poverty was a virtue involving desire. Curbing the desire for things of the world allowed simplicity in one's daily life. Too many material possessions only bogged down the spirit. Without these encumbrances, we would be able to focus on the important work of serving God and his church. After a while, I did not miss having cash in the bank or a checkbook. I was clothed, fed, had a roof over my head, and could go to school.

A few months of wearing the black skirt and cape seemed to

wash away my initial discomfort of looking like a weird cross between an almost religious nun and a puritan. We all wore the same outfit, and I saw myself coming and going.

Every day I walked a short distance from the Motherhouse through a breezeway to Siena Heights College, an all-girl school run by our order. The college was situated on the grounds of the Motherhouse, which was home to some of the teachers.

Taking classes throughout the year helped me to indulge in my "book fix" and, I must admit, my love for school and learning. Even my text on philosophy of education was a book. How could I not be interested in the why and how of bringing knowledge to children? Would I have loved a twenty-dollar per month book allowance? Absolutely.

Yet, at this point in my life, with prayer, an obedience, classes, and my evenings filled with an hour of recreation, I had very few minutes left to indulge in an extra novel of my choice.

The second vow we "almost" studied in our morning homeroom class with our postulant mistress was chastity. Sister Therese was brief, and the definition was simple: To be pure in mind and action. Did we ask questions? Of course not. None of us wanted to hear the details. We could figure things out without a lecture.

Sex was always the taboo topic in our religion classes from seventh grade till twelfth grade. The stand-by line to describe sins against chastity was "impure thoughts." To the sisters in school, that seemed to cover it all, but we knew it didn't. This special virtue seemed to be the secret one, the one most of our instructors did not want to discuss fully, including our postulant mistresses as I observed in our discussion of the vows.

Yet back in 1963, sitting in a classroom with the other postulants, I was relieved. I did not totally realize what I was giving up by taking the vow of chastity because I had never experienced the act that chastity forbade. Not only that, I wasn't sure if I knew what the entire act involved (I was definitely in the minority here) since I had only experienced parts of it. My visions of the sexual act were vague, and "sex talk" with my girlfriends encompassed only what was termed "foreplay" back then.

Our mistresses didn't seem to want to teach a hundred young, idealistic girls sex education, so that we would properly know what the vow of chastity encompassed, and that was fine with me. My twelve years of Catholic education had sufficiently denounced anything that hinted at sex. I was already convinced of my guilt in having impure thoughts, indulging in French kissing and letting a guy touch my breasts. I preferred to try to leave all of my impure thoughts and actions behind and move on.

If chastity and poverty were not the big ones, obedience certainly was. This vow had to do with God's will, not my will. Obedience was all about spiritual logic. I was placing my life in Christ's hands when I freely chose to live as His servant and do His work here on earth, and not that of my own. Therefore, His will would command me. How was I to know His will? My superiors and teachers would express it to me, by the large and small decisions made for me by those in charge. I was relinquishing my independent spirit, my personal choices, so that God (through his representatives on earth) might direct my life in service and love toward others.

Obedience: this was the difficult one. I had learned in my months as a postulant that everything was assigned to me: my seat in chapel, my bed in the dorm, my seat at the dinner table, my classes at the college, my form of recreation, my companion for visiting day with my parents, my time to write home, my time to pray, my week's supply of clean clothes, my duty and jobs cleaning and caring for the Motherhouse; in essence, every section of my day was regulated by my superiors.

This would continue when I became a novice; in fact, the daily regime of my life would be even more controlled. After my novitiate year, I would be given my "assignment," a job teaching somewhere in the country or out of the country. I would be told which grade I would teach, be given duties to care for the convent, and on and on.

At eighteen, this was a huge sacrifice. One wonders, perhaps, how anyone so young would be prepared to accept such a situation. I wasn't ready, and I knew it. Yet continuing on was the only acceptable option for me at the time.

Indeed, I wasn't alone. Sixty-nine of our original one hundred and ten postulants prepared for reception as novices. Since I wasn't able to speak with most of the forty-one postulants who left the convent before novitiate, I speculated that some of them wanted to work at jobs that would allow them to make and manage their own money. Others might have realized that they wanted a family—a husband and children. And then many of those who left may have felt crippled by the vow of obedience; adjusting to some superior's choices for their daily and long-term life was too large a sacrifice.

I don't have a general explanation for my willingness to forego my personal freedom, but, coming from a Catholic family, I wasn't exactly raised with unlimited freedom. Perhaps the change wasn't as drastic as it might have been for a truly independent, free-spirited kind of girl. From my experience, after the first year of being told what to do and when to do it, I had acclimated myself to the routine. I felt that spending one more year in the convent, a year in which I would be semi-cloistered, would help me to understand what religious life was really asking of me. What was one more year when so much was at stake?

For many of us, it was too difficult to walk away from our original commitment without a thorough evaluation, which meant giving our vocation a chance. Realizing that I wouldn't be the only one going forth with serious doubts and questions actually helped me. It seemed normal not to know for sure, to have a sinking feeling inside; but, ultimately, I felt my uncertainty alone.

I thought about it alone at night and wondered if it would ever go away. Misery may love company, but after all the talk, all the consoling with a few friends who felt as I did, I was still fraught with fear. It was a dilemma without a good answer; no clear choice.

So, I chose without choosing, but at the time, I didn't think of it quite so clearly. I simply moved forward because moving back to my family right then was still too much like turning my back on God.

Another visiting day much later in the winter of '64.
My father and aunt sit near me.

CHAPTER 16

Big Sister Is Watching

THE POSTULANCY PROVED TO BE an excellent breed-
ing ground for paranoia. The soil was nurtured often, and
the roots spidered out their tangly fingers and took hold. Once,
I was walking down the hall in the Motherhouse, my mind
miles away from my feet, when I looked up to see one of the
mistresses studying me. A tingling of fear awakened my senses.
My back straightened, my hands took cover under my short,
black cape, and my eyes found refuge on the floor. A hot swipe
hit my neck and forehead, while droplets of sweat oozed onto
the collar of my blouse. Immediately, my legs felt like rickety,
unbending sticks, jerking me along as I walked in erratic bursts
of stiffness. The mistress didn't say a word as I passed her; all
she offered was her quiet, museful watching. For hours I'd be
frozen in a fruitless mental game: What was sister thinking?
What had I done wrong? Why did she study me like that? Did
she see my lack of focus, know my thoughts, know how I felt
about things?

We postulants were always watched and studied. At eighteen, many of us were still self-conscious, insecure adolescents.

We already studied every move of our bodies and each word from our mouths for the sin of stupidity. For me, the scrutiny of two extra sets of eyes was almost more than my psyche could take. I could ignore, with rolled eyeballs and a sigh, the criticisms of my parents and the suggestions of my teachers, but this careful examination by the mistressses—every day and every moment—was ripening the soil of my weakest tendencies where fear grew in prolific abandon.

For the most part, our mistresses were scrutinizing us during those first six months because we had been instructed to leave the silly school-girl behavior behind and conduct our bodies befitting one of God's servants. This turnabout of the natural bent of our natures did not come as easily for some, and the term "proper decorum" had for sure not been a part of our daily vernacular. Those of us who had encountered this Victorian warning from a teacher during high school would have blown it off as a fuddy-duddy kind of concept, one that might have been valid in our great-grandmothers' time but certainly not in the twentieth century. Rock and roll had paved the way for words like "decorum" to fall on deaf ears. Luckily, I had attended an all-girl Catholic high school, and, therefore, knew what decorum meant. At least I thought I knew. The new and unabridged definition of this word, according to our convent handbook, would take up a half page in the *American Heritage Dictionary*. The rules for decorum as given to us in our many mornings of instruction were:

- *Never run.*
- *Never hurry or rush, even when late.*
- *Keep eyes lowered at all times.*
- *Keep hands under your cape or scapular.*
- *Laugh and talk softly.*
- *Walk with a brisk step.*

☞ *Never slouch in a chair or while standing.*
☞ *Eat slowly and moderately but sufficiently.*
☞ *Always defer to an elder.*
☞ *Be moderate in joy as well as in sadness.*
☞ *Offer a peaceful, pleasant face to others.*

And on and on. Some postulants couldn't help but violate almost every decorum rule during that first year of our training; their lively personalities were the antithesis of proper decorum.

Linda, my high school buddy, was one of those unfortunate exuberant individuals. While Linda was eating lunch in the refectory one afternoon, a messenger arrived and delivered a note to the postulant mistress nearest her. Since we all watched with eagerness these deviations from the steady drone of our meal-time postulant reader, Linda's eyes were fastened on the interruption and our mistress. To her surprise, the mistress beckoned her with her finger.

Linda rose up with her usual flair, knocking the table in her rush to get the message. She was told that she had a visitor, a favorite teacher from her grade school years, who was a nun. Linda's joy could not be contained. She left the mistress and careened down the aisle between the wall and the row of tables at such speed, she resembled a bowling ball weaving down the lane.

And her face. Linda's face, when happy, was a virtual symphony of expressions, all tumbling out like an endless candy jar spilling out its goodies. I remember holding my breath to see if Linda would make it out the door and up the stairs to safety. But just as she came to the exit door, our postulant mistress rapped her ring on the table and summoned Linda. Linda stopped as if the sound of the ring's knock had stabbed her back; she turned and walked slowly up to the mistress, her face collapsed with the realization of what she had done.

I'll never forget what happened next. Instead of a short

reminder or scolding, with Linda leaving to see her visitor, she was told to walk back to her seat and exit properly. Down the long row of tables and the sea of faces of her postulant friends she went, her body deflated, her face red and shamed till she found her place. Then, just as slowly, she walked the entire way back and out the door. I couldn't believe that she didn't cry; others would have.

While nudging the pieces of food on our plates that afternoon, many of us felt the injustice of Linda's punishment, yet we clearly understood the message given to each of us who hadn't been called from the room.

Another rule of decorum that puzzled us, as many of these new rules of behavior did, concerned friendships. Around the half-year mark of our first year in the convent, our postulant mistress looked at us with her signature sideways glance, which seemed to be uncharacteristically full of importance, and told us we would be discussing *particular friendships.*

Our warning was sketchy, a few sentences delivered in a slow, deliberately clipped enuciation. We should avoid friendships in which we single out just one person for our attention. We should share our gifts with all of the postulants, and pay special attention that we do not always seek the company of the same individual. At the end of this explanation, so short and somber, I understood only one thing—that this was a forbidden and very shameful type of friendship.

Eluding me at the time, however, was the exact nature of this offense of being particular in my choice of another person. Each of us had particular friends; girls we enjoyed more than others, who made grotesque faces at morning meditation or whispered gossip while we walked to our duty or just listened when we thought we could not bear another day of the loneliness. We were thrown together by our daily duties, or college classes, or any number of pulls that bring certain people to enjoy each other's company.

By this time I had found a group of about twelve girls that I sought out during the recreation hour of our day. Yet, my encounters with them, whether we shared laughs or stories or disappointments, were never what I considered to be shameful or unusual.

In my years of Catholic education, shame was usually associated with two things: sex or dishonesty. In the '60s, we did not openly acknowledge sexual friendship existing among women. Such behavior was not even spoken of in my high school circles, so this assumption of particular kinds of friendship was way beyond my comfort level.

Yet, sister had definitely insinuated by her choice of words and severe tone a shame attached to this kind of friendship. Rather than delve too deeply and perhaps avoid the discomfort of a shameful type of friendship, I ventured a safer guess about what sister meant by particular friends. I came up with offenses like separating oneself from the other postulants by enjoying the company of one special person, avoiding the larger group during recreation hour, meeting the same person for study in the library, or walking alone with the same postulant to and from college classes. Whew! Now each of us had a new catalog of possible infractions to worry about at night in bed. We had an entire day's activities to examine, to sort through and to fret about.

Within a week of the particular friendship announcement, our small group of twelve friends was confronted with an accusation. Two of our friends had been summoned to our Mistress, and each was advised to enlarge her circle of friends. They were told or warned that having a best friend was not acceptable in the new life each of them had chosen.

It didn't take long to notice a huge change in two of our friends. Jenny and Paula slumped around one day; their eyes would not meet ours as we searched their faces in the college halls. After all, we were the foreigners in the university, with our Puritan black and whites and black laced-up heels, and we scanned the halls for another postulant for a minute of conversation before our lectures.

But Jenny and Paula offered no pithy comments about classes or knowing smiles of collusion. In fact, we didn't even see them walking together! It was quite unusual. That evening at recreation, they sat alone on opposite ends of the large room. We tried to engage each of them in conversation, bouncing from one side of the dance-hall-sized space to the other. Jenny offered only monosyllables and seemed uncomfortable, while Paula averted our questions, her eyes pools of sadness.

We were too much for them, however, as the weight of our concern brought them to talk with us. What did they tell us? They could not be alone with each other because they were in danger of forming a particular friendship. It was beyond horrible to watch our friends stumble about in such an obvious, shameful display of what all of us must avoid. I couldn't believe that these two bright and sensitive women had become our physical lesson of the week. Our fear for them gave way to anger, and our idealistic young hearts, so carefully formed by our schools and parents to protect and defend justice, were charged into action.

We did not speak to our mistresses. That would have been too naive for even the youngest of us. We did not dare tell Jenny and Paula to ignore the warning. Our plan was less direct, and so much easier. We felt that we could shield them in our group so that they could be together while not alone together. Even though they could not sit near each other, they could still talk and be friends. When we walked to class, or to an open field for a sing-a-long, or sat in the study hall, they could be together with a group of four or six of us.

As if on cue, one or two of us would always appear next

to them if we found them alone. Later, more postulants, even myself and Linda, were also warned that we spent too much time together. We looked at each other in shock since both of us had good friendships with at least three other postulants, and I could not remember that we had isolated ourselves from others. I did not feel shamed by the warning, however, because at that point a good number of postulants had been admonished for the same offense. It seemed to be too epidemic to take seriously.

Besides, our convent regulations would jump from warnings of being with just one sister exclusively, to throwing us into situations where we had to have a chaperone. The first time I had to visit the dentist, I discovered that another sister would be accompanying me. I could almost understand the logic behind this chaperone; I might not know the way or I might need assistance coming home because of pain or discomfort. However, the constant tag-along postulant for every Sunday visit with my family and any trip which took me away from our home grounds became a burden. I felt as if I had to entertain this poor postulant who had no choice but to follow me everywhere. I've never liked human shadows; people who are always at my heels so that if I happened to turn around abruptly, we'd have a collision. I put up with it; I had no other choice.

The mistresses' reading of both my incoming and outgoing mail eventually left me resigned and rather nonplussed, but even that did not compare to one particular "big sister is watching" practice that was beyond my understanding. We were warned during our morning instruction class that our little space in the dorm was not our personal property. Our mistresses might search them at any time. The warnings, however, were quite subtle. We were told, "Postulants, be sure your dressers and beds are in order." Or, "If you just couldn't leave that one picture of your boyfriend home, this would be a good time to make the break and let him go." I wondered who would have brought such pictures and found out, to my amazement, that many postulants had. How little I knew of the fierce drives at work in some of my friends. I didn't have a real love to pine for so it was not difficult for me.

One evening, when I came back to my dorm, I saw beds with articles strewn over them. A dresser drawer lay on its side next to the items. After my initial shock, I realized that our dressers had been examined. With relief, I saw that my bed was empty and untouched. As I looked around at all the overturned drawers, I thought myself very fortunate.

Karen was not so lucky. To me, she had all the fun qualities I felt I lacked. She jumped into situations with both feet flying and her mouth going while I usually watched and waited before I joined most activities. Karen warmed up to everyone right away; there was no holding back, no sizing up the situation, just full-scale friendliness. Her laugh was husky and boisterous, and I can't remember one time when she might have giggled behind her hand. She never seemed to cower inside when our mistresses scolded us or pointed out our "collective" faults, and, yet, she didn't respond in secret with sarcasm. If we happened to grumble about reading aloud in the refectory during dinner, suffering the badgering of one of our mistresses when we made a mistake in pronunciation, she would only remark, "I don't agree with criticizing someone in public." Invariably, our conversation would turn to lighter topics when she joined us—that is why her sudden departure shocked all of us.

Linda was one of the only postulants who had an opportunity to speak with Karen right before she left. It was not a planned meeting; Linda just happened to be leaving her dormitory, late to class as usual and rushing around a corner, when Karen appeared. At first, Linda was shocked because Karen should have been going to class as well. When Karen tried to avoid her and whisk by, Linda reached out an arm, pulling Karen's cape till she could see her face. Linda was like that; she would have never let Karen go past her, figuring she could talk with her later. Karen's eyes were dazed, incredulous, as if she had been stunned by some terrible news; her face was crumpled, and her body moved ahead like a lost, disoriented child.

"What happened? Where are you going?" whispered Linda, pulling Karen into a door frame.

Karen studied Linda's face carefully, as if establishing where she was, and Linda waited without a word, knowing this was serious to see Karen all beaten.

"I'm being sent home. My parents are on their way."

And then, prompted by Linda's head shaking back and forth in disbelief, "They found a picture of my brother and his friends in my dresser. They had bathing suits on. I forgot it was there."

That was all. When Linda insisted, her arms flailing about, that Karen go back and talk with them, tell them how she felt, beg them to let her stay, Karen repeated, "My parents are on their way. I have to pack."

I wonder as I am writing this how I would have reacted to Karen. By now, a few of my friends told me beforehand that they were leaving. They were happy; ready to go home to their parents, family and friends, not to mention their comfy beds and homes and streets. I had a chance to say goodbye to them, knowing this was their choice.

Usually, however, the postulant or novice was sworn to secrecy and removed from our midst until she was safely gone. It happened with great swiftness, like big companies who shuffle the dazed worker out the door within minutes of her firing. Except these postulants and novices—young girls—were not employees. They were impressionable women offering themselves to some higher cause. They expected no salary, no raises, no employee benefits. It seems to me that their fellow postulants really should have gathered around them the night before they left. We should have hugged them and spoke of how we'd miss them, how much they meant to us, and how we wished them happiness. These women were too good, too special to have to go out the back door of our lives in covert escape.

CHAPTER 17

Puff the
Magic Dragon

WHEN WE POSTULANTS WOULD LEAVE our Motherhouse quarters for the park near us, or the field behind our buildings for a bonfire and singing, I used to wonder what if someone who knew very little about nuns or the church were to see us filing our way— all one hundred or so in our group— into the late evening air. How might he make sense of us? I don't think I ever saw anyone standing around observing us when we left after dinner and stayed until dark, but I couldn't help imagining what he— always a he—might be thinking.

I anticipate that the reader might guess that I was one of the mournful postulants whose voice howled with sadness during our singing. Yet, even though I had always sung this way, diving into the deep well of pain or loss in a song, our campfire song-fests always left me with a confusing mix of emotional release and yet more intense longing so that it might take days for me to recover from my melancholy. But enough, I will tell my story.

The light of day had begun to fade and summer's ripeness

hung seductively in the air, when our procession of postulants in long black skirts and capes wound its way to the park near the Motherhouse. To a casual observer, one not acquainted with the practices of a religious order, we could have seemed a gathering of ancient priestesses, weaving our way to the altars of the harvest sacrifice. On further examination, however, the onlooker might notice a lack of seriousness, a skipping or twirling of the body here or there, a sudden laugh, a rush of voices and, most telling, a large brown guitar toted by a young girl (not a priestess at all now) who appeared to match the size and girth of the instrument. The diminutive girl with the guitar seemed to be the most animated and bouncy of the group of girls (without a doubt, not priestesses either).

The sheer number of postulants would have piqued the interest of the imaginary viewer, standing in a small grove of cottonwoods on a gentle rise at the very edge of the city park. He might have wandered here innocently enough, enjoying the delightful expanse of fields and woods, when to his surprise he happened upon our clusters of black veiled heads snaking through the trees and tiny hills for perhaps as long as two city blocks. He might have estimated our numbers to be a hundred or so. At the head of this now very loud and almost unruly procession, he would see two brisk leaders, in contrasting garb of white long tunics and black veils. The entire entourage might evoke curiosity now of another kind: Who are these rambunctious, loud young women (definitely too tall and shapely to be mere girls)? Why are they wearing such unattractive clothes? What are they up to?

The imaginary onlooker's musings might be interrupted by the sudden organization of this very large group of women into a circle, which involved much turning and scooting and spreading out so that all could be seated in concentric rows around a clearing. The leaders, chuckling and pointing and genuinely appearing to enjoy themselves, sat in chairs, which had seemed to appear magically underneath them, above the now high-pitched screaming voices of the black-skirted ones who were seated on the ground.

This process of seating took an inordinate amount of time and the viewer, fascinated with the spectacle before him, might have been acknowledging this when, without warning, the night field was jolted by the unexpected burst of voices in song. It happened instantaneously, without an initial strum of the guitar or even flick of a leader's wand. The sound, rich and sweet with the lightness of youth, was lifted on the now shadowy night air up to the observer whose eyes might widen in approved amazement. The song was "Five Hundred Miles," and the viewer would have had no way of knowing that the group always started with that particular song. He could not be prepared for the emotional charge of it; the sheer wail of the tone, the cry of being left behind in each girl's voice raised as one. It might trail after him like a river in the air for the rest of his life, the sadness and beauty of that music and its melody like the loneliest train whistle he had ever heard.

Eventually, the moon would rise on this odd little concert in the clearing; and a rustle of black skirts would light a small fire in the empty space in the middle of the circle. Ah, now those priestesses might come back to the man's mind, and he would smile that his first analogy was rather intuitive. As darkness flooded this rather mystical setting, the observer would see the fire lick the air with yellow leaves of light.

The singing would resume and the man might wonder if every song must have been seared into the girls' memory, because they needed no words before them. The little guitar player encouraged them along, with her bobbing head and expressive face. She, alone, seemed not to let herself walk into the words and hold herself in the "lonesome valley" of "Tom Dooley," or the "longing for the far away troubles" of "Yesterday." Nor did she appear to show a bit of rebellion, of 60's protest, of the freedom that was soon to descend upon society when she led them in "If I Had A Hammer." She was not a child of melancholy or passion, it may have seemed to the bystander. A simple girl, her freckled, youthful face never wavered from its steady, happy gaze whether she strummed the tunes of "Where Have All the Flowers Gone?" or "This Land is Your Land." She seemed not to possess a complicated nature as many of the others girls might suggest, with their bodies swaying wantonly, their hands pounding their thighs or beating the air, their voices hitting the notes with a howl of unbridled longing.

The guitar player knew just when to change the tempo, too. After the mournful mood set by "The Cruel War," she would tilt her head, a sparkle in her eye, and strum vigorously the beginning chords to "Gypsy Rover," while the mist of sadness still hovered above their heads. The viewer might notice that some of the young women did not jump right in and embrace the new humor set upon them by the song. A few of them simply sat staring dully at the fire, watching the light dancing, and ruminating, lost in some state of delicious ennui.

But the little one with the guitar would not give up. The viewer might wonder if she had orders from the leaders, the two who watched everyone so closely from their chairs above the girls, since she seemed so insistent that all be together in their focus and spirit. And, yes, wouldn't the observer have noticed that she had one song, one that was bound to capture even the remotest black clad and sad girl?

While he watched, perhaps now worried for this delicate group of young girls (sweet and tender girls, he might now feel), didn't she transform and brighten their mouths and eyes when she strummed "Puff the Magic Dragon?" It would probably be quite a shock to the spectator when he considered the nature of the song, with its subtle reference to weed, which brought them into shades of joy. But then, he had no way of knowing that most every girl belting out the words to this mythical tale truly believed that Puff was a dragon, that Jackie Paper loved Puff and took care of him tenderly, and that Puff lived by the sea in a land called "Honah Lee." It was all a wonderful mythic tale, of course.

CHAPTER 18

Storms Inside
and Out

MY FIRST RECOLLECTION OF THE night was waking up to a room whitened by beams of ragged light, illuminated as if by a spotlight, giving me a glimpse of ceiling high overhead or a slash of dresser hugging the wall. A collage of unrelated parts flashed in the blackness, fragmented by the darkness around me. It took my mind a few seconds to adjust to the scene, but then, in violent eruption, a stream of thunder cuffs followed the bursts of light and exploded in my ears.

We postulants slept on the second floor; our tall, paned windows looked out at the friendly arms of tree branches, which now flailed about like giant claws. The rain attacked those lovely old windows in pelts of water big as golf balls, and the panes seemed to shake from the force. It felt as if the dark, rolling clouds of the storm had descended ominously onto the roof of our second-story brick structure, moving and churning the air like a pressure cooker about to explode.

In minutes we were all starkly awake. We sat upright, our

hunched, white-gowned bodies flinching with every new attack. Someone asked, "Do you think a tornado is coming?" None of us answered. We were too frozen by the unrelenting stream of booms that filled our room, vibrating our twin beds. I worried that one of the trees might be sliced in two by a lightening strike, and that half of the trunk with its towering branches would crash into a long pane of window and onto us in our beds. It was rare that anything woke up all of us in the black of night, and I wondered if we should be taking cover somewhere.

Then, a figure appeared in the frame of our doorway, a ghostly white apparition, and hurried down the aisle between our beds. It was Marianne, one of the older postulants who had completed college before she entered. She sat on the last bed in the row, the one right next to mine. She told us that she had to get to Sister Catherine Ann, a professed sister who was our dorm mother, something like a resident assistant in a college dorm. Sister slept in the room right at the end of our aisle of beds, one bed from mine. The door to sister's room was right next to the bed where Marianne was sitting.

All of us liked Sister Catherine Ann; she smiled at us with genuine sympathy or understanding when she passed one of us in the halls. Plus, she was younger than the usual sister living at the Motherhouse. We came to know, however, that she had an inoperable brain tumor and needed to be in a quiet and calm place.

I was intrigued with her, but so busy that I did not speculate too much on her past and present situation. She had a very quiet way about her, and I would not have approached her to talk, other than a short greeting, because we simply did not chat with the professed sisters who lived on campus. I rarely saw her come in or out of her room, and her door was closed on this night.

In spite of the storm, Marianne's voice rang out plaintively, "I have to get to her. She's afraid of storms. She told me tonight that she was afraid to go to bed because we were going to have a terrible storm."

I tried to understand this. When had Marianne talked with Sister Catherine Ann? How did she manage this? None of us had a friendship with a professed sister at the Motherhouse. Sister Catherine Ann had obviously confided in Marianne, and I wondered in awe how this situation, in which she pursued a friendship that was not sanctioned by our postulant mistresses, came to be.

We heard the fear and worry in her voice when she turned her body to face our beds and cried, "I know she needs my help, someone's help! She shouldn't be alone in there."

The postulant in the bed where Marianne sat said quietly, "How do you know she's in there? Maybe she decided to stay in chapel during the storm. She might be in chapel."

Marianne considered this for a few seconds and then turned to stare at the door. To our horror, she rose and grabbed the doorknob to open it. The jangling of the locked door added a new and frightening dimension to the situation. I felt each of us intake a gulp of air and freeze. What now?

Marianne looked at us, looked at the door as if it was a completely astonishing object and croaked, "She never locks her door. Something is wrong. She's in trouble."

At this, she began knocking and calling Sister Catherine Ann's name. The storm still raged outside our windows, but we could hear the thin cries of Marianne, her lips touching the door as she spoke.

"Sister Catherine Ann, it's me, Marianne. Open the door. Please open the door. I'm right here. I know you're afraid of the storm. Please let me in."

We waited. Marianne continued her pleas. We watched the door like in the story from high school: *The Lady or the Tiger?* Nothing happened.

She turned from the door, her eyes and hands wildly darting

about. She sat again on the mattress, clearly shaken, and asked the postulant on the bed, "What can I do? I have to get to her. I know she's frightened. I have to get her door open."

This was too much. I wondered if every postulant was thinking as I did at that moment, which was: How can this be happening right now? And, then, thank God she's not sitting on my bed and asking me this question.

Several moments passed. We heard Marianne's sighs and sounds of distress. Finally, tentatively perhaps, because even she did not believe it, the girl beside Marianne offered, "Well, she might be sound asleep. She could be fine in there, just sleeping through the storm. Maybe she took some medicine to help her sleep. She wouldn't hear you then."

It was pretty lame and Marianne did not buy it. "I'm going to Sister Louis Edmond. She has to have a key. I have to get someone to help me."

A low, audible gasp rose up from the ten or more beds in our room. Marianne stood, looked at us all in a sweeping motion as if to ask for help or sanction, and started for the door.

Donna, the postulant in the bed directly across from mine, looked around at all of us to see if we would let this pass. After all, Sister Louis Edmond was one of our postulant mistresses. In desperation, she put her arm out and said, "You can't do that. You can't get Sister Louis Edmond up in the middle of the night for this. You've got to wait till morning."

Marianne stopped then and said to no one in particular, "It's all right. I know I'll probably get in trouble, but I have to do this." And she was gone.

Sister Catherine Ann's room was on the other side of the wall behind my headboard. In the heavy silence that now hung over our heads, I tried to figure out what might be going on beyond that wall. Was Sister Catherine Ann there? Was she too ashamed to come out and let us see her all disheveled and frightful? Was she concerned about getting Marianne in trouble since she had confided in her? I wished I could do something to help, but at this point, I felt very unsettled and didn't want to think of the possibilities beyond the wall.

None of us spoke. Donna caught my eye once and shook her head back and forth, a grave look on her face. I figured that at any moment Sister Louis Edmond would march into the room, and we might be severely admonished for this bizarre commotion so I dared not talk. I could tell from the faces around me that we all waited in fear, for the sister behind the door and for the appearance of our postulant mistress.

Of course, we would all feel somewhat guilty about this nighttime disturbance of profound silence, as if we had approved the incident merely because it occurred in our room. Besides, many of us had experienced Sister Louis Edmond's stern response to nonsense or disobedience.

Eventually, we lay back down and waited, eyes opened, ears perked for any sound. I felt so spooked that if the unmistakable click of a lock had jangled at sister's door, I might have screamed or hid under the bed or run from the dorm. I actually welcomed the sight of Sister Louis Edmond as she walked swiftly into our dorm in her nightgown; her head focused hard on the ground before her as she approached the locked door.

Marianne followed closely at sister's elbow, her eyes searching for the door; her face creased with concern and remarkable determination, considering the boldness of her request. I wondered just what words she used, what approach she took to get Sister Louis out of her warm bed on this menacing night. Sister Louis jiggled the doorknob and called for Sister Catherine Ann a few times. She waited, her head still down, never once glancing our way. She called her again, somewhat louder. Apparently, she did not have a master key for the building.

Finally, she turned to us and said, "Sister Catherine Ann is not answering. We all need to calm down and get some rest." She took Marianne gently by the arm and they left our room.

Morning couldn't come quickly enough for me. When I awoke, my shoulders were tightened into my neck and my hands were clenched. The little rest I had came only after I talked myself into accepting that Sister Catherine Ann might be fine after all, snug and asleep. I walked into chapel that morning like someone in a time warp; the night had been surreal, but here we were, ready to close our eyes in our pews and try to connect with God, try to experience his love and grace in our hearts during our half hour of meditation.

My eyes fastened on the choir stalls at the front of the chapel. I searched for Sister Catherine Ann's place, wishing with all my heart that she would be kneeling there, her hands calmly in her lap. But it was empty, a glaring void in that fortress of white and black. She didn't appear either, when we stood and turned as one to face each other and chant Matins, our beautiful song of praise for the Lord's new day.

It was then that we hunted for and held each other's eyes—those of us who had spent part of last night with Marianne in our dorm—the pall of doom framing our red and tired lids and the dread of Sister Catherine Ann's absence pulling our minds from the comforting Psalms of David into the frightening possibilities now taking shape.

After Mass we filed down to the refectory for breakfast. Sister Catherine Ann had not made it to the most important part of our day. What could be so wrong that she had not even come down to chapel for Mass?

My stomach, wide-awake now and very empty, churned with rising alarm. We all knew that although sister might have lain awake during the night with the storm, she would have at least tried to attend Mass.

After breakfast I walked out of the refectory, still musing over the night and Sister Catherine Ann. I caught Donna's saddened eyes and recalled immediately that it was our week to dust and sweep the dorm. I stopped abruptly, mouthed, "Oh, my God," and leaned against the wall.

Walking into the dorm and confronting the scene of our fearful night was the last thing I wanted to do right then. Donna hurried to me and linked her arm under mine. Her round face, so open and kind looking, always reminded me of a gentle, wise grandmother. She had the permanent worried look and bustling movements of a mother, yet she could laugh heartily like a young girl.

She bowed her head and turned toward me, her arm taking charge of my steps as we made our way up the stairs to the first floor.

"Let's get our cleaning over with. I'll be with you the whole time. We'll be OK," she said.

Neither of us wanted to enter the room. We huddled at the entry, our eyes scanning the empty and ominously quiet space. Even in our fear, we were drawn to sister's door and there on the floor sat her breakfast tray: the stainless-steel lid over the plate; the coffee covered with a small saucer; the orange juice; the carton of white milk. It hadn't been touched.

We backed up at the sight of it sitting there so hauntingly, as if it were an armed bomb. I grabbed Donna in panic and begged, "We don't have to clean the dorm now. We can skip it for a week, right?"

She looked around at the dust balls on the floor, the smudges on the dressers. I saw the tension lining that creased, pudgy face.

"Let's clean fast and get it over with."

She handed me the dust mop and I whisked it under beds and dressers, my eyes darting back to Sister Catherine Ann's door and the breakfast tray after every sweep. Donna wiped the dressers, lifting each object hurriedly, clanking it back down in her rush. We never said anything, but both of us seemed to know that Sister Catherine Ann might not be alive in that room beyond our dormitory wall.

Later that afternoon, someone heard that a key was secured and sister's door was opened. By evening our mistress told us the sad news that sister had died.

Sister Louis Edmond seemed especially reserved and sad, but did not mention a word about the warnings of Marianne in our room the night before. In the two days before her funeral, we talked endlessly about how the sisters found her.

There were two versions of her position in death. One was that she died standing up, her arms above her head holding the wall—the wall behind my bed. The other, just as chilling, had sister kneeling toward her headboard with her hands clutching it. We never knew for sure which one, if either, was the true vision of her in death, and we never knew what caused her death; neither of our postulant mistresses discussed it at first.

We attended her funeral in chapel, walking in the procession to the graveyard beyond the infirmary, and said the prayers for the dead. That was supposed to suffice, I guess, in soothing any sadness or grief we might have had at her passing. It was the philosophy of the time. The best cure for disappointment or sadness was a stiff upper lip, busy hands and quiet meditation. Talk only expanded the sorrow and led to self-pity and self-involvement.

Marianne became awfully quiet; she held her grief inside of her like a hurt child, very carefully and protectively. We sat and talked around her and tried not to leave her alone.

In small groups, we whispered our theories of sister's death, a topic we were unable to exhaust. Did she die of fright, her heart pounding and thundering right along with the storm until it could take no more? Did she have some premonition that she would be in trouble with the tumor—some sign like a terrible headache, or nausea, or pressure that pushed on her scalp? Is that why she confided in Marianne? Did the tumor hemorrhage in a great burst of light in her head, which caused her to grab the wall or her headboard?

I wonder how many of us who were in that dorm might still be as haunted by sister's death as I am. And even though I have always wished that Marianne had been able to open that door, I understand, too, that Sister Catherine Ann did not want Marianne to enter her room.

Perhaps sister had pangs of guilt later that evening and wondered why she had involved such a young woman in her secret terrors. We'll never know if sister heard us, if she was still alive when her door rattled with knocks, if Marianne might have come just in time to be with her and offer comfort. Mysteries like this one are never easy to let go.

CHAPTER 19

A Postulant Vacation

A T THE BEGINNING OF JUNE, after our classes at the college were finished for the semester, and our crisp white muslin habits had been stitched near to perfection, we headed to an island for two weeks.

It was a real island with a summer camp owned, to our surprise, by the sisters of our order. I never really understood how we could "own" something with the vow of poverty and all, but figured someone gave us this camp. So, what could we do but take it?

Imagine: two whole weeks without a rigorous schedule, without classes, without duties, without all the pressures of getting ready to take the habit in August. We would get to wear shorter skirts rather than the ones that hit our ankles, different shirts (which were not our standard black, long-sleeve kind), sneakers without socks (no brogans), and a modified, shorter veil.

And, if that wasn't enough to send us over the top, we found out that this island sat in the middle of Lake Erie, so we would have to take a ferry to get to it! It was pretty amazing stuff for girls who had not left the convent grounds except for dentist and doctor appointments and walks to a park just off our campus.

I am fortunate to have many photographs that my parents took because they drove a car full of us to the ferry. The photos tell the tale; without them I would not have guessed at our actual childlike frenzy from the deck of the ferry before we took off. We were girls gone wild with excitement. Like a nest of birds, our mouths were open, either yelling or talking or laughing, and we appear to have the energy to burst through the black and white images into the real world of flesh and blood.

There is constant movement on the deck: our bodies going every which way as we lean over the railing, bunches of us two-deep, wide-open smiles breaking through the bobbing faces. We look so much younger than our years; it surprises me.

I'm not sure which I was more excited about—the two weeks at Kelley's Island or the drive with my parents from the convent to the ferry.

My parents and I left the group as we waited for the ferry to depart and explored the surroundings, climbing up some of the huge white rocks for which Marblehead got its name. My dad and I stood in the middle of these giant boulders while my mother took our picture, and I hoped she would leave us after the click of the camera.

As if she could read my thoughts, she did just that. Some places can carry the heaviness of memory and import, and this trip up the rocks was one for me. My dad and I looked out at the rocky lake for a long stretch without a word. The sun and breeze were enough for us to take in, and my dad was never one for probing.

Finally, we spoke a few quiet words about the lovely day, the lake beaming back at us, the sun on our faces—clearly, neither of us wanted to break the spell. It was one of those spots of time. I had never felt so close to my dad, so much a kindred spirit. While it is quite difficult for me to describe the experience, it is not difficult to know when it is happening.

I have a picture that has stayed in my mind of myself at Kelley's Island on my hands and knees on a wooden floor. I'm in the parlor of the old mansion, which dominated the buildings on the grounds of the camp. It was no secret that we came to the island as hired help. Someone had to get the camp ready for the young girls who would come to the Catholic girl's camp for part of their summer. We postulants cleaned the cabins and bathrooms situated near the main building to prepare for them. And where could the sisters find a crew of sixty-plus young, healthy, able-bodied women who were willing to work for free?

We cleaned every speck of lawn, every activity building, all the camp dorms, the dining hall and every room of the main building. The entire estate reminded me somewhat of Miss Havisham's gritty old overgrown tomb of a house. Paint was peeling, floors were darkened by years of use and abuse, and the yard was a mess of leaves, tree limbs, and winter's debris.

Just as we were assigned duties at the Motherhouse, we were assigned a job on the island. The very lucky ones got the chapel, where they floated around with dusters and prepared the altar linens, the candles, and the flowers. Actually, they probably scrubbed floors and polished pews, too, but after a few days of my job, I grew irritated at their "chosen" status. The "lighter" jobs were almost always bestowed upon the older, calmer, and more serious postulants.

The rest of us raked the yards or trimmed hedges. We turned the ground for planting grass or flowers, painted buildings inside and out, cleaned each and every room and cabin, hung curtains, made beds, and even drove to the island's dump with the piles and piles of rubbish.

I would have loved an outside job; at least that way I could be in the sun, laughing and talking while I raked or gathered debris into small hills. Linda was lucky enough to be an outside worker. She spoke of loving the yard work and being outside, wishing that her mother could see the lovely rose gardens on the grounds.

In one letter she told her dad that he should hire the postulants to do the landscaping and painting of their home because they were so good at it! The fact is we knew that the sooner we were finished with our duties, the sooner we could play and have fun. We had the purest form of motivation.

While Linda was enjoying the sun's warmth on her back as she raked the yard, my days were spent looking at a wooden floor, my head only eight inches from its surface. I held a round tangle of steel wool in my right hand and rubbed the outer layer of darkened dirt off each plank, cleaning off the rubbery pieces of grime with a cloth and water.

The room seemed like a roller-skating rink from my vantage point. I did look up occasionally from the floorboards; I would let my eyes scale the heights of walls and ceilings, finishing with the crown molding. But when I dropped my head back down, my eyes would sweep past the baseboards and on to the endless floor stretching out in all directions.

My partner in this beast of a job would work from one side as I did the other, making sure we would end at a point of exit from the room. Every half-hour or so we'd sit cross-legged, holding and massaging our arms because they would just get too shaky to continue. I'd get light-headed, of course, from the pain, the heat, and the exertion. Truly, this might have been one of the nastiest jobs at the camp, and I was undeniably a complaining wimp through it all.

The next day we took our positions again, this time to sand the boards down till every spot was removed and the wood shone again in its pristine, unfinished state. Our buckets beside us, we then washed away the very fine particles of sawdust, which took quite a bit more effort than the steel wool grime. I wonder to this day if this is where I developed my true distaste of heavy-duty cleaning—big jobs like washing thirty or more screens or sanding and finishing furniture.

On the third day, we were ready to buff the same floor until the wood looked smooth and clear. The buffer machine was a hulking, gray monstrosity with a huge rotating brush that had a way of spinning out of my hands. The T-formed handle would press into my waist while I gripped the shafts with every bit of strength my puny form could deliver. I danced around that parlor while the machine veered left and right like a swerving car, pulling me along as I tried desperately to steady its jerking mass of metal in my hands. My stomach ached almost too much to laugh, but I often dissolved into giggles, at which time, seizing the opportunity, the buffer would skate away from my hands and career about in circles. Catching the wild, untethered buffer resembled roping and tying a greased pig.

In spite of my labor-intensive job, which did happily come to an end, there were some wonderful perks to this vacation. By far the best change was getting up at 7:15 instead of 5:10 every morning. We walked to the chapel, had a short Mass, and chanted the Office, omitting the half hour of morning meditation. We even skipped noon Office. We talked during meals and, I promise, the food tasted better.

Some of us, charged with this overabundance of freedom, forgot to set limits. Linda remembers that on the second day of camp she and another postulant decided to go touring the island on a couple of bikes they had found. Leaving the grounds of the camp, they were "lost" for two hours. Most of us had no idea they were gone, but the two-hour foray into the "wild" ended with a severe scolding for the two wandering postulants. That evening we were greeted with an announcement—we could leave the camp only with permission.

Although we had our work responsibilities, like helping in the kitchen for one of the meals, cleaning bathrooms, or some other necessary task, we did have many hours to play. Lake Erie awaited us right in the front yard. And just like our new outfits of colored shorter skirts, short sleeved tops and rubber-soled tennis shoes, each of us was handed an appropriately fitting bathing suit.

Who knew that the sisters had boxes of "civilian" clothes packed away somewhere for this trip? I wondered how they acquired them, and just where they bought them or found them. It was a strange, but happy, mystery, and I can't remember if anyone asked.

We did spend afternoons jumping and swimming through the waves in our bathing suits as we'd done for all of our growing up years. For me nothing had ever given a feeling of freedom and abandon more than riding the swell of a wave or diving into and through it like a sleek arrow. Linda told her mom that we "exhausted ourselves" in the water. I remember the prickly feeling of a burn on my face and shoulders in the evening at dinner, feeling sleepy and whipped, the smell of the lake still on my skin.

At times it seemed quite unreal, this quick change from the dutiful postulant/almost nun person I had been, to the girl on the island who wore a bathing suit, skipped pebbles, and walked around in bare legs and sneakers. Did I dare engage myself fully? I always had a difficult time changing gears with ease; besides, there was the sense that our fun was controlled and scheduled, not spontaneous. Spontaneity was the result of grabbing the moment, and I'm not sure that I allowed myself to do that as easily as my friends.

After dinner we gathered for some kind of entertainment. At times it was a long walk along the island's shore, but at others, it was a loosely prepared skit by some members of our group. We might sing some songs, recall a few of the funny incidents involving our friends by acting them out, have a talent show, or some kind of "campy" style production. Of course, I worked on one of our shows, but in true fashion, it did not raise any eyebrows or cause too much of a ruckus with the girls. No inside jokes that the mistresses couldn't understand but knew that they should.

Not to worry: enter Linda. She was the master of ceremonies for one of our productions about the camp. I can still find that long-ago image of her up in front of the cafeteria where we put on our shows. She was certainly a natural at comedy, but my picture of her is a wild one, as she elaborated on the various skits, mimicking our duties, the camp itself, or the restrictions imposed upon us. She laughed and forged ahead without a speck of censorship. It was, of course, wonderful and terrible all at once.

The next day at our morning meeting after Mass and breakfast, she was asked to stand up at her place. Her humor was pronounced to be inappropriate. This was Linda's second misstep at Kelley's Island, quite a feat for anyone. She did apologize for making us laugh at comments not suitable for us, but I did not notice a lessening of enthusiasm in the days we remained at Kelley's. Linda had probably accepted her fate by this time—she was simply unable to think like a reserved, prudent-sister-in-the-making. I admired her and worried about her at the same time.

One evening after dinner, our postulant mistresses announced that we would be going on an adventure, a walk along the rocky shore of the lake to see what we could find.

Our group of rather oddly dressed campers straggled along the white rocks, having fun jumping to the next boulder and climbing up the groups of larger ones, all the while checking our footing when the rocks created a challenging walkway. Chatting, laughing, and stopping every now and then to examine some interesting specimen on the ground, our progress was halted in this natural manner. So relaxed and easy, we blended with each other and the flow of our progress like so many birds flying together, leaderless yet in tune with the smallest shift of motion around them.

I can see the rocks under my feet even today, probably because I replayed that step so many times, the one just before my shift off the rock where my foot wedged itself, curling my toes in half. My entire body plunged over and onto that foot, stuck and reeling with pain. I took off my shoe and massaged the bottom of my foot beneath my toes.

One of our mistresses appraised my foot for a few minutes. "Looks like you've just sprained it. Keep walking and it'll work itself out."

I've already admitted to being a wimp and a whiner, but have I said that I was pretty much a safe kid, one who avoided disaster in the form of breaks and hospital emergency rooms? I'd never had this kind of pain that surged up from my toe in rhythmic spasms. Later that night in bed, I elevated my foot on pillows, but sleep did not come nor did any relief from the "toothache" in my toe.

In the morning, I was assigned to the kitchen and I dreaded walking into the cafeteria on the heel of my left foot, a real cripple who would drag down our team. When the cook saw me hobbling, she stopped what she was doing and ordered me to sit.

"What have you done, my dear?" she said.

After examining my long middle toe she said, "Well, I think it's broken, but there's not much you can do except avoid standing on it."

She brought a chair outside the kitchen door, asked a postulant to bring another chair, helped me sit down, and gently lifted my leg to the chair like my own mother might have done. Before I knew it, aspirin and water were in my hand.

"Take two every four hours and try to stay off that foot."

I sat outside in the sun with a pot of potatoes to peel—my contribution to our lunch or dinner. It was funny, and I've found this to be universally true, that even though the pain abated somewhat after the aspirin, I really felt so much better about dealing with it because of the cook's few minutes of attention.

Our two weeks at Kelley's Island came to a close and, within hours, we were back on course to taking our vows in August. My schedule was full with summer classes, and, in addition, I was plunged back into the details of our reception: the intricate planning with my parents, as well as the particulars of the ceremony itself; including the music, the Liturgy, the protocol associated with entry into the chapel, change of clothes, re-entry into the chapel, positions I would take and ceremonies I would participate in during reception.

Our mistresses spent most of our morning instruction classes briefing us on the details of the ceremony, but practice in Lumen Chapel would consume hours and hours. Time was snatched here and there when I first began practicing, and after my classes were finished, we practiced for longer stretches of time.

I wonder if our morning instruction classes and the hours spent practicing in Lumen Chapel amounted to a total of sixty-six hours. If so, that would be one hour for each bride on our large wedding day.

This rigorous schedule left me little time to think and worry about what I was doing, and the campus was full of so many sisters, young and old, many of whom I knew. The distractions proved a good thing, I guess. I would only have continued to fret about my choice, and I would not have changed my course in spite of the worry.

The reception train was chugging, then moving like a bullet, and the idea of getting off was lost like the flashing windows of my days' activities.

How many brides jump off that train? Not many, and not me either. When I wasn't studying for my classes or practicing for our reception ceremony, I could get lost in the beauty of summer at the Motherhouse. I really allowed, chose even, to be pulled into the smells and sights around me when I had a chance to be outside. The huge trees swayed in the breeze, and the flowering bushes lit up the sidewalks. I found a few times in my busy schedule to just sit on the lawn and breathe in the air. Nature gave me a peaceful place to fall when I needed to get away from those all-encompassing hours of practice and planning for reception into the novitiate, a reception that I both anticipated as well as dreaded as the days closed in on me.

CHAPTER 20

The Final Stretch

March 13, 1964

Dear Miss Linda Brandies,

It is a great joy for me to learn that you have decided to apply for admission to the novitiate, and I am enclosing all the forms to be completed and returned to me with the other documents....

...I am sure that you are deeply grateful for the precious gift of your vocation and that you are eager to do all in your power to make ready for the service of the King. Earnest prayer, frequent reception of the sacraments, obedience to your confessor's directions, and daily offering of yourself to God are the means that will increase your love for Him and prepare you for the day of your consecration....

Sincerely yours in Christ,

Mother Mary Jean

If Linda's mother had not saved documents like this one—
a letter confirming Linda's application to become a novice—I
may not have remembered that we actually had to apply (and
could be refused) for entrance to our second year of training
as a semi-cloistered novice. I did not include the entire letter
and I changed the names, as I have been doing throughout this
memoir, but the wording is exactly as it occurred back in 1963,
five months before the day we would accept the habit and veil
of the Sisters of St. Dominic of Adrian, Michigan.

Your "consecration;" the enormity of that word: "To dedi-
cate solemnly to a service or goal" is how the dictionary defines
it. We understood the idea of consecration because we had been
baptized, made our first Communion, our confirmation, and
our first confession, but those were only baby steps of commitment—not like marriage and certainly not like giving ourselves
totally to God. Accepting the habit and veil was a major step;
it was Holy Orders. We would live a life of holiness dedicated
to God's will and not our will, live in an order of like-minded
people, and take direction from our superiors. How could we
even begin to grasp what this meant?

My friends and I talked secretly about our anxieties, and I
remember feeling a mixture of sadness and fear when the shaki-
est of our group confided that she didn't think she could do it.
Through that summer before our reception and taking of the
habit in August, I was beyond confidences, except for a very
few close friends. It was much too frightening to speak aloud
the words I perceived as weak. The hint of failure loomed large
above me, of being thin-skinned, spineless. There it was, the real
issue—the dreadful stigma of leaving.

The brave ones spoke with our postulant mistresses about
their doubts, serious doubts, but they usually stuck it out.
I never wanted to share my instability with our mistresses. I
heard what happened to others, a little nudge or severe sermon

would bring many of them back to piety and faith in God who had asked this sacrifice of them. One of my good friends who wanted to leave several times during our postulancy was told over and over how selfish she was. She stayed and, selfish or not, she did leave years later.

So, did we ever have moments of real spine-tingling joy and ecstasy, a feeling that we were infused with light; the light of God? Yes, some of us made this claim. I wanted so much to feel love, to know the whole of giving, that I would create a warm fire inside me and make it be Christ who touched me. Could my vocation be real if I never felt his love lifting me, choosing me? I needed a few signs, some spiritual glow to keep me going, and if it didn't just surprise me and happen spontaneously, I generated my own rapture.

Divided as I might have felt inside, there was no way I could desert my vocation after only one year as a postulant. I couldn't turn my back on God so quickly. For me it would be like someone leaving a marriage in the very first year of living together, after all the showers, the presents, the huge expensive ceremony, and the generous involvement of family and friends. What kind of person does such a thing? Who gives up so easily, without a backward glance and hours of consideration? Hadn't we been warned about this all of our lives? The answer was easy: a childish, immature, and selfish person does such a thing.

Fortunately, we were distracted from these periods of exaggerated angst with a few mundane concerns that had to be addressed before reception into the order—but not before we made a ten-day retreat. Very soon after we received our letters of acceptance into the novitiate (I don't think anyone was refused), we were plunged into ten days of silence. Our retreat was a requirement of canon law, and if nothing else could bring us to a decision; these ten days might make or break us as members of the church's elite.

In her letter home, Linda seemed amazed by the prospect, "Ten days of silence...imagine that." I'm sure my parents could not imagine it. I, who had spent hours on the telephone with our party line interrupting me in desperation to make a call, who lived for my friends and outings that left endless words and sentences riding the wind at my back. How could I be silent for even one day? Well, I could, but maybe not with ease and joy.

Nonetheless, I would be silent and alone. A proving ground for the strongest of us, I had nothing to do but ruminate, hash over all the shapes of my indecisions night and day. This retreat cemented my insecurities for the months to come.

Finally, a real distraction came in May. We were informed that we would have to take a canonical test. At this point, any relief from introspection was welcomed; I had sunk pretty low when it came to happy diversions. With eagerness, I jumped into the task of memorizing the one hundred plus catechism questions, which each of us had to answer as preparation for the exam.

Again, Linda dropped a line in one of her letters, "I never knew women had to take a test before receiving the religious habit." How innocent and childlike we were. Everything about this life was new and incredible to us.

Who would have guessed that we'd need a dowry before our reception? We were about to vow our love to Christ, our bridegroom; to wear a white gown; to receive a new name. Shouldn't we follow the social customs of most marriages, minus the honeymoon?

Our year of training as a Postulant was completely funded by the Adrian Dominicans. My parents did not pay tuition for college at Siena Heights or for room and board at the Motherhouse. I recall that my dad was happy to give the fifty dollars to marry me off, but Linda worried about the strain it would put on her parents with such a large family.

She tried to make it easier by suggesting to her mom and dad,

"I will need very little from you before reception. I do need fifteen dollars. This is a dowry. It is required and must be received before reception day. If you would like, I can have the remaining amount of money from my income tax return transferred to my dowry. It is about thirty dollars."

This arrangement only amounted to forty-five dollars, so Linda must have had five dollars lying around. We had to tell our parents that this was "required" and "must" be received before we were to make our reception and become novices. Would any of us have been kept back if the check didn't arrive on time?

There was more to come, however. The "very little needed from you" grew. I needed a black belt for my long tunic, a very plain belt to circle my waist and keep me from tripping on the gown. My parents also needed to find me a bathrobe to cover my body more fully from neck to heel, quite different from the skimpy one I wore as a postulant. The robe had to be floor length and white, no colors in the novitiate cloister and no skin showing, except my face and hands. This cumbersome bathrobe for the novitiate was a night-time "habit," welcome in the winter months when leaving my bed brought a shock of artic air to my body but most undesirable when I was soaked with rivulets of perspiration in the middle of the summer. I had to explain and describe in letters all of these directions to my parents concerning the additional items. I planned my wedding long distance, and thankfully, my parents came up with the goods.

As the summer languidly offered long days of warmth and blue skies, I continued to dash off letters to my parents with additional requests. One request was the rosary we would wear from our belts; the ones I always loved to watch swishing back and forth on the belts of the sisters in grade school. A long chain of black beads ran up and down at the side of their habits, and then only chain, and back to black beads, over and over again for what seemed like miles, with a huge cross placed right in the middle of the biggest loop. It was the only jewelry a sister had permission to wear other than her ring at final vows.

For some reason our rosaries were to have been made by the sisters at our high school who were also Adrian Dominicans. It may have been a welcoming tradition to do this for us as new novices, or simply a gesture on the part of the nuns who had taught us. At some point our mistresses were informed that the sisters would not make them this time. We had quite a few girls entering the order that year, and it may have been too daunting a task to take on for all of us.

So, in my hurry-up letter home, I gave all the particulars for this very specific kind of rosary. Most rosaries are only five decades long; this one had to be fifteen decades! In addition, it had to have a Dominican joiner and a black ebony wood crucifix with silver-plate edging. I guess our rosaries, like our new lives, were one size and shape fits all. Imagine if some of the sisters had gold and jeweled crosses, beads that shone like Swarovski crystal.

Linda said in one of her letters that my mom knew where to purchase our "special order" rosaries, which is amazing to me. I wonder how long she had to search and how far she drove to secure mine.

The best part of our preparation for the novitiate did not require money, religious articles, or clothing from our parents. It was the simplest, yet most exciting preparation of all; we were required to decide on three names we would like for our life as a sister. Our Mother General would choose only one of them for us, of course, but we had a real say in the matter. Think of it: we were each given the chance to rename ourselves without any bad feelings from parents who might feel a sting of rejection in the betrayal of our baptismal name, and without raised eyebrows from friends who might think we had suddenly gotten an attitude. For sure, it had to have "Sister" in front of it, but that was expected.

My baptismal name, Patricia, was just fine, but no one other than the nuns at school called me that, especially my Latin teacher, who loved to declare over and over that it meant "of noble birth." Patty was all right as well. My family had chosen this as my nickname, I guess. But kids in the neighborhood soon found rhymes to taunt me, like "Fatty Patty." Of course, my eight-year-old plumpness didn't help. By high school, I was Pat, only Pat. Like "pat of butter" or "pat on the back." It stuck. It was short and easy, and I never really liked it.

Here was a chance, a gift sent to me, to find something dramatic, something more like me, something theatrical. It was all so easy, a no-brainer. In high school I had discovered through my Latin classes that the name Peter, leader of the apostles, was *Petre* in Greek. The feminine form would be *Petra*, with a long *a* in the first syllable. Not only was my dad's name Peter, but this was a name I loved! I said it over and over. Sister Petra. Sister Petra. Petra. My dad might be touched, and I would be reborn.

We had to write down, however, three different names for selection by our Mother General. We were cautioned that another nun might take one of the names we had chosen, and one might not be suitable. So I found another name I could live with, but not love as much as Sister Petra. I chose Sister Marie Jeanne for my mother whose name was Marie Pauline Jeanne. Now I had both of my parents covered. My final choice must not have had any significance to me because I have no recollection of it. Perhaps out of desperation I wrote down Sister Petra Jeanne or Sister Jeanne Petra. Luckily, I did not get my third choice. I had to wait like everyone else to find out which name I would have, but in my head it was always Sister Petra.

Linda was not as excited about choosing a name as I was. In fact, in one of her letters home she complained that she was bothered by this practice. She wanted to keep her own name! She wondered how we could so easily discard the name of our baptism, the name that actually brought us into God's family. Why would that name become less important? I am amazed that this part was not censored.

Eventually, Linda settled for her oldest and youngest brothers' names. She asked for Sister Paul David or Sister David Paul. Her third choice could have been a name that she knew someone else already had; that way she would be less likely to get it. Her choices would be a reminder of her strong connection with her brothers and a tribute to them as well. Although I admired her sentiment, I would never have wanted a man's name and chose Petra because there was a feminine form of the name Peter in Greek. Taking the vow of chastity was a big enough sacrifice, why would I need to take a man's name to boot, as if I were now a person with undetermined sexuality?

On the day before reception into the novitiate, Mother Mary Jean gathered us together to give us our names. Our postulant mistresses did not think it wise for us to hear the bishop pronounce our sister name for the first time in front of the entire congregation; a packed house with all of our families and friends. Considering our heightened state of anxiety, tears of distress or jumps of joy would be distracting and even embarrassing for everyone. It was much better to give us a night to get used to our future names; we could try it out hour after hour and lessen our heartbreak, if that was our response.

So that morning we stood outside on the Motherhouse lawn, our young, eager faces raised up to Mother Mary Jean as she stood on the top step in front of those huge oak doors. The sun was shining and she appeared to me like some goddess all in white who would bestow upon us our new selves. As always, she looked at us with great kindness and patience. We fidgeted and bounced around until she began, and then, with control we didn't know we possessed, we listened to the names, noting our friends' names with a turn and wide smile if it was the preferred one, or a furrowed sad brow of regret and concern if it was not. But, through it all, we were really waiting for our own turn. At least I didn't have to wait till the Zs.

I realized without the least bit of guilt that a lot was staked on this decision. Would I feel less dedicated as Sister Jeanne? Less likely to stay? Who knows? I heard her say Pat O'Donnell and then I heard "Sister" and "Petra," but something else had entered the space between them and it stopped me. Did I hear a "Marie"? My friends were smiling wildly at me so I knew they were happy for me. I was disappointed but tried to hide my feelings with broad smiles to those near me. Inside, I really felt that the Petra would be tainted with a Marie before it. What could have been wrong with just Petra? Yet when all of the names had been given, I noticed that some of my friends had been given a name they hadn't even listed. I didn't dare complain now.

When the final name had been pronounced, our mistresses excused us, and we let loose upon each other. Most of us were satisfied, and the thought that in just one day we would be using these names to summon our friends made us laugh and giggle until the final bell of the evening tolled and we kept silence. It had all the earmarks of my days of creative play—those lovely years of pretending, a little mother taking care of my dolls, a teacher bossing my teddy bears in class. Was I really going to walk into a church as Pat O'Donnell and come out with a white habit, a veil, and a new name? Was this the ultimate game of pretending?

After the naming ceremony, a group of us was walking across the lawn to the cafeteria for lunch. I looked up from our revelry and noticed Sister Louis Edmond watching us. We were huddled together as usual, the five of us who hung around, trying out our brand new names and attempting "nunly" poses.

When we approached her, she looked at me with one of her signature hard stares and remarked, "I hope you won't be like the first Sister Petra. She left after only a year."

The smiles dropped from our faces, and we looked at each other in confusion. What was she saying?

I looked at her stunned and surprised, "I didn't know there ever was a Sister Petra."

"Oh, yes," she said. "She was a very bright and talented girl. We had high hopes for her. Perhaps you will keep the name."

A light beamed in my head and I couldn't believe I pushed her untimely warning further. "Is that why I was given Sister Marie Petra instead of just Sister Petra?"

She smiled then but didn't answer me. Her body turned briskly on the path, which was her way of indicating that the conversation was over and we needed to move along. We followed her like little chicks, running almost to keep up, our earlier excitement and fun dissolved. I felt like a marked specimen. Who knew there was a history to this name? Four years later, when I had decided to leave, I thought of her veiled prediction. Was it a simple warning, advice to keep me on track? Or did she see something in me; something she saw in the other Sister Petra?

After my initial feeling of being slapped in public, of being singled out in front of my friends, I settled down a bit. Our postulant mistress had said that the first Sister Petra was talented, didn't she? And intelligent? Well, though I might not be in the league of an Evelyn (who was one of the smartest women I have known and one of the most modest to boot), I wasn't a total dunce either. It took some of the edge off her words. I wondered back then if the first Petra had loved literature, poetry and the theatre. I wondered if she too planned and directed plays. If so, how eerie it must have been when I asked for the same name. What are the odds?

We may have been giggling about our names the day before we made reception, but that was only a reprieve. The long journey to reception began with the details, and they could be crushing. None of these matters was handled on the phone or in person, of course, so we had to be writing home constantly in the months of June and July. We needed to know which members of the clergy our parents wanted to attend the ceremony other than the pastor of our church at home, who was automatically invited. We had to have a list of all of our family and friends who wanted to attend.

Linda, who had a big family, asked the mistresses for eight tickets. She instructed her family to be at the chapel (a very large church, actually) an hour before the ceremony in order to have good seats. We had to have a list of folks we wanted announcements to be sent to following our reception. We instructed our families about where they would eat after the ceremony (without us, of course) and when they could meet us.

Linda wrote without a hint of nonsense, "I will join you after dinner. We have to straighten our headgear, practice walking and handling a fifteen-decade rosary." God forbid if one of us tripped on the thing half-running to the outstretched arms of our parents!

The full extent of our shaping and formation into "religious-minded" beings is evident in a comment Linda made to her mother about our impending reception—clearly one of the biggest deals on our journey to sisterhood. I hear in Linda's words to her mother the unqualified change in her attitude from the high school girl of seventeen to the soon-to-be-sister-in-training at eighteen.

She scolds, "Mom, the ceremony for receiving the Dominican habit is called 'reception' not 'investiture.' This is not the Girl Scouts. It's called 'investiture' when a brownie becomes a girl scout."

The inference is blaring; we are seeking a higher and loftier state, and you must learn the language. It was a lot to ask, and our parents accepted their humble servant roles completely. How was it that now our lives dictated to them what they should do? Who were we to demand such attention?

I cringe at writing this now, but I know without a bit of doubt that my parents would have done anything to secure and further my vocation. My vocation was a call and a blessing from God for *all* of us in my family, as my father viewed it. My parents would have walked through fire if asked. I took it in stride as my due, as expected. I was still somewhat a child after all and had yet to learn many things about life and sacrifice, even though I was soon to be considered one of God's "chosen."

PART 3

Novice

Reception ceremony in Lumen Chapel when I took my vows and the habit. I am in the middle of the row of novices.

On the Motherhouse lawn with Fr. Schurman and my mother after the Reception ceremony. The tall priest talks on and on.

CHAPTER 21

He Has Set
His Seal upon Me

"He has set his seal upon me, to claim me for his love; to claim me for his love."

A LTHOUGH WE WOULD NOT KNOW it when we awoke on reception day August 4, 1964, the morning would soon shower us with a blazing sun and the bluest sky. In photos, my sisters Maureen and Margaret, and our friends were in short-sleeve or sleeveless tops, and bright rays fell everywhere; on our skin, our clothes, the grass, and the buildings behind us. It was the kind of day every bride might wish for.

Our reception service in Lumen Chapel was at ten in the morning. We would march in wearing white bridal "dresses" and veils, march out, and then reenter with our "sister" clothes: habits with headgear, veils, and footwear.

Each of us was assigned a room for dressing and then undressing and dressing again. We had help; that was the good

part. After taking off my very black Puritan-style postulant outfit, I slid over my head and shoulders the plainest white satin,
long-sleeved top, which felt cool and sleek against my skin—
quite a change from the nubby black shirt I had just removed.
Then, I stepped into the floor-length, gathered satin skirt. I had
no belt to cover the elastic at my waist, but I didn't even consider the idea of becoming a fussy bride, demanding belts and
other adornment—ruffles on the skirt or sequins and a bit of
lace, maybe a lovely pearl necklace as many brides might want.
It would have been a worthless, not to mention worldly, desire.
Would God care if I had a belt to cover the plain expandable
waist of my skirt? And would he find me more acceptable if my
gown were trimmed and my neck adorned with jewels?

Our helpers, the outgoing novices who would soon be
leaving for parts unknown as full-fledged sisters, were fussing around us, pulling on our blouses and skirts, securing our
buttons and then poofing up our veils. We were attended by
serious, deliberate faces, as if the novices had been told to keep
a religious demeanor, so that we wouldn't dissolve into hilarity
or something worse, like excitement.

It was not the wedding dress I had seen other brides wear, but
what could I expect? I was one of sixty-nine brides in this community marriage. Yet, the very basic quality of the gowns and
veils disappointed me, and one of my friends still remembers a
stain that dripped down the front of her white skirt. Regardless,
since our hair hadn't been cut yet, we actually appeared pretty
normal looking under our uniform, white net veils. Young and
thin, we did shine in the photos, innocent beauties with make-
up-less faces and natural-looking hair.

The high-heel shoes were the killer. They were very high
heels. Before I entered the convent, if I had even worn such
shoes, I did so infrequently. They looked like foreign objects,
pointing out dramatically in front of me. I wobbled horribly

as I prepared to attempt the walk to the chapel. It was clear to me that one false move and I'd see an ankle turn completely and some poor bride would crumple into a white mountain on the ground, grimacing in pain. How amusing it was to see a few brides leave the line for some lessons from another, more capable, heel handler.

The high heels were quite a risky choice for all of us, since our postulancy footwear for the past year had been the typical nun shoe—black, tie-up, leather brogans with thick, short heels. I wondered then, as I do now, just why the high heels? Wouldn't plain white flats have worked as well?

Perhaps the point had to be made that we were leaving behind the sexy and luring apparel of our past, worldly lives. Certainly, the dress did not send that message, but for sure those high, narrowed-to-the-sharpness-of-a-bird's-beak heels did resemble to me the chattel of the world. I had seen shoes like these in many magazines, models posing in very short skirts advertising the desired look—long, shapely legs.

In my case, it was inconsequential: before I entered the convent, I hadn't seriously tried to look sexy. I tried to impress a few guys, but not in overt showy ways as other girls did with low-cut blouses or short, tight skirts. I flirted with words or looks, but not often because I was quite shy around guys.

Our entrance into Lumen Chapel must have been like an otherworldly experience for our families and friends. Marching through the doors at either side of the altar, we traveled in single file down the outside aisles to the very back of the chapel, and then we continued, two abreast, up the middle aisle. I was toward the back of our long line.

This bridal procession of white-clad, angelic-looking women—eyes cast modestly to the floor, hands holding a white Missal neatly in front of them, faces starkly serious and devout—must have seemed endless and rather heavenly. If I had

felt before this ceremony that my impending marriage was surreal and something far away and distant from me, when I was
beckoned by the words, "Come, O promised bride of Christ;
receive the crown Our Lord has destined for you from eternity,"
I was awakened soundly to the stark reality of the moment.

The choir began to sing the beautiful words of Psalm 44, and
in one sweeping movement, each of us postulants was sprawled,
facedown, on the floor in the Venia, the practice of lying face
down and kissing the floor. A swish, a drop, and a muffled thud
were all those in the chapel might have heard or seen. When I
reached the tiles below me, I could hear an audible sigh of shock
and wonder from the congregation. My face and body, so close
to the tile floor, could not relax, and we lay there for so many
minutes. Only the words of the Psalm gave me something different to ponder, other than the heat of the chapel and the drops of
moisture falling to the very small space between my face and the
now wet floor:

Hear, O daughters, and see and turn your ears.
Forget your people and your father's house.
So shall the King desire your beauty.
For he is the Lord your God.

Such romantic words should have brought me back to my
commitment, back to the marriage theme. Still, it was a very
long Psalm and my submissive gesture was becoming painful.
Eventually, after my contact with the tiled floor had reached
the status of a long-term and most undesirable relationship, the
music of the Psalm ended.

I rose from the waist first, as we were instructed to do, and
brought my left knee up, my hands clearing the long white skirt.
Finally, I pushed off with my right foot, my head facing forward
confidently, until I stood, shakily at best, on those pencil-thin
heels. Our rise from the floor, in this completely prostrate

position, was supposed to be one fluid movement, and we practiced it over and over until every postulant could lift herself from
the floor without tripping on her skirt and falling with a thud
back to the floor or worse, becoming entangled in the skirt so
that she could not move.

The ceremony was two-hours long, and we had a full Mass.
We received Communion from Archbishop Deardon himself,
our hands folded against each other in perfect symmetry. At the
end of Mass, each of us approached the altar, walking to the far
left side where the archbishop was seated. Young second-grade
girls who looked like mini-brides in their First Communion outfits of white lace and ruffles (more elaborate than ours for sure),
led us one-by-one to the sanctuary, a small plate in their hands.

I waited my turn before advancing toward Archbishop
Deardon and Mother Jean who was standing beside him. As
I moved into place in front of the archbishop, my young girl
beside me, Mother Jean softly gathered a few locks of my hair
in her hands and held them out for the archbishop, so that he
could snip them. The curl of hair was dropped onto the plate
and, as I turned to walk back, my hands folded like an obedient
servant, the young girl slid the strands into a large urn.

While I was wearing the wedding gown of an earthly bride,
performing this final ritual signified my withdrawal from all I
had known. I was leaving my family and friends, and spiritually
I was leaving the world, its possessions, desires, and values. From
now on I would be cut off from the possessions and charms of a
secular society.

Returning to the same room in which I had dressed in my
wedding gown, I found my habit (the very one I had spent the
summer sewing), hanging as neatly pressed and folded as I had
left it back in May. Another flurry of arms and legs ensued as I
discarded the now sweat-stained blouse and wrinkled skirt for
an even heavier fabric. For the change into the habit, there were

layers and layers to put on: undershirts that covered my arms; the tunic or gown which hung from neck to toe; the long scapular, draping down to the hem of my tunic; and the wide collar covering my breasts. And this was the easy part.

Waiting for me and my sensitive forehead and cheeks was the headdress with the cotton *guimpe*, which the novice pulled up from my chin and attached at the top of my head. The sides of the guimpe covered the sides of my face in a straight line from my jaw to the outer line of my eyebrows. Then she placed the hard plastic headgear on my forehead where it immediately dug into my skin. Finally, she pinned the veil to the top of the guimpe fabric. I felt like I was trussed and all tied up. The novice pulled the material of the guimpe so tight, it was hard to move my jaw, and the collar around my shoulders had a two inch neck cover, which she fastened so snugly that I had trouble swallowing.

Yet there was one bright spot for me in this anxiety ridden makeover. I never would have thought when I purchased those ugly leather brogans back in the summer after high school graduation, which had me laughing at home with my friends as I modeled them that I would be relieved, happy even, to fling off those high heels and put my aching feet instead into their soft, leather-sided soles. At least my feet would feel happy.

I'm not sure what the congregation did while I was struggling with my new attire, but there had to be a ten-minute lapse until the last bride left the chapel to be twirled into her new habit by every helper available. I imagine that the choir softened the interlude with lovely music, while our parents and families might have felt excited, even a little nervous.

Was my mom wondering if her little girl would really look as if she were a nun, someone like the sisters from church or school? And would she worry a little bit if I might still be the huggable kid she raised? Would she wonder if she would be able to really talk with me again, the way we always had?

I was rustled into my multiple layers with assembly-line precision—including the black belt, the very long rosary, and, believe it or not, a full-length, heavy black cape in August—and hustled out to the waiting line before I had a chance to see myself.

But I saw the effect of a guimpe on other postulants. I saw cheeks projecting out of those guimpes like hardy peaches. I saw all the marvelous magic of a crown of hair, which had previously softened the faces of some of my friends, become glaringly absent with the headdress. The natural beauties in our group looked angelic and pure and lovely, while the rest of us, those like me with large faces and features, lost any contrasting interest we managed to gain with our thick manes. Good thing I hadn't seen a mirror.

With my hands at my side under my cape, I marched into the chapel for the second time that morning, looking much the same as before except for my habit. When all of us had entered the chapel and taken our places in the aisles, our entire group descended to the floor in another even longer Venia.

This time, my headgear stopped my face from touching the floor, but after five minutes of pressing the hardened plastic to the tiles in such roaring heat, I felt its rounded forms begin to cave-in and crumple as I lay there. I had to lift my head to stop the denting, and then worked desperately to get my fingers under the plastic to push it back out. All this time I was lying on the floor and my neck ached from raising my head up from the tile and fussing with my plastic piece. Yet, I could do nothing but carry on.

Eventually, I rose and took my seat in the assigned pew, waiting my turn to approach the archbishop who would declare my new name to the congregation. Before this, however, the archbishop turned to us and said:

"O God, bless these veils which for love of you and of the Blessed Virgin Mary, we shall place upon the heads

*of your handmaids. Under your protection may they pre-
serve inviolate chastity of soul and body, so that in the
day of judgment they may deserve, as prudent virgins, to
follow you to the wedding feast of everlasting joy."*

My turn came and this time I stood alone, listening to his
words of solemn commitment and warning:

*Receive this veil, Sister Marie Petra, and carry it without
stain before the throne of Our Lord Jesus Christ to
whom every creature is subject in heaven, on earth,
and in hell forever and ever.*

I cringe at the harshness of this "prayer" to God to bless our
veils. No one had to tell us how we might "stain" our veil, but
back then, none of us would have thought of such a thing. Were
we better off entering this marriage with warnings of dangerous
consequences rather than a celebration of our commitment?

Soon, however, in unison, our group would recite the lovely
words: "He has set His seal upon me, to claim me for His love;
to claim me for His love." The mixed messages, of warning and
blessing were rampant but, luckily, they were probably lost on
most of us.

Barbara, a friend who left the convent a few years after I
did, amazingly expressed what I felt. She wrote in a letter, "I
didn't feel like I was feeling anything, more just numb and out
of it. Everything felt extremely surreal...like an out of body
experience."

However, the prayers continued to admonish us of the seriousness of our vow of chastity. We declared toward the end of
the ceremony:

*I love Christ, and I shall be His bride. Born of a Virgin,
conceived of the Spirit....Chaste in love, pure in touch, vir-
ginal in contact with Him. I am sealed with His ring, and
adorned with His jewels, and adorned with His jewels.*

Another prayer asks that the Lord bless us so that: "By your protection may they carry it [the veil] without stain before your throne...."

We were cautioned over and over to live without the stain of impurity, but the actual vow of chastity was not alluded to until our final prayer:

"May the protection of Thy loving kindness guard
Thy handmaids, O Lord. May they preserve inviolate by
Thy assistance the vow of chastity they have taken by
Thy inspiration."

This recurring drumbeat of the words *pure, chaste,* and *inviolate* during the reception ceremony is quite the opposite emphasis from the church's doctrine we studied in our classes. In class we focused on the three vows—poverty, chastity and obedience— the most important of which was obedience. Yet, our prayers on reception day mostly stressed purity, in both sexual thoughts and actions. It was as if a few of us might escape the walls of the cloister, run feverishly toward the city of Adrian (in or out of our habit), and wantonly search for a man.

I can only conclude that the church's centuries-old preoccupation with sex was shining through in our service, and that in some unnerving way our marriage to Christ, our spiritual bridegroom, was to be clearly distinguished from a physical marriage of a mere earthbound man and woman. Love and devotion were rarely mentioned in our marriage ceremony, when in reality, these two commitments were the goal of our life's work and discipline.

After the congregation uttered their last prayer and *amen,* I marched out of the chapel, away from my family and friends. No one threw rice. No one greeted us with hugs of joy outside of the chapel.

We had work to do, I guess, because I do not remember any lessons in handling our habit right after the ceremony. We had to practice walking? My rosary was hanging on my belt just as the novice draped it. The only thing I eventually learned was to make sure one of the loops did not drape too low. If it did, I might trip on it. The long slip and tunic were quite a bit of fabric swishing around my legs, but again, I realized after a few steps that I would not be running in this outfit or walking too fast. Getting our headgear straight took a long time with all of us, so on reception day I may have pulled it to the right or left to get it straighter, but I wouldn't dare take out a pin and have the whole thing fall off!

Eventually, all of our families found us, as Linda stated in her letter: "After dinner they [the sisters] will take you to the visiting area we have been assigned to. Some families will be on the front lawn of the Motherhouse and others will be in the back. There is nothing like Dominican hospitality."

If you had known Linda as I knew her, you might have found this last sentence totally out of character. Perhaps this was her way of apologizing to her family for the obvious separation of her life from theirs. Didn't the Psalm at the beginning of our reception tell us to "forget your people and your father's house"? Well, if that fact had not yet been driven home to either our families or us, it was sufficiently manifested in the logistics of this day.

Assigned to the Motherhouse lawn, my family and friends sat in a casual circle of lawn chairs. Some of the chairs looked familiar, and I figured that my parents brought them from home. I was uncomfortable being the center of attention, but they had all come to see me. In one photo, I had in my hands what appeared to be congratulatory cards. Cards. What might they have said? It was really quite unreal—all of it.

For instance, the women's clothes: every single woman wore a dress, the kind that was proper for afternoon luncheons, parties, or church. My sister Margaret looked serene (Wasn't that the way I was supposed to look?) as she sat next to me, her features soft in a steady smile, and my mother looked lovely in white and yellow. My aunts, who had come from Detroit and Windsor, were in a photo as well. I was touched at their effort to be with me, since they both had health issues. With them on either side of me, I appeared less stilted than I did in other photos, and I smiled broadly. Both of them strong Catholics, they hailed my choice and approved the more serious, less flighty change in my demeanor.

Yet my friends, my dear friends who supported me through each milestone in my journey to sisterhood—what could they be thinking? Gone was the girl from high school, and in just a matter of a year. Photos do not lie. In one, some of my school friends looked away at different scenes on the lawn, others seemed to work valiantly at conversation; it was clear that they were now on the outside, trying to find some common ground.

Father Schurman stood next to me in another picture, listening to the words of a tall priest. Right now as I write, I want to interrupt the priest and pull father aside. I want to tell Father Schurman how I really feel. Inside my stomach flutters and dips uncontrollably; I'm in a stunned state, watching myself like on a stage. I'm wondering why I'm here; if this is *me*, I don't know who I am. But I said nothing. I listened instead to the drone of the priest, my face almost pouty and sad. Taking any action would have been a giant leap for a girl frozen in place. And I was afraid, hanging on the large cord of the missionary's words, knowing that I had to go on. I had to give it a real try, not just the half-way try of being a postulant. I had to become a novice because it was the real thing.

Later that night, the ceremonial snip of one lock of hair by the archbishop would become a chop and drop of chunks of hair, all falling to the floor in thick circular curls or wide ropey wedges. I knew it was coming, the doom of it all, as I walked to the cutting room in profound silence; a silence I had kept since the evening bell had rung. There I took in the scene: my friends sitting in chairs spaced four-to-six-feet apart, heads down as if hiding, while one of the older novices, one of the same sisters who had so carefully helped us with our habits in the morning's quick change-of-dress, grabbed a swath of hair and clipped it clean from each novice's head.

I stumbled to my seat to wait my turn. I watched in shock as one of our group, a gal with the most beautiful, long, reddish-blonde hair—her signature feature for all of her eighteen years—sobbed loudly into her hands, her body making convulsive heaves while the novice forged on with her scissors until her head was a mass of stubby shoots.

I sat, hoping and praying that I'd get one of the better novice barbers, till I received a nod to be next in the cutting seat. Yes, some novices were kind and gentle, and clearly did not enjoy the task given to them. With relief, I noticed that my friend Dawn had a compassionate novice, who patted her shoulder and smiled encouragingly in between cuts. Dawn was crying openly but trying to stifle her sobs, and I hated to watch. Yet, I felt surprised at how many of my friends, including Dawn, who had always seemed indifferent when it came to their looks, were so very devastated by this final good-bye to their worldly, perhaps pretty, image of themselves.

My memory of this event, therefore, is more of watching than of participating. For me, the damage had been done already; the headgear and guimpe, which would now surround my face, had effectively "cut off" the thick, wavy mass that had framed my head for eighteen years. Losing my hair with the clip of the scissors was anti-climactic, because my face without hair already plunged out of the headgear in the starkest reality. Besides, with wavy hair like mine even the worst cut was not a tragedy. The unfortunate girls with straight hair suffered the most; there was no hiding the tufts that stood out like spikes every which way.

The real deal seemed to be this: During those twelve months as postulants, when alone in the bathroom in front of a mirror, we could always take off our short veils and strike a pose, turn our head to the side, our hair falling into our eyes, and look demurely into the face gazing back at us. Well, at least I did. My hair, peeking out around the veil, was the last vestige of femininity I could hold onto, since my breasts and young curves were shrouded in the black cape and the gathering folds of my skirt. Imagining that I could still be pretty in the postulancy may have been a major avoidance of reality on my part, but this new loss was clearly different.

When my last curl had fallen to the floor, the novice barber handed me a small, white bonnet to cover my head at night (since, as novices, our hair was not to be seen from now on). Hiding my butchered hair did nothing to heal the reality of my diminishing recognition of my female-self. It seemed as if I were now a different type of woman. Only my face and hands would be seen; everything else would be covered, my long lean body, my legs, my hair and curves. The parts of my body that enabled me to attract a man as well as have children were no longer important, and everything about my new habit reinforced this weakened status of my womanhood. At first, I had only glimpses of this change, but over the year, my sense of this very different female I had become would grow and trouble me.

I would not have children, not know the wonder of feeding my child from my own body. I would keep my eyes down in modesty and purity, avoiding the gaze of men, and never bring attention to myself. Most difficult of all, I would still be married. Married. I would never see the person I married, never touch him, never look at his eyes while we talked. He would take care of me though. I guess. And somehow I would try to *see* him—to grow in my love for him.

Yet, as I came to my dorm and sought out my bed, my white cap with the elastic ruffle resting on my forehead, I had to giggle quietly at what I had come to—a young woman sleeping with a granny cap. I looked around to see my friends likewise bonneted, and the sight of them seemed so utterly incongruous. We had all become the "mama in her kerchief" from the poem, *The Night Before Christmas*. I lay in my bed with a smile at the absurdity of our transformation. It was only the first day. I didn't want to think about the other remarkable changes we would all accept in the days and weeks to come. Fortunately, I was just happy to be quiet and alone, all curled up within myself. And no matter how I looked, I knew that I wasn't a bit like a grandma, whether I wore a nightcap or not.

*At the Motherhouse with my sisters, Maureen
left and Margaret right. They always dressed up
when they came to see me.*

CHAPTER 22

Sealed and Delivered

M Y RETREAT FROM MY PARENTS and friends on reception day was quite a different one than the previous year, when I walked up to the oak doors, struggling to hold back tears. This time I said good-bye right where my visitors sat. It was not a remarkable departure; in fact, it was a rather ordinary one. I had become used to saying goodbye to my parents and family when they visited me the year before. And even though I trembled inside at the thought of another year, I knew how things worked. I knew the ropes of religious life. I felt that even with some doubt and hesitation about my true vocation, I could handle just about everything I was asked to do.

I suffered from a strange case of over confidence. How could I find this year any more difficult than that first year of all firsts, I wondered? Given this over confidence, I was destined to be disappointed. In the sunny bath of the day's events with my family and friends around me, youth and optimism took over to give me false hope. I wasn't really ready at all for this life of cloister, so dramatically diverse in tone and purpose from the year of postulancy. But I would discover that in due time.

Since we left our families and friends in late afternoon, we had time to get acquainted with our new lodgings. So, after entering the Motherhouse in our brand new habits, we were asked to gather all of our belongings in a bath towel and cart them off to the novitiate. I opened my drawers, and sure enough all of my clothes, my toiletries, and my personal possessions fit into the sling of a regular-sized towel.

I walked with my fellow novices through the closed walkway to the novitiate for the first time. There I found my own special place—a bed and a small dresser. Hanging in my alcove was another habit; an everyday habit. It had a yellow cast to it. It wasn't white and clean like the one I had on; the one I sewed in the postulancy. From now on we would save our reception habit for special occasions like visits from our parents or church officials, and holy days like Christmas and Easter.

Some of the everyday habits, which we were told to wear immediately, were too short for a few of the novices; some actually had holes and others had stains. We may have been the brides of Christ a few hours ago, but now we were clearly his servants.

Well-worn and dingy as our habits might have been, we still had to learn to arrange them on our bodies. The long, flowing sleeves of the habit had to be pinned at the beginning of the week (we wore a habit for seven days), and each sleeve took eight pins to hold the cuffs and folds in place. I never figured out why we had to have six-foot sleeves so that we could fold them at least twice and stick pins in them to make them smaller! Since our sleeves were very wide, we always wore an undershirt, a long-sleeve undershirt—summer and winter. It would be indecent to show our forearms. Sisters who dared to omit their undershirts in the summer were severely reprimanded.

Seven days seems like a long time to wear the same outfit, but I know that I would not have wanted to do all the pinning and fitting of the headgear more than once a week. It took so long. I would get spots on my collar or scapular, but muslin is easy to clean, and I would wash out the stain and let it dry overnight. I *could* change my undershirt every few days and my socks and underwear every day.

Our muslin fabric had a distinctive smell, clean and a little wheaty, so I came to actually like it. Summer was the only time that a few sisters had trouble because they would perspire through their undershirts onto their tunics. And really, is that a surprise? Our undershirts were a killer in the summer.

We also had to face our headgear each morning, literally. Standing in front of a mirror, I tugged this way and that, pinned and unpinned until, in frustration, I sometimes settled for a skewed look. A sister helped us for a while but eventually we were weaned off our assistants.

In one of her letters, Linda, now Sister Paul David, told her parents that she had been pinning up her own headgear but was far from efficient at it; in fact, she said that one week it could be crooked and the next straight.

I recall that some novices never seemed to get the hang of arranging headgear on their heads. Their guimpes and veils were always pointing east or west, depending on the day. I used to wonder if it was the shape of their heads. If there might be some heads that weren't made for a guimpe and a plastic forehead band.

We learned that we would now have a new birthday, since we had changed our names and our lives. Instead of a celebration in March, I would have one on June 29, the feast day of Saint Peter, my new namesake. Just like that I was supposed to forget the day I was born and latch onto the twenty-ninth of June. The new day felt foreign; as if I had been adopted and suddenly found out I had celebrated the wrong birthday because of a mishap. I loved my famous actual birthday because it had a literary past. None other than William Shakespeare mentioned it in his play *Julius Caesar*, when Tiresius warned Caesar to "Beware the Ides of March."

We had to inform our parents of our new day so that they would know the correct time to send cards or gifts. If my mom sent me presents on my regular birthday, not only would I not receive them, I would also be questioned about whether I had told my family about my new "name day."

This was a mystery to me. Why wasn't the day of my birth and my baptismal name important any longer? It seemed that a Sacrament as integral to the Catholic faith as baptism was demoted in favor of my vocation, and my parents' part in giving me life and naming me was likewise undermined. Why couldn't my parents celebrate the day of my birth and call me by my baptismal name, while the sisters celebrated my reception into religious life on my name day?

How strange Linda's explanation of our new name day seems when she wrote to her parents, "In the convent you celebrate your feast day instead of your birthday. On your feast day, before Mass, your name is announced. All the sisters pray for you."

She was so matter-of-fact in the way she introduced this policy. Later, in another letter, she told them that their gifts arrived early and that she was given permission to open them. "The contents were all very practical and will be useful."

If it sounds like Linda had gone through a bit of indoctrination, she probably had. We felt pressured to accept the sacrifices of religious life, and to present a serene front to our families. We could not verbalize our internal conflicts or struggles, especially outside the walls of the novitiate. In this way, our families became further and further away from the daily reality of our experiences, which was intentional. We were told that like Saint Peter and the early apostles, we had to leave our families and devote our lives to the service of God's holy work.

To illustrate my growing retreat from my family, I was allowed to write home only once a month instead of every week as I did in the postulancy. This was actually a relief; I had nothing new to report. My schedule was daily prayer, chanting, Mass, meditation, my obedience, and classes. I found it challenging to find something unusual to write to them and, even more, to attempt enthusiasm in the telling.

The real crunch came when our visits were limited to only three or four a year. We were so cut off from the rest of the world that I felt a bit forlorn or withdrawn when I actually did meet with my family. We had so few points of reference. Could I talk about my class on the rule and constitution of our order? Would they be interested in hearing about my one hour of recreation, how we played Scrabble and other board games? We all tried valiantly, but our words dropped like stones in the air. It was just plain tough to take up a topic and run with it.

I looked forward to visits from my family but how disappointing they were in reality. I wanted everything to be the same. After I left, my sister Maureen told me that she wondered if I felt funny with everyone focused on me all the time. She asked me if I thought I had to keep the conversation going, or if I felt I had to act holy? And this really surprised me, she worried that I might be able to sense that she had partied the night before and necked with her boyfriend! I was amazed that she felt the strain of the conversation because no one acted as though it was an ordeal, just tough to find points of interest.

They embraced me, held my hands, and looked at me with such pride and joy in their eyes, but each of us wore proper white gloves, as if we were at a fancy gathering. No teasing about my dingy, brown-spotted habit, my undershirts sticking out from my sleeves (which should have been a huge joke with my sisters). No asking to peek at my hair under my headgear. No teasing about my grades (my family used to carry on about my good report cards).

Now it was expected that I would do well; I had chosen this life and I should want to do my best. Amid protests from me, my dad used to remark that I'd be mother general of the order some day. It could never be the same; they had adjusted to me as Sister Marie Petra, and I wouldn't dare confide in them that I still struggled, still wondered if this was a life I wanted.

CHAPTER 23

Veiled In and Out

THE BIGGEST SHOCK OF BECOMING a novice, other than dealing with the multiple parts of my new habit, was the silence. I was used to silence in the morning—actually appreciated it—and I adjusted to the end-of-the-day silence. It gave me a chance to slow down from my busy schedule of classes, studying, and taking care of my duties in the infirmary. However, I was not prepared for endless silence, a silence that was only broken during classes or my single hour of nightly recreation.

My new residence in the novitiate was tucked away from the activity of the Motherhouse, my home for that first year of the postulancy. I was now in a cloistered section of the campus where other nuns or people from the outside did not enter. If a nun came to our quarters, she had a class to teach us or she might have needed to see our mistress. We were truly insulated—even from the safe world of our Adrian campus and the Motherhouse.

The Motherhouse now seemed like "normal" to me. No longer would I bustle down the wide, tiled halls of the main building into the huge gathering room, with windows that reached to the ceilings and light that showered down upon everything. I wondered if I'd walk up the marble steps again, or more accurately, rush up or down those familiar stairs, late for class, prayer, or duty.

The cloistered section where I now lived was darker, with fewer windows and more closed to the outside. The rooms, with low ceilings and rather cramped conditions, were meager in comparison to my former home. One might have thought that the smaller size would have helped me feel more comfortable and secure, but that was never the case for me. The intense quiet and seriousness had nowhere to go, and eventually, I felt the weight of it descend upon me.

I left my giggles and my husky laughter at the novitiate entrance. I could no longer pretend that I was a college student who happened to wear black instead of colorful slacks and skirts because now, instead of the college, my classes were held exclusively in the novitiate. I slept there, studied there, and had recreation there. I was so hidden away that I had to enter the Motherhouse through musty underground passageways, mazes with huge furnace pipes overhead that must have been like the catacombs. I took a back stairway to the chapel for meditation, Mass, chanting of the office and meals, hiding my entry from even the professed sisters. I seldom entered the main section of the Motherhouse at all except for the times I knelt in vigil over a sister's remains in a casket. My life was bubble-wrapped and sealed with silence from which there was no escape, which was, after all, the entire point of a cloistered life.

I learned to keep my eyes down, my hands under my scapular. I walked softly, slowly, as if life had paused and stretched out the hours for me. Indeed it had; hours and hours of silence while praying, eating, working. I heard my heretofore-familiar voice only during the chanting of the office, occasional responses during Mass, and at classes and recreation.

When I noticed a friend's freefall into a state of anxiety, which left her closed and withdrawn, I had only an hour a day to talk with her and try to coax a smile or lighten her mood. Really, what could I do when my own nerves were wound so tight they were ready to pop like the boom of a fireworks display?

I tried to talk with Sister Paul David, the Linda whose walk was once a bounce, whose face was a bright sunflower whenever I saw her, but she became defensive. She felt I was ignoring her and wasn't her friend any more. Of course, she was hurting. She wanted to tell me all about it.

I had avoided her, because really, the change in her scared me. Her devotion and seriousness were over the top; she was trying so hard to mold herself into the good novice, the bride of Christ. How could I help her when I was worried about my own fragile state of fitting in, my confusion and fear that I was not going to make it? What did this mean—the joyless, somber wintering of our once buoyant natures?

Luckily, I found solace, perhaps even escape, in my classes—an old pattern with me from that very first year at Holy Redeemer. In the novitiate, my courses were easier than they were in the postulancy, but that was by no means a guarantee that they would be interesting as well. Sitting through God and His Creation, Church History, Dominican History, and Theological Virtues wasn't exactly stimulating stuff; but these courses were a distraction from the weighty questions hovering over my conscious thoughts each day.

I relished Cosmology. The study of the entire universe helped to diminish the huge importance of my minute universe, and gave me a chance to hear about Genesis again in a unique format, where Galileo's findings were not challenged but accepted and discussed.

Psychology, Logic, and Introduction to Metaphysics, which, according to the *Catholic Encyclopedia* is "the study of being as being or being as immaterial being," fascinated and amazed me. Our study of logic was a necessary prerequisite for metaphysics, since we employed the scientific approach to come to some conclusions about the existence of the soul, the spirit, and the creator.

I can remember these courses as some of the few that opened vistas for me in my years of schooling. Of course, I was only nineteen, impressionable, full of myself, and ready for all of the world's knowledge. In this way, I was a typical college student, ready to explore and discover my own truths and discuss the "meaning" of everything till the wee hours.

Even though my freedom was curtailed, I could ruminate on these mind-bending classes all I wanted while I sat through Patrology: the study of the writings of the church fathers concerning faith, morals, and discipline. I have almost no residual knowledge of this class now, but I remember it offered me an hour each day to dream about the wonders of metaphysics.

Since I was not taking the generic academic classes, such as Botany, Survey of Civilization, or Writing and Research as I took during my postulancy, I thought I could breeze through God and His Creation, Church History, Dominican History, and Liturgical Latin, which seemed like light weights compared to the "real" college courses.

Consequently, looking back at my transcript, I can't understand how I managed to receive a C in God and His Creation. The only other C on my transcript for the years I studied in the convent was in Elementary Spanish, and I confess to a lack of commitment there. But God and His Creation? Wouldn't this be about Genesis? Or maybe a metaphysical look at the nature of God and the creation of the world? In any case, how could this subject matter (well, what might have been the subject matter) be beyond my comprehension, whether presented as factual data or figurative, spiritual ideas?

For me, it was difficult to earn a C grade. I figure I would have had to be inattentive during lectures and unwilling to take the time to study. In other words, I blew off the course. I didn't care, which would have been out of character for me. This is a mystery and a surprise to discover so many years later. Perhaps this C was an eerie premonition back then, if I had chosen to see it, of something missing, some earnest, whole-hearted acceptance of religious life.

If, as postulants, we were the green, untried new members of the order, as novices we were almost sisters, and certain privileges came with our heightened status. In fact, we were actually elevated to the stalls in the front of the chapel, the high-backed, throne-like chairs that ran perpendicular to the pews. No longer would I sit in the long lines of wooden seats as I did as a postulant. Like monks and sisters had done throughout the ages, I would stand at my chair and sing the divine offices five times a day. As novices, we were now in charge. We were the cantors, and each of us had a turn at leading the singing. The amber, muted lights of early morning or late evening were my favorite times to chant the office. The high, lilting sound of our voices lifted like tiny bells to the vaulted ceiling.

My life was now devoted to prayer; serious prayer. As in the postulancy, I chanted *The Little Office of the Blessed Virgin*, but in this special year of devoted study and prayer, I rarely missed a single chanting of our Psalms. I chanted every office; there were no breaks because of classes at the college. Every single bowl of cereal, sandwich or casserole was served to me only after I had chanted my office.

Fortunately, the Psalms of David were poetry for me. They were musical and mystical and full of longing. If I ever truly prayed while I was in the convent, it was during the chanting of the office because that was when my soul sang with my body.

In the morning, before our half-hour of meditation while the world was still dark and waiting for light, I chanted Matins and

Lauds, the first of the hourly prayers we observed according to the Rule of our Order. For me, these words would beam through my sleepy senses and awaken me. From Psalm 62:

> *"O God, you are my God whom I seek. For you my*
> *flesh pines and my soul thirsts…Like the earth, parched,*
> *lifeless and without water: thus have I gazed toward you*
> *in the sanctuary to see your power and your glory."*

I wondered sometimes if the science and math majors amongst us loved the Psalms as much as we English majors did. I did not ask them, but I know that if any one thing fastened me to this restricted pattern of days, it was the mystical pouring forth of King David's supplications five times a day. Without these words, which I could sing aloud, I wouldn't have the relief I needed, if only from the fog of silence I lived within. Singing David's songs and hearing his pain, his struggle to stay devoted to his God, helped me. I knew that even the mighty king became despondent; even he had doubts.

Before lunch I again stood to face my fellow sisters in their stalls to chant Prime, Terce, and Sext with our voices answering each other, one side chanting from Psalm 120: "I lift up my eyes toward the mountains. Whence shall help come to me?" Then, the other, "My help is from the Lord, who made heaven and earth." Back again, "May he not suffer your foot to slip. May he slumber not who guards you." And in answer, "Indeed he neither slumbers nor sleeps, the guardian of Israel." Here was the soothing balm, the protection and promise that brought me hope. I did believe in it, while I chanted. Every word. Like David, my soul was surely fragile, and like David, God would strengthen me.

Our dinner hour followed the chanting of None and Vespers, which included one of my favorite Psalms, Psalm 129. Hungry and weak as I might be for actual food, when we echoed back and forth "Out of the depths I cry to You, O Lord; Lord, hear my voice!" I felt a satisfaction, a kinship with each sister begging for mercy. Later, when I had grown accustomed to my sadness, these words, strangely enough, lifted me. I can still recite the first four lines of the Magnificat, Mary's canticle to her cousin Elizabeth, who knew the moment she saw Mary that she had been chosen by God. Mary's answer to Elizabeth's greeting, a prayer we chanted at Vespers, is a manifesto of humility:

> *"My soul magnifies the Lord, And my spirit rejoices in God my savior / Because he has regarded the lowliness of his handmaid, for behold, henceforth all generations shall call me blessed / Because he who is mighty has done great things to me, and holy is his name."*

I might say it on beautiful mornings when I feel especially blessed. For sure, Mary's words apply to any of us who see the light in our lives.

Finally, after our evening recreation, I finished the day with Compline, the evening song. How fitting that Simeon's song from Luke should be my final chant for the day:

> *"Now you dismiss your servant, O Lord, according to your word, in peace / Because my eyes have seen your salvation, which you have provided in the sight of all the peoples."*

Simeon believed he would see the Lord during his lifetime, and upon seeing Jesus in the temple for his circumcision, he felt he could leave the world with peace and joy in his heart. I, too, could leave the chapel for my bed, wondering what shape the joys in my life would take to bring such a feeling of fulfillment here on earth. I have kept this prayer with me, first recited in the Latin Mass as the *Nunc Dimittis*, for occasions of great happiness and have recalled it throughout my life.

As I write this, I think about the winding paths I have taken. If I had stayed in the convent, I would not have had the chance to bear children. My daughter, from the time she was five years old, looked at the world with eyes of awe. She'd stare at the stain-glassed windows in the church and whisper to me, "So pretty." She loved to read, loved words and poetry, and when she was older, we'd read aloud to each other. Her own poetry is richer than mine, and her openness to others continues to amaze me. Likewise, my son and I are very close; his warm smile and easy manner always bring a smile to my face. We have always had an instant rapport, no matter what the circumstances might be. It is a wonder to me now how this circle of interests and personality is formed without a purposeful design on our part. I know that both my children and my step-children, who have brought so much to my life, are my very own "Magnificat," my special song of rejoicing for the family I always wanted.

In the morning, a half-hour of meditation followed our morning chant of Matins and Lauds. I could sit there and get back to a semi-sleep state, remembering dreams or actually dreaming new scenarios. It was no longer funny when someone's head dropped down in sleep as if chopped off at the neck. We were all bobbing helplessly, except the truly devout, because we were so very tired. I had moments of concentrated effort, quieting myself so I might hear God's voice. But I really had no idea what I was supposed to do during meditation. Not many of us did.

Back then, however, I figured that some novices had been chosen for holiness and inspiration. Some were given grace: a kind of fairy dust that God gives to those with whom he wants to speak through meditation. I wasn't one of them. I even created a "voice" inside my head, low and soft, that talked back to me, giving me advice and comfort. Most of the time, however, I would think about my classes, my family, my faults, my fears...oh, the list never ended. None of my attempts remotely resembled meditation.

I may have eased my anxieties had I really learned to empty

my mind of thought, which I understand today is what those who meditate try to do. They attempt to empty the mind so that the self can be felt and known. Now, I sadly realize that fifteen minutes of a blissful absence of thought could have worked "miracles" on my stress level.

Daily Mass concluded the triumvirate of prayer I faced every morning. It was a relief to stand up, stretch, and do some walking, as I had to walk up to the Communion rail to receive the consecrated host (the unleavened, flat, round bread).

It was an even greater relief to know that, in just a short half hour, I would be given food to silence my groaning stomach and light-headedness. I must say that this early hour of rising and the two hours of basic inactivity without food almost brought me to my knees, or worse, the floor, from feeling faint. I was not the only one. Some of us needed just a bite to get through till breakfast, a few grapes perhaps.

However, my devotions were not complete until I had walked and prayed the Stations of the Cross in chapel. Our novice mistress, Sister Charles, a wise, twinkling smile forming on her face, would tell us that this was one of our most important duties. Walking the fourteen stations and reliving Christ's passion and death was the best antidote to self-indulgence or pity. Ah, so she had actually noticed our forlorn, dark, and desolate faces, I thought. Since I truly came to believe that sister's mind existed on another plane, it amazed me when occasionally I witnessed it drop down to earth and her young charges.

I skipped my stations often. I did not worry about a reprimand because Sister Charles did not watch us all the time as our postulant mistresses did; in fact, I felt that she didn't pay much attention to us at all.

First, the Stations of the Cross depressed me, though I knew in my heart that this was the self-indulgent problem Sister Charles spoke about. Second, I wondered what to think, what to pray at so many of them. The first station gave me a glimpse of the horror to come. Christ stood there, his robe falling off his shoulder, his hands tied with coarse rope, a "crown" of long, pointy thorns shoved onto his head. Blood was beginning to drip down his forehead. I could pray that I was sorry; that I wished he could get a break from Pilate; that it would only take one brave soldier, struck by a kindness he didn't know he had, to help him. Of course, this would all be silly blabbering.

When I was in first grade, my very first religion teacher told us all the sad stories of the crucifixion. First grade was my initiation into the dark side of life, including not just the crucifixion, but evil, sin, hell, and whatever other horrors I had been heretofore blissfully unaware of. When it seemed that we could not take anymore of the scourging at the pillar and had reached an alarming state of distress, our teacher would quickly comfort our trembles with a sweeping justification for Jesus' suffering; "Oh yes, it is very bad what the soldiers did to Jesus, but he knew that this was his Father's plan for him, and he accepted it." Now we could feel sorry for him and love him for what he did for us, and put the misery aside. Jesus was supposed to suffer. He wanted to suffer.

As a young first grader, my more innocent mind was eager to throw off the horrible thing that happened to Jesus a long time ago. So it didn't take much for me to giggle at the girl next to me when her leg stuck to her wooden seat, making that blunt-rubbing-of-skin-on-wood bellowing sound. From there, I could think of what to do after school and my paper dolls waiting in the pink box where I laid them, all neat and organized. I could think about whether to play "Monkey in the Middle" or "Four Corners" in the empty field next door. I could leave behind the images of Jesus' cross gouging into his shoulder on the journey to the hill, his hands skewered by nails and his broken body bowed over on the cross.

Likewise, years later in the novitiate, I would perform my duty walking the fourteen stations through chapel, distancing myself from the real story, never quite finding the stomach to dwell on misery with devotion. Except for a few stations that always broke right through to my heart.

I could never walk by in a hurry at the fourth station. Jesus is walking the uphill road where he will be killed, and in the crowd of people, he sees his mother. She cannot hold her grief, and she goes to him, knowing she can do nothing to stop his pain and suffering. His mother, helpless, yet there with him. A woman, in the midst of angry mobs, unable to stop Herod Antipas, Pontius Pilate, and the Roman soldiers from carrying out the cries of the people. I have always been drawn to Mary and her quiet resolve when I pray. From the time I heard her prayer of greeting to her sister Elizabeth when she visited her, I wished to be like her. I knew that opposites attract, and yet, I prayed that a little of her wisdom would rub off on me.

I stopped at all of the stations with women: Veronica with her towel to wipe the blood and sweat from Jesus's face, the women of Jerusalem who cried for him as he stumbled by, and Mary, again, at the foot of the cross as he was placed in her arms. All of them were offering acts of love, of light. I could try to imitate them each day with my fellow novices and the sisters in the infirmary.

It always seemed to me that the light of Jesus's life was far more compelling than his death. His kindness to the blind man, the dying child, the lepers, and the harlot at the well offered a way to live. That is what I needed then, and still do now. I want to remember to look out, to listen rather than talk, to bring a little joy to the sad or troubled. I want to look for the light. It has never failed me to look for a way to love.

Finally, after I had prayed, chanted, meditated, attended Mass, and walked the stations of the cross, there was one more requirement in my daily regimen of prayer: I was to spend a half hour a day in adoration before the Blessed Sacrament. After Mass, the priest would place a large consecrated host in a *monstrance* (usually a golden receptacle for the host), which sat on the main altar of the chapel. This host, consecrated during the Mass, was an outward manifestation of God's spirit living with us at all times. Every hour of the day, a novice needed to be present before the host, which to Catholics is the body of Christ.

Linda wrote in a letter to her parents, "Daily, every novice has a half-hour adoration period in front of the Blessed Sacrament. We schedule our own meditation time around our obedience, classes and instruction." Her words sound matter-of-fact as if she accepted without a hitch all the parts of prayer and work and study that our mistress directed us to do.

I am amazed to think of just how much we had been formed into our religious habits, both physical habits and behavioral habits. Since I have very few recollections of keeping vigil in front of the Blessed Sacrament, I wonder what I thought about as I knelt there. I imagine my meditations were not easy since I could not see the human element in my adoration. I was limited, perhaps, in my need for story and connection.

Then, to truly understand the import of our gradual acceptance, whole and complete, of our mission and purpose, my friend goes on to say, "We are told that our novitiate year is the most important year of our lives. It is to be a year spent with God."

Today, I wonder how we could fathom the task we were given: A year spent with someone we could not see, hear, touch, or talk with, but nonetheless, we were expected to learn to know and love. If only our superiors had tempered these high expectations a bit and laced them instead with the language of possibility, of effort, of a journey never finished. There was pressure on us to grow in our love and devotion to God. Yet I felt that I needed spiritual guidance to get there.

What happened? In my case I carried around with me a secret too awful for others to know. I didn't know if I knew God, and I didn't know if I truly knew how to love him. Because of this secret, I really needed a God to save me, and that became the mantra of my prayers.

When I felt unable to face another hour of recreation, playing some game that might have brought shrieks of laughter to other happier novices, I made up excuses to skip dinner and recreation. I lied to my novice mistress several times. Told her I thought I was getting the flu and felt all achy. Other times it was my stomach.

Once when the sisters who had just left the novitiate came back to the Motherhouse for the summer session at Siena Heights College, I was at the time so riddled with anxiety, I thought I might break down and cry if I had to stand in a group and listen to their glowing reports of living in a convent and teaching. My stomach was truly dipping and swooping so badly that my hands shook, and inside it felt like electric currents were charging off, making me jump and start at the slightest noise. Sister Charles, as always in my sudden cases of sickness, nodded sympathetically when I asked to go to bed and sleep.

That night while all alone in the dorm, I left my bed briefly, and I looked out from the window to the patio below. For a few minutes I listened to the excited voices, watched the faces— all smiling and fully engaged— and I wanted to run, anywhere. The urge was so strong that I ran back to my bed and curled up under the covers and told myself to keep calm.

When no other help came to shake up the malaise of my spiritual situation, I found help from what may have seemed the most unlikely place. It came from the beautiful, vulnerable sisters at the infirmary; the women to whom I brought food trays. These nuns were sick, weak, alone, and perhaps even dying. Every day they quietly and heroically accepted life in a small room with a bed, a sink, and a chair.

The infirmary was away from our cloistered quarters, and there, not only did I find a world beyond the novitiate, I found a place I could hear my voice. I couldn't wait to see their faces light up when I stuck my head in the door. I might find a patient sitting in a rocking chair looking out the window or lying in bed napping, praying, or reading. Most of the time, I found the patients ready to talk. I loved to fluff their pillows, fix their covers, and fuss over what they were served for dinner.

"Look. It's *Jello*, your favorite," I said. Or, "Now, remember, you can't eat that chocolate cake until you've had all your lima beans."

They loved to be teased, to have a ritual of small talk about simple daily happenings. And, many of them wanted to hear all about my life. What are they teaching you these days in the novitiate? What will you study when you go on to get your degree? This would bring them back to their early days in the convent, a flood of memories that they trusted me to hear: the "old" days and the days of their teaching, the places where they lived, the few children they never forgot, the sisters who were their friends. They saved me. I saved them. It was a beautiful, wonderful thing. For this, I will be forever grateful.

I was one of the lucky novices who had a chance to get back into life. I may not have succeeded at meditation, the Stations of the Cross, or adoration of the Blessed Sacrament, but I did succeed in finding a way to cope. It took the shape of these wrinkled, gray-haired, bent or crippled nuns whose kindness and peacefulness enclosed me whenever I walked into their rooms. Perhaps finding what I needed on my own was the answer to my many "failed" attempts at prayer.

I had an easy obedience. I carried trays to sick women. I did not have to keep a chart on their progress, administer medications, or take their temperature or blood pressure. I just had to be a happy face in the vast sea of hours in their day. What could be better than this kind of "work" for a troubled novice, made brittle with the hours of introspection and prayer and desperate for human contact?

CHAPTER 24

Sister Mary Gertrude

I WAS ALWAYS BEING SURPRISED BY something at the infirmary. Really, even in what might be considered a rather static environment with so many sick women waiting to get better or to die, my daily walks through the halls, stopping and peeking into rooms, was never dull. Those walls would harbor some kernel of the unexpected, and I knew it might pop up anywhere. It might be in the elevator, or a sister's room, or right away when I walked into the kitchen, or even right beside me in the wide and long corridor I traversed each day.

Sister Gertrude was simply deposited at the infirmary overnight, I suppose. I first saw her in the hall, near my clinking tray cart, my gray, metal moving-banquet-of-breakfasts kept warm with stainless-steel covers and arranged neatly on the many rows. She walked up to me, leaning on a cane with every step, yet gingerly, not strenuously. Her face seemed so young for this quiet passageway to another world, and her energetic smile and rosy cheeks startled me.

During that first meeting I tried to make sense of her appearing in the infirmary as a resident. I wondered for a moment if she was a nurse or director, someone assigned to our sick house. Alas, no, I soon discovered that Sister Mary Gertrude had come simply to greet me and walk with me as I carried her tray to her room.

Her voice was lovely, resonant and full as she introduced herself and asked all about me. Where was I from? What was I studying? Her face glowed with delight when I told her my studies were primarily in literature. Why, she had taught high school English for many years! I cannot remember one incident during my year of novitiate that comforted and soothed me more than this angel who found me in the infirmary hall.

I lingered in her room all those bright days of her stay with us, and why not? She, alone, was up and about; looking out the narrow window of her room; visiting a frail, paper-thin sister or reading quietly in her chair. When I arrived, never did I find her perched in her bed among pillows and coverlets, a quilted jacket on her shoulders, waiting sleepy-eyed like a cat ready to nap. Always when I approached she gathered me to her, a mother hen, folding her wings around me.

Certainly, she must have remembered the parched silence of her own novitiate year. I wonder if our bubbling stream of words were meant to water my soul especially, because I found such joy in every conversation.

We talked of authors, of course: Jane Austin, the Brontë sisters, Thomas Hardy, (my very favorite for the moment,) and many more. She listened, a comrade-in-arms, as I related the happenings of the previous day or night: How sister so-and so tripped on her cloak when rising from a genuflection and spilled over with giggles, covering her mouth as she shook down the aisle to the safety of the chapel door; how another one of our group choked on the rutabaga (served for the second time that week much to our dismay) with awful gagging noises, red cheeks filling, and finally, some sputters, gulps of water, and a blessed look of relief, pain, disgust...it was difficult to tell; how sad I felt when one of my friends left, and how much I wished I might have said good-bye. She laughed heartily at my tales and listened carefully to my concerns.

I loved Sister Mary Gertrude for her boundless energy in this place of death that sometimes made me tremble, but mostly for the gift she gave to me of "normal." She did not speak of vows or prayer or devotion, though I felt she held all of those dear in her life. Sometimes she took me to her window, spreading her arm out to show me the beauty beyond the glass—the trees beginning their sage-colored flush of new leaves, the sky blue beyond the tops of the trees, and the grass greening before our eyes. Sometimes she rushed her way down the hall, a smile flashing her teeth at me the entire time. She'd place her arm on my shoulder to share some funny story, usually an incident from the day before. But when she brought me news of the world, I would stop and savor every word, question her until I had more and more of it. She was my only link to the outside, and I know that she realized how much I longed for it.

What a gift she gave me in the days I knew her. She helped me to remember what sane was while I lived in the cave of the novitiate, which seemed to bring me into some netherworld of my soul where, like Persephone, I might eat the tainted food and never return.

One day, about three months after she came to the infirmary, she asked if I could go with her to the "trunk room" and get some of her things. We descended to the dark belly of the building, where huge black leather and fabric trunks lined the floor in row upon row. The trunks were much the same as the next, yet not the same at all since each contained a sister's possessions: special mementos, photos, books, clothes...all the trappings of a life spent with a vow of poverty.

Sister Mary Gertrude didn't say much, nor did I. There was something sad and lonely about those dark trunks and the way they were buried in the very bowels of our buildings. Perhaps they reminded me of waiting coffins. For her part, sister seemed simply intent and thoughtful as she followed the maze to her own trunk.

Most every trunk had a removable shelf on top, sectioned off to hold smaller items. We looked down now at Sister Mary Gertrude's shelf, lined with a pretty blue flowered fabric. I felt I was gazing, intruding really, into her very private collection of important loved and cared for items, and I had the good sense to keep quiet, backing away to give her some room. She was always one to put me at ease, as she lifted up one lovely piece after another. Finally, she placed in my hands some of her special belongings. She looked into my eyes, gently yet firmly, and said, "I want you to have these." I was so shocked; I almost dropped them. They were valuable to her. I could tell.

In my confusion and surprise, I moved her things back toward her, "No, you can't give these to me. They are too special...I can't take them."

She urged. I protested. And then, very quietly and tentatively, she said, "I won't be here much longer."

I searched her face for some further meaning, some verification that "won't be here much longer" meant she was leaving to go back to teaching.

I uttered a shaky, "What...what are you saying?"

She did not move, her eyes a calm blue sea meeting my own. No words, just a look, with her hands on my arms, warm and alive.

Her dying was difficult to swallow, and I was so young, just nineteen, not yet accepting of the random, lottery-ticket manner in which death chooses us.

Indeed, I argued with her as if I could talk her out of it, "What do you mean? You are young. Healthy. Your cheeks are rosy...." I stammered on until she helped me out.

"I know. But I feel my body fading inside, weakening every

day. I can feel the life going out of me."

Then, her face opened in a lovely, wide smile and a little laugh to ease the seriousness of it all. "It will be all right. I'm ready to go. I'm not afraid."

Each week I noticed small changes. Her rosy color faded slightly. Eventually, she took on a light gray tone with masks of darker gray around her eyes. Her walk slowed considerably, and after a few weeks, I watched with alarm as she moved with difficulty, even pain. I had to be careful not to stare, or look frightened when I spoke with her. Somehow I became used to the slow changes, and our conversations, although altered by her change of energy, continued to be full of fresh ideas, as if a window had been opened right near us.

Then one morning her room was empty. She had been taken to the hospital, and I knew I would never see her again. Her loss was so final. She was so quickly removed from her room that I felt terribly angry. For some time, I thought about walking out the doors of the infirmary and finding her. Foolish, I know, but I was still trying to make sense of death. I suppose my anger gave me some purpose, which was delaying the sadness and fear rising in me.

Sister Mary Gertrude died about a month after she left the infirmary for the hospital. In all the time that we were together, I never asked what was eating away at her life, and she never told me. It didn't seem to matter. I cried at night in my sheets and blankets for a few days. She had been so good to me, sought me out in spite of all her troubles, and it seemed unfair that she should die so young when she had so much to give.

Even today her memory brings me to tears, but not so much because she died; I have grown up and know that we will all die. Instead, I mourn those few belongings she placed into my hands years ago because they are lost, gone the way many physical pieces of our lives are gone. I would like to hold them carefully in my hands again, touch and keep them warm for a bit, but mostly, and worst of all, I want to know what they were. The mind loses things, too, and that is sometimes the hardest truth of all to reconcile.

CHAPTER 25

Winter Walk to Duty

IN THE HOARFROST OF EARLY morning, we huddle-walked to our infirmary duty; our breath stopped in the icy air but not our words. Our bent heads bobbled and bounced together as one body, our black capes flapping in the wind in spite of our efforts to pull them close. We stepped with a jerky rhythm in reaction to each bit of delicious news, complaints or stories. We might have resembled a flock of geese, short stepping it this way, then that, as if joined at the necks. These walks were our five-minute purging of all the feelings and worries and even laughs we couldn't share in the silence. Yes, we were supposed to keep silence, but I guess we figured that we would be talking the minute we came into the infirmary, so what could be wrong if we simply began on the way?

We followed the sidewalks lined with trees too old to be surprised by anything we might say, and the walk was beautiful even in winter's wind or chill. The moon's glacial film would still be lighting our way past large tree trunks comfortably marking the path. The quiet was lovely, if only for those brief moments when we slipped out of the back door of the Motherhouse where we had just eaten our breakfast in the refectory with the other novices. We were always hushed at first by the still-ness outside, but especially in winter, when overnight the snow magically muffled the air and insulated the ground.

We usually waited to get down the steps and a good twenty feet away from the Motherhouse before we'd let loose, some-times all at once, sometimes with a rush and peak of intensity that set each of us into riotous giggling. Other times, the words seemed to leak out and gather momentum, leaving a fluttery sensation in my stomach; like the morning I heard about Sarah.

After a minute or two of silence, Sister Marie Ann whispered that she had seen Sister Sarah's bed that morning and Sarah hadn't slept in it. It was still all smooth and tight. She peeked in Sarah's nightstand drawer before she left the room for cha-pel—nothing was there, not one safety pin or pencil. It was as if she had been removed right out of the air around us. I searched Ann's face for more, but she had no other news, and each of us walked on with Ann slouched into herself beside us.

So, she finally did it, I thought. Even now, I can still see her in my mind: her straight-blond hair, her thin, angular body, her slow-eyed smile. I remember the crazy way she could trans-form herself into all kinds of characters. None of us had the chance to say good-bye, but I knew that Sarah's dropping out of sight was particularly difficult for Ann. I used to imagine a conversation I would have with a friend who left. As I walked quietly with the other novices, I probably thought about what I would tell Sister Sarah.

I might have hoped that when she walked into her safe and familiar home, she would smile again. And, eventually, perhaps not right away, her blue eyes would level someone with a mis-chievous look, and she would drop a remark that caught the absurdity of a situation. It was this wonderful, ironic humor that drew me to her. I knew that she would be herself again, put on some weight and fill out the sagging skin around her eyes and cheeks. She was better off, even if each of us would miss her.

Our quiet thoughts of Sarah brought us all the way to the entrance of the infirmary. The five of us picked up emotional currents as if electrically charged wires connected us. The air pulsed around us in waves of tension, but we knew we had to put this incident away for now and we walked into the warmth of the steamy kitchen, loosened our cloaks from our shoulders and waited to begin our daily round of trays. I never found the right words when someone evaporated like this. Like death, it was a complete cutting off, only I didn't have a body to grieve over.

Some time later, a group of us made a pact and vowed to tell each other if we were going to leave. We would break the promise our mistresses shamed us into making. We would not leave under cover like a common criminal. Funny, as it turned out, none of us left the convent until after we had taken vows and were assigned teaching jobs around the country. Yet, the idea that we decided to break the stigma of leaving makes me proud even to this day.

When we arrived in the infirmary kitchen, which smelled of home with whiffs of cinnamon-laced oatmeal and buttered toast, usually we saw only Sister Alphonsis's ample back and hips. Her figure never seemed to change. She was tall and upright, and most mornings we found her stirring oatmeal or boiling eggs at the large stove. Her face struck me as ancient; her eyes drooped, heavy and dense with pouches like overnight bags reaching down to mid-cheek. She was the sister most like my mother; her impeccable radar could detect the slightest change in any of us.

Sister Alphonsis never seemed to mind that we burst into her kitchen talking, even though she, too, was a novice once and knew we were supposed to keep silent. In fact, sister seemed to enjoy our busy chatter bouncing around the kitchen as we settled into the space by the door. She would shake her head back and forth, taking in our flutter of energy as she waited to give us a few instructions for the infirm. She'd direct her face at me and say, "Sister Ann George is not feeling so well today. Don't make a fuss if she isn't interested in her tray."

To another novice she would remark, "I'm trying oatmeal today for Sister Josepha. Her stomach's been acting up. Let me know how she does."

And, for one of the sisters who often balked about a special diet that included prunes for breakfast, she'd remind one of us, "Be sure she eats the prunes. You know, she forgets she's been put on this diet to help her, not to punish her."

Sister Alphonsis knew her patients at this place for sick or dying Adrian Dominicans. She visited with them in those interludes between meals. Perhaps she was dietician and cook in one person; I was not sure, but I did know that she knew, not only their individual ailments, but also, the nuances of their personalities. She wasn't just a cook who spent all of her time behind the doors of her domain; she was a caretaker, a nurse, who cherished each of the wrinkled women she served. Even the cranky ones, the sisters she never really pleased...maybe she loved those sisters more than the others.

That particular morning, she turned sideways to welcome our bustling bodies. After we settled down from hanging our cloaks and taking off our boots, she appraised us quietly, walking slowly from her position behind a large silver pot as we huddled near the trays waiting for her instructions. Her sad eyes took us in, but she concentrated on only one of us. She walked directly to Sister Marie Ann and put her hands on her shoulders, standing full in front of her. Sister Alphonsis's eyes scanned Ann's face like a doctor who was looking for symptoms of illness.

"What is this worried look I see?" she said. "Come, now, your troubles can't be as bad as that face says they are." And then her strong, quick arms enclosed Ann, enveloping her in the draping habit of her sleeves. Ann was like a child falling into a cushy chair of solace. Sister Alphonsis patted her back a bit, and then stood away from her with a slight smile, looking directly at Ann until she had coaxed a smile in return. She never probed us for information or explanations. Somehow, she seemed to know that what we needed was not to talk but a more physical remedy.

On other mornings, Sister Alphonsis would not turn to us immediately from her pots at the stove. On those days our trailing whispers or giggles would seem boisterous in the vast kitchen, framed by the silence of her still form and her head bent at her work. We would wait for her then, hushed and quieted, our gaze never leaving her back.

I could always tell when someone had died; I think each of us could. Sister Alphonsis's eyes would be immobile, staring, her expression level and flat. All of us would wait, poised for her announcement. Very softly, perhaps as she lifted a dish from one counter to another, she would turn to our little group and say, "Sister Marie Henry will not be needing a tray today." Her eyes, held sadness like a precious orchid for each sister who left us that year. She grieved inside, as if death never became commonplace for her.

None of us ever got used to it; only one of us would have fewer trays to deliver, but each of us felt the exactness of death. We'd search each other's eyes to see whose sister had gone, and still silent, we sent waves of concern to the novice who found a closed and empty room that morning.

We mourned each loss together, gathering our carts with trays, and made our somber journey to the service elevator. It changed me a little every time we lost someone.

I approached my ailing sisters more tentatively because I

knew, that just as the heat surrounding a sister's body blew in from the floor vents, the news of a sister's passing from this life would reach them as well. I'd linger a bit longer, making conversation about the weather or whatever I could muster up to fluff the air in their rooms. I'd try to soften my voice, and after I had placed the tray on my sister's table, I would place my hand on her arm and give a little squeeze. "How are you feeling this morning?" I'd ask. "Did you sleep well while the snow fell?" In almost every case, I saw the sister change. Her eyes would wake up from the pall of silence in the room and she would carry on a bit about the state of her body and her night's rest. I often wondered how many times sister had a chance to hear her voice during the day.

I realized that, even with death waiting behind each door, I had the best duty of all the novices. I was able to feel for someone other than myself every single day, to reach out literally from the spiritually laden heaviness of my novitiate training and know the soft touch of another warm and living body. This was the unexpected gift that caring for the sick and dying brought to me. My infirmary duty kept me from drowning in the flood of self-doubt and misery I had nurtured in my weakened state; it kept me in the novitiate. I loved delivering trays to these calm women whose peace radiated from their eyes every morning, afternoon, and evening that I knew them.

CHAPTER 26

Acquainted with the
Night and the Dead

B EFORE I DONNED THE HABIT and, with the best of
intentions, seriously gave myself to God, I was really only
playing at nun life. I was a child who hadn't been told there was
no Santa. My world became smaller and darker; it was more
unusual, heavier in Liturgy, rituals, and ancient practices. I had
crossed over a bridge to the novitiate, and the river was wide
that kept me secluded.

A few in our group may have known beforehand of these
ancient practices, the more attuned and alert, of course. I was
not one of them. Would I have gone through with it had I known
that I would be expected to kneel on my own small kneeler
called a prie-dieu in the wee hours of the night, watching over
the dead body of a nun in her casket? Did I realize that very
soon I would find myself plunged into medieval practices that
would make the Venia seem tame? If I did have some inkling of
these ritualistic devotions that would open the door to what it
really meant to be a nun, I might not have believed the stories,

or if confronted with proof, figured that I would deal with each one as it came.

Fortunately, I was spared the suspense of waiting to discover the truth about at least one of these "secret practices." When a sister died, our novice mistress instructed us in the sacred practice of keeping watch over her body and praying for her soul. This was an honor bestowed upon us as servants of our older sisters. It lasted for two days and two nights. Four of us at a time knelt on our own individual prie-dieu near the casket for a half hour; two of us knelt in front, nose to nose with the lit candles and the body, while the other two knelt behind. During the night, when the half hour was up, two of the novices walked back to the novitiate and woke up the next four novices. Only two novices left at a time since the body always had to have someone in attendance. Nighttime vigils were the only ones I remember, but we kept a presence both day and night.

The middle of the night was always a creepy time to walk down the long, hollow halls. After the shock of someone's hand tapping my shoulder, or in some cases rocking or thumping my shoulder until I awoke, the awful realization would hit me that I'd have to get out of my warm bed and stumble around in search of my already laid out cloak and headgear. It was never easy.

I would grab my black, full-length cloak, pulling it about me to cover my nightgown. The real challenge, however, was getting on my headgear and veil in the dark, especially in that first month or two of the novitiate when this task was difficult enough facing a mirror with lights to help me pin and arrange all the parts of my veiled look. We were warned to hurry since four sisters needed to be praying over the body, and two equally tired sisters were waiting there on the kneelers for us to arrive and rescue them.

Worst of all, when I had half opened my eyes, I knew I would have to face the cave-like walk along the creaky wood floors and echoing walls of both the novitiate and the Motherhouse. It was a long walk. I always thought I should have held a candle, like in the old days, to light my way through the narrow halls, past the groaning doors, and the ghostly forms of statues or furniture taking shape around me. I never made the journey alone; my partner and I shuffled together, our shoulders bumping as we walked. We yawned and moaned with our surroundings... real live ghosts creeping around in our stupor.

Some of us never truly woke up, and the sight of a novice dragging herself into the "funeral parlor" with her headgear sideways, like she had tackled someone on the way down, brought smiles or snickers to those of us waiting to go back to bed.

These midnight vigils were like a haunted history for me. The stage was set for the unusual or the frightening to occur. If roaming through the cavernous Motherhouse in the middle of the night didn't get my adrenaline going, the sight of that darkened parlor, lit only by candles that illuminated the face of a dead sister, would get my nerves prickling for sure.

Linda, who always seemed to be present when one of the more bizarre episodes happened, told us about the time Sister Mary Ann saw a mouse skitter across the floor. (It stands to reason that anything moving anywhere would be cause for alarm, but Sister Mary Ann was really afraid of mice.) She let out a yelp that could have wakened the entire Motherhouse, flailed her arms about like she was going to fly, lifted her cloak and nightgown, and jumped on top of the kneeler of the prie-dieu.

The other three sisters, deep in prayer or some other activity, screamed involuntarily with her and stood up ready to fight or run. By this time, Sister Mary Ann had shouted the word "Mouse!" several times, her finger pointing to one wall and then another as the frightened mouse looked for cover.

Linda said that although she and the other two sisters eventually resumed their places on the prie-dieu, Sister Mary Ann stood on her kneeler, studying the floor until her watch ended.

In one of her letters, Linda told her parents that we had been told by our mistresses, "There is only one thing better than being a dead Adrian Dominican and that's being a live one." If this sounds a bit morbid, the second part explains. "It's good being a dead Adrian because you have the whole congregation praying for you."

I wonder what Linda's parents and sisters and brothers thought of this. Would they be happy at her death, knowing that she had the prayers of the entire congregation lifting her up to heaven?

The "happy" death sentiments were difficult for me to accept, and I thought often about dying as an Adrian Dominican. Even then, kneeling at a sister's casket, I wanted her other family to watch with her as well. Yet, we were now her family; we, who hated getting up in the night, who had never met her, and who would never love her like her blood family had. Death for a nun seemed cold like her poor body, and I shivered at the thought of my own face looming from my headdress while inside a wooden casket.

Nonetheless, I am pretty sure I was in the minority with my death vigil. I stayed awake and alert. I imagined what the sister's life might have been like. Did she teach? Most likely she did, since ours was a teaching order of sisters. How many different classrooms of students did she guide through her courses, watching them grow up from one year to another? Which students stayed with her, tugged at her heart, turned her mouth into a smile? Which young faces were still vivid for her after years of absence? Who were her friends? Where did she love to visit? What were her simple joys? Even though her life may have been restricted, it was her life, her only one. It was real for many who came to know her.

I forced myself, at first, to look at the heads shrouded in their headgear. It became easier and eventually seemed a betrayal of sorts if I did not study their features. Some looked kindly, all rosy and round. I could imagine a twinkly smile, inviting like a generous grandma. Others had sharp, wedged features, deeply creviced making it difficult to imagine a happy look. Mostly, the faces were pasty and puffy, since no undertaker colored their cheeks and lips and very little sunlight had bronzed them. I guess it was all right this way; they went back to the earth the way they came into it—natural and untouched.

It was a fully awake novice who smelled the burning material and rushed to beat out the fire in another novice's veil during one of our night vigils. The story was whispered through the halls and rooms of the novitiate the next morning. Most of us knew that two of our novices, Sister James and Sister Judy, had acquired a real dislike for each other. They hid it from our novice mistress, Sister Charles, or it may never have continued. Our mistress was truly a saintly person, and she did not appear to notice her surroundings as other sisters did.

The novices who had lived in the novitiate the year before us spoke of Sister Charles as a mystic. She glided when she walked, and her mouth was always upturned in a Mona Lisa smile. I knew for sure that if God were to talk to anyone in our midst, it would be Sister Charles.

On this particular night, Sister James bobbed her heavy head all the way down onto the armrest cushion. Her veil came dangerously close to the lit candle right in front of her, and in seconds, the material began to smoke, eventually igniting into small flames. Luckily for her, Sister Judy, a wiry wisp of a gal and Sister James's archenemy, wasn't nodding off. With the speed of Hermes, Sister Judy rose and batted Sister James's head back and forth with a fury of slaps.

In the meantime, a shocked, and then very angry Sister James stood up and let fly her own strikes at her assailant. The parlor-room brawl lasted for some ten seconds or so, words sputtering forth and arms swinging, before the two novices behind them broke them up. I wonder what those sisters' thoughts might have been as they witnessed, from their somnolent states, a full-grown battle going on in front of them!

There was no apology forthcoming from Sister James when she realized that her assailant had saved her from severe burns on her face and possibly her body. Only the acrid smell of burnt fabric remained in the air, and sister had a damaged veil to wear and explain to our mistress, for which she would probably receive a hefty penance. The fight was never mentioned to our novice mistress; she only knew that Sister James had avoided major burns by waking up in time to put out the flames.

Eventually, the "burning veil" became the stuff of legend, lavished upon and chuckled over at many a gathering as we continued into our professed years and beyond. What a blessing that the poor, dead sister, who during her entire religious life had been assured that lovely young novices would lift her soul to her eternal home with their prayers, had laid still as a stone, oblivious of the commotion.

Death seemed to be all around me in the novitiate. Before I entered the convent, I had experienced only three deaths that truly affected me. One was my grandma. I didn't know her very well because she spoke just a few words to any of us kids when we visited her in Canada. I don't remember ever seeing her walk around. When I came into the dining room, she was sitting like a Buddha in her big chair while we stood before her and took her hand. I do remember my mom sitting all alone in our dining room after she answered the phone call from her brother about her mother's death. She cried into her hankie for a very long time. And she didn't stop when we sat near her and patted her shoulder.

When I was older, my aunt died in our house on New Year's Day. I saw her dead body lying in my mom's bed, her face crushed in where it rested on the pillow. I hurried away from that awful image of her broken-looking face and was haunted by the idea that she died in the room right next to mine.

Then, one of the nicest guys I ever knew died when he was fourteen in an automobile accident. He was with his mother, a simple trip to the grocery store, when someone hit them. He died instantly. I stayed in my room for a whole day, trying to fathom the fact that I would never see him again. I thought of all the times my friend, Joy, and I told him to leave us alone when he came around. We teased him for wanting to be with us. He always came back though. His death was the worst of all, and I am sorry that I couldn't bring myself to go to his funeral.

I would tell him I am different now. That, even though I didn't stand before his casket to look at him one last time, I can still see his freckled face and earnest eyes as he walked up to Joy and I, hoping we'd let him stay around while we carried on about the silliest things. I remember how he always made us laugh and how he'd stroll over to where we sat on Joy's porch, his face all eager and happy to see us, a crazy greeting coming out of his mouth.

Yes, I am different now. My year in the novitiate acquainted me with death, and I no longer stay away from the funeral parlor or a tribute ceremony for someone I used to know. I held two kitties I had loved for years while the veterinarian put them to sleep. I watched their eyes close, and their bodies slump into a quick stillness. I could never hand them over to die alone without me beside them.

I saw my father right before he died. I wanted to stay at the hospital that night because I knew death was imminent. His heart was failing and I heard the nurses say his heartbeat would keep rising until it gave out. I didn't want to leave. I wanted to be with him. My family said that we should go home; we were all tired. "We can come back in the morning when we are rested," someone said.

"But what about dad?" I asked. "He may not last till morning."

"It's a long, slow death," I heard, "and he will probably last till morning."

I left with them. My baby girl, just eight weeks old, was staying at my mom's with her brother who was almost three. They would need me.

We arrived at my mom's home, and within five minutes, the hospital called. My father had just died. Alone. I've never forgotten it. When we rushed back to the hospital, his body was very still, but I looked up, hoping his spirit was still there in the room, watching us. I talked to him while my family recited the Our Father and the Hail Mary. And I knew inside that he heard me. He was listening.

CHAPTER 27

The Liturgy of
"The Death"

FOR CATHOLICS, CHRISTMAS OFFERS THE most joyful, lovely Liturgy of the church year, and the traditions
accompanying this season, the presents and mail from home
and festive dinners, brought happy smiles to my now more serious face. I didn't mind waiting for the letters and cards that
must have been piling up in some box for me. Even as a child,
I loved the Advent Liturgy, the readings in church of Isaiah's
promise of a light to come. Christmas was about a beginning,
about a small baby and two very poor and alone parents. It
never became old and worn for me. And with the addition of
joyful music for Advent Mass and Christmas Mass, all written
by famous composers, my heart swelled like a child who learns
the Christmas story for the very first time.

Lent, however, had surprises that surged beyond the ordinary Catholic experience. By this time I should have been
seasoned and nonplussed about my daily and liturgical schedule; yet this section of the church calendar, Passion Week during
Lent, was revved up and expanded beyond anything I could
have imagined.

Yes, I had given up candy or talking back to my parents or soda
or something I thought was a big sacrifice during Lent when I was
growing up. I received ashes on Ash Wednesday; attended retreats
hosted by missionaries from very far away who tried to help
me get my soul in order; was taken weekly to adore the Blessed

Sacrament in the evenings; and went to Mass on Holy Thursday, giggling as grown men got their feet washed by the priest.

I also attended Good Friday services, where I heard the entire reading of The Passion of Jesus by the priest and some church members, fidgeting and scratching until my parents gave my sisters, brother and me "the look." And just when I thought I could endure it no longer, I would walk up to the priest, holding the large cross at the front of church, to kiss Jesus's feet along with everyone else. It felt good to do something for Jesus, to show that I cared.

On Holy Saturday, I joined our Polish and Italian neighbors with their baskets full of Easter breads, coffeecakes, hams, and sweet potatoes to receive a blessing from our pastor. How could any other practice seem more ritualistic than these from my past? Walking around with a black smudge on my face, washing feet in church, kissing feet on a cross with hundreds of other faithful parishioners, and bringing food to be blessed for a meal? I was in church all the time it seemed, and I actually became used to it.

Clearly, even with these practices, I was not prepared for the novitiate practices surrounding Lent and Easter. In my wildest imaginings, I could not have envisioned General Chapter, which took place on Ash Wednesday or some time early in the season of Lent. Our novice mistress tried to prepare us for this Lenten exercise during our instructional period, and after we adjusted to the shock of what we were asked to do, we could not quell our foreboding and fear.

Sister Charles's eyes leveled us with the seriousness of the task. We must examine our conscience fully, bore into the center of our soul, find the truth and declare it openly. We needed to purge our hearts of actions and thoughts that kept us from accepting our savior and his call to be saints. This inner search was between God and ourselves, and we dared not discuss it with anyone.

So what was General Chapter? It was a confession; each of

us was to ask for pardon from our other novices and sisters for our faults and unkindness toward them...aloud. That was the killer—alone and aloud.

On the day of our General Chapter, I stood against the walls of a large, rectangular room waiting my turn with the other novices. I kept my head down while others confessed their sins. I wouldn't dare look up. The Mother General of our order, whom I did not know personally and whom I had considered almost equal to the Pope in my mind, sat at the front of the room. Our novice mistress stood beside her. When it was my turn to confess, I was supposed to approach Mother Mary Jean and stand a distance away but directly in front of her chair. Before confessing, I would face the chapel, lie facedown on the floor in the Venia, kissing the floor and showing my submission to God and my penitence, and then face Mother General, with a medium-inclination bow, and begin my list of misdeeds.

Each squeaky voice croaked out her sins while the rest of us waited, pale, sweaty and pretty much close to fainting from misery. What if I forgot my sins? What would everyone think when I admitted that I felt impatient with some of my sisters? What if our Mother General questioned me or asked if I had more sins?

I remember this as one of the most frightening ceremonies of novitiate. I used to get worked up telling the priest my sins in the confessional, and he wasn't supposed to even look at me. I made sure he didn't, watching him with my left eye as I turned my head to the right so I couldn't be seen entirely. Most of the time, he didn't move much. Sometimes he held his head in his left hand, obstructing any view of me. I appreciated that. I hated to think that he actually knew me! How could I face him when he knew that I had "bad thoughts" and lied to my mother?

It must have been a blessing from heaven itself when, in the middle of this soul baring, one of our novices took the edge off the tension for a brief moment. She was from one of the small countries where our sisters had set up missionary schools, in this case, the Dominican Republic. I admired her courage. She had left her home to live in a new country where she had not completely mastered the language. Her eyes lowered in a smile whenever she greeted me, and her face bore the innocence and simple goodness of a life that differed remarkably from mine.

After many admissions of serious faults from the novices before her, she took her place before our Mother General and began her own litany. Somewhere in the middle of her list, while I was probably repeating my own faults in preparation for my turn at confession, I thought I heard her say "break" and "toilet seat." I looked at each sister next to me in amazed confusion. Did I really hear what I thought I heard? Yes, apparently I had, since every novice next to me and across the room had awakened, heads raised. We were all alert.

Sister Monica had confessed to breaking a toilet seat that morning. Each of us stood there, wide-eyed and waiting, peering at the little novice, who was looking around the room as if ready to run for it, and then, to our Mother General who was looking down at her lap, chuckling a bit and shaking her head back and forth. Instantly, we erupted into longed for laughter, and relief, thankful for the childlike novice's misunderstanding of the word *fault*, and her uncensored approach to public confession.

Of all the unusual practices, General Chapter seemed to be the most medieval. Standing along the wall of the large room, watching as one of our sisters confessed her sins openly, as if she were on trial, and lying prostrate before another human being— how might any of us avoid feeling shame and fear?

My heart may have been pounding in terrified anxiousness while I waited my turn to confess, but I also felt anger. Were we so awful that we needed to be degraded before all of our sisters? If the practice of General Chapter was originally formed as a means to an end for religious candidates, what might possibly be positive in the end result? I know that the better applicants for religious life who stood against the wall that day were able to shrug off the ritual as soon as they walked through the door. I was not one of them. I felt tired about feeling bad about myself. Was there no end? I really wanted a spiritual awakening, but this path of guilt and shame did not bring me to it.

Yet, each time I held back and criticized our training or the rituals we were asked to perform, I felt worse. I simply had no where to go with them.

It would be Holy Week, the week preceding Easter, which would bring me to my knees and my body to the floor...literally. I observed silence during this entire week with no hour of recreation. I sacrificed during meals. On both Good Friday and Holy Saturday my breakfast and lunch combined could not be greater than my dinner. Since there were few physical pleasures in the novitiate, food took on new heights of importance.

I suppose that when distractions are at a minimum, many of us looked for other ways to highlight our days. Along with nourishment for myself and the other sisters, food became a steady and satisfying pleasure. Our meals were bountiful feasts with some type of meat or protein dish, a potato or rice side, a vegetable, a salad, plus, the big bonus—dessert at lunch and dinner.

I never ate this well at home, and in the '60s, my mother cooked most evenings, so I was accustomed to some pretty substantial suppers when dad came home from work. The difference? In the convent all of my meals were prepared for me, breakfast, lunch, and dinner. All I had to do was show up. Each dish was served "family style" in a bowl large enough for ten people rather than six, and seconds were coveted.

When I was presented with plates of hot-cross buns on Good Friday morning, it was no wonder that I wished for the next course. None arrived. I had to rethink that extra bun as well. First, I was supposed to eat smaller meals. Second, if I ate too much for breakfast, I'd have to really skimp on lunch. Our two meals of breakfast and lunch were to be smaller than our evening dinner, and that meal was reported to be rather lean.

I remember hearing about the tradition of these buns with the little crosses on them—frosting crosses. They were very good, sweet tasting, and I could slather mine with butter. Even though my meager bun did not ease the rumblings in my stomach, I appreciated the history of these breads, which had been served in England since the fourteenth century to represent the crucifixion, and I was eating my one and only bun now, so many years later.

When I finished my frosted roll, a novice came to our table and used a crumb grabber to clean any particles of bread left behind. This device looked a bit like a shovel, and the novice moved her tool over the tablecloth until she had captured most of the crumbs. We couldn't help smiling at the absurdity of it. There were very few "crumbs", and this practice seemed like something a waiter might do at a high-class restaurant. But our mistress had told us that the tradition of collecting crumbs was supposed to be a reminder of the poor who always had very little to eat (not just a few days a year as we did) and hoped for the remnants from the tables of the rich.

Holy Saturday was more of the same: small meals, praying, and silence. All of us wore our long, heavy black cloaks the entire day to cover our white habits. Our cloaks were to remind us of Christ's death the day before. Even the chapel was shrouded in black. I was feeling a bit weak and somber from Good Friday's fasting and sorrowful Liturgy, but I didn't think of complaining. I was only one of this large group of very serious sisters; we were paying homage to one whose sacrifice was immense compared to our meager denial of food and days of prayer.

Yet, I must confess to feeling something akin to despair in the time before and during Holy Week—at times darkness would come over me heavily; my stomach would drop, my skin prickle and my whole body tremble. The drone of death was everywhere I went.

Our days were now full of silence— no hour of recreation. The chapel and halls looked dark as well; and, the Liturgy echoed the theme of Christ's trial each day. Even our meals were somber with smaller portions of food and readings that asked us to look deeply into our hearts for the sin of pride.

I wanted to escape, but I didn't know where I could go. My head reeled with tension, and I feared that any minute I might break if I didn't control myself. I had reached a deep pit when I looked inward, and it frightened me. I didn't even think of leaving—I was too sad, too far away from myself for that. I wanted only to hide somewhere until I felt better. I lived for night when I could slip into bed as soon as possible and hide under the covers, turning my face into my pillow where no eyes could see my fragile state.

At our lunch on Holy Saturday (we skipped dinner that day altogether), we were instructed to place our plates, utensils, glasses, and napkins on a tray. Our novice mistress then informed us that we would eat our meal on the floor. I watched as she proceeded to find a spot near her chair and, without an adjustment of any kind or a break in movement, calmly folded herself and her habit onto the floor. The room was full of quite a bit of confusion. Each of us turned in unison, stunned but obedient participants, hitting each other with our trays; our meager food offerings ready to topple to the floor before we did.

It didn't get any better. It turned out to be quite a feat to kneel, balance a tray, and then attempt to slump into a position on the floor while four other novices were intent on settling in the same spot. Our elbows and knees jabbed each other until we had shimmied ourselves into an opening, our legs spread out in front of us like puppets.

By the time I had settled somewhere, I had poked or bumped the novices near me so often, mouthing "sorry" repeatedly to my right and left, that the somber tone of the meal had disintegrated into pure, yet restrained comedy. I never regained a semblance of piety and humility, which seemed to be the point of our lunch on the floor.

Still, only the hardest heart could say that after all this preparation, there was not a brief reward. It came to us that very evening as we celebrated the Easter Vigil Mass at nine or ten o'clock. The chapel had lost the shrouds of death, and wore instead the white of life. Each prayer we sang at Mass, like the *Gloria*, the *Sanctus* and the *Agnus Dei*, was a special, more vibrant version from a famous composer.

At the moment the priest consecrated the large host, we flung off our black cloaks in a rare demonstration of pure abandon. Instantly, a sea of white habits drenched the chapel in light. This is as wild as it gets, I thought. Here we are throwing off a garment from our shoulders.

However, the tiny crack in our window of opportunity proved too much for some of my friends. Cloaks went flying over pews or into someone else's face. Nonetheless, it was a most beautiful, joyous sight.

The bells at the consecration, which had been silent for Holy Thursday and Good Friday's Mass, increased in number and pealed thunderously for an entire minute. It was a rock-concert frenzy right there in our chapel. Best of all, I knew that very shortly I could talk with my friends, and when we entered the refectory, we would be served a meal that even a king might envy.

A magical dinner it was. We ate in the middle of the night, the rows of tables lit only by candles. Serving platters were piled with meat, and bowls and bowls of side dishes were mounded over with vegetables and potatoes, breads and salads and desserts. I didn't even feel tired, and it was close to eleven p.m.!

After the long darkness, I wanted to hold the memories, like candles, forever, recalling my friend's faces in their golden light and feeling the mystic secrecy of our meal in the dungeons of the Motherhouse.

Was my joy emanating from the true cause of our celebration, Jesus's resurrection and conquest of death? Yes, for those moments in the chapel when everything turned bright and the silence of the week broke with the bells, it was. Later, the beautiful meal in the late night and the release of my spirit from the trail of somber, black and heavy silence, of days alone with only my inner voice, well, that was what really brought me to a rarely-experienced blissful state. I went to bed with a full stomach, and an almost calm heart.

CHAPTER 28

More Lessons in Dying

SISTER WAS SITTING UP IN bed, propped up by several pillows, the covers pulled up close to her chin. Her small face stared out of her bonnet, eyes the hardness and flatness of granite, mouth a clamp of anger. This image confronted me in the somber gloom of her room's dusky light; the tiny circle of her face rising from the enormous bed and flicking darts of tension which pierced the air. I remember feeling physically assaulted, although she obviously never delivered a blow.

She watched me with those steely, fierce eyes every step of my journey to the tray table with her lunch. I smiled uncertainly, not daring to talk. However, the moment I began to roll the table over to her in the bed, she barked, "Just leave it." My hands flew up from the table in shock and surprise, but sister was unmoving in her furious inner struggle. There would be no chat, just her stare, boring into me until I fled the room as fast as my long skirts would allow.

I had sisters who lay in their beds—powder pink, crocheted bed jackets around their shoulders, their heads covered with little white bonnets, stray silver locks peeking out from the edges—but when I brought their trays, no matter how sick or tired they seemed, they'd muster up a smile when I stopped to talk. Even the sisters who sat in their rocking chairs looking vacantly out the window could be brought around. I could find some way to interest them, some way to get a hint of a smile to clear their cloudy eyes.

This sister was different, however. Even though I felt intrigued by her rigid adherence to an angry solitude, I would have to fight my own terror when I entered her room.

Her bitter anger was at the cancer that struck her body so ruthlessly and consumed every inch of her. Anyone would rail against such a sentence.

Yet, at the same time, I wondered about her. Wasn't she supposed to look forward to the *next* life? Look forward to seeing Christ, her heavenly bridegroom? Didn't she realize that this earth and all its trappings were transient, fool's gold? How could she show such little faith in God's mercy and his place for her in her *real* home, her eternal home?

I was steeped in the philosophy of religious life then. Every day our classes of Sacred Scripture and Christian Dogma stressed the world of the soul, the work of God, and the many ways we would be comforted by giving our lives to him, bringing his message to humanity.

This particular sister had not felt that comfort; she did not truly *believe all of this*, I thought. The unusual fact of sister's wrath at her imminent death was almost as frightening to me as entering her room.

Her bedroom was the last one on the left down the hall, larger than the others. It was very dark—so unusual in this hospital that tried to create an atmosphere of cheer. The window shades were down and the curtains pulled, so I had to pause a moment at the door to orient myself. At first, I wondered if this were deliberate, if sister's illness caused her eyes to be light sensitive; but I was told that her eyes were fine, that she wanted the darkness; demanded it. Nothing more. Unlike many of our ailing sisters, she did not come to us in a state of semi-health, writing letters to friends, knitting, reading, or venturing into the halls with canes or walkers. This sister had come to die.

Every day churned into a challenge. When should I deliver her tray? Should I take it early and get over the frightening task, or should I wait till her tray was the very last on my cart, fretting over the unavoidable while I delivered the other trays?

I had learned to say "Good morning" or "Good afternoon," regardless of her silence, leave the tray, and then scuttle out the door. My nervousness would get the better of me at times. I'd do silly things, like turn abruptly into the tray table rather than away from it, jarring the contents of her breakfast or lunch so that her drink spilled onto the place mat. She'd snap an exasperated click with her tongue and teeth, while I'd almost fall over my feet and skirt heading for the door.

I only heard her voice a few times but it, too, stays embedded in my memory. The second time she bellowed at me, after only a week of our acquaintance, if one could call it that, I pulled the door to shut it as I left, which I never, never did with any sister. Sister, whose eyes assaulted me every minute of my brief excursions into her chamber, boomed, "Don't shut it!"

I turned sharply, struck by the thunder of a voice from one so small and mysteriously quiet, and asked stupidly, "The door?"

Her eyes widened then, her voice softening strangely. "Yes, the door. I want it open."

Walking away down the hall, as I reviewed the scene in my mind over and over, a thought struck me mid-step. The voice that shouted "Don't shut it!" was not just angry, it was completely afraid. That voice did not want to be alone. It was a human voice, after all, and those squinty black eyes terrorizing my heart held terror as well. An interesting calmness came over me. I could deal with fear, being fairly well accomplished in experiencing it often in those first years of my convent training.

Now I wanted to know all about her. What did she do? Where did she come from? Who was this sister who seemed to be made of steel instead of flesh? There had to be someone who could give me a bit of her history.

That person, of course, was right in the building. Sister Alphonsis, our sister in charge of the kitchen, would tell me. From her, I learned that Sister David Thomas was a lawyer for the congregation—a renowned lawyer. She had been one of the few women, and a nun to boot, who had tackled the male-dominated law profession in the early part of the century. A pioneer in this field, she had earned the respect, as well as the business of many patrons, and her talents were sought after for both speaking and teaching. An icon in our congregation, sister was a model for the strong force we all could be for God and our community.

Wow, I thought, no wonder she had trouble accepting death; she had so much more to do. Disease had infiltrated her body in the very prime of her profession—her mission.

I brought Sister David Thomas's food to her for a brief time, perhaps three weeks in all. Her demeanor changed a little toward me, but I had found a bit of understanding that eased my discomfort. I looked at her directly now, smiled, and offered a remark like, "Here's your food. Shall I bring the table to you?" She would nod weakly and I would leave. We never had a conversation, only a few sentences, really.

During the third week of delivering her trays, I noticed small changes. She seemed to slump lower and lower into her pillows, until a few times she was lying down completely, as if asleep. When I came back to see if she had managed to sit upright and eat, she had a companion near her bed helping her.

The last few days of her life were different, however. I had never witnessed anything like this in the year of my work at the infirmary. During those days, I found a group of sisters standing in half moons at the side of her bed, and chairs were brought in for them to sit on. I couldn't see Sister David Thomas anymore. She was shielded from me. I knocked slightly on the door and a sister came to take her tray from me with a soft "thank you." I thought then, as I do today, that they came to help her die. They came to calm her, to soften the hardness of her fear and anger with their love and presence, day and night.

The sisters must have had shifts, because each day I found them keeping vigil in her room. I don't know if anyone tried to talk with her, but she had to know that they were there—standing, sitting for her. It was the quietest and simplest act of love I had witnessed as a sister.

One morning when I entered the kitchen, Sister Alphonsis left her position at the counter and came up to me. She rarely did this. I had walked over to my cart to see if it was ready for delivery and she met me there. I looked up in surprise. Her eyes held mine for a few seconds before she spoke. Then she told me softly, "There's no tray for Sister David Thomas today. She died late last night." I watched her face, searching it without speaking, and then, as if she knew what I wanted to ask, she continued, "She died peacefully, her heart calm, and she was not alone."

Sister David Thomas and I never had a conversation of any kind, except the two that I have mentioned here, but she has never left my mind. I know that every death I have experienced, even in the impersonal way as her death was to me, has formed a cloth of understanding around me.

Eventually, I began to comprehend, as any of us can do only imperfectly, sister's anger and her fight for life. If life is sweet and we are given this body and this soul to enjoy family, books, nature, music, and food, to name a few of life's pleasures, why would any of us just lie down and roll over? If we have held the beauty of our time here in awe and gratefulness, why wouldn't we feel the terrible finality of all we have loved?

At fifty-three years old, I, too, faced the possibility of dying. I had stage three breast cancer with at least four lymph nodes testing positive with the disease. The tumor was invasive, and I had to have my breast removed. Yet, that operation and the others I had during my treatment were not the worst part of dealing with cancer. Neither was the chemotherapy or the radiation. My challenge, like Sister David Thomas's, came from fear, the fear of leaving my husband, my children, my step-children and grandchildren, my sisters and brother, and of course, my friends.

I spent time in my room, sitting on the couch and reading books about accepting cancer, about choosing a positive attitude, and eventually, about looking squarely at the possibility of my own death. According to one of the books, I had to imagine my own death. Imagine how it might look and what I would want to happen during my final days.

It took weeks to even attempt to consider this end of me: of my view out the windows, the lake stretching out from our grass, my garden so full of the plants I loved, my times on the back porch watching the birds, books that I had yet to read, the touch of another person, words I would not be able to say to those I loved. I would start to imagine and get only as far as me lying in a bed, which I realized was the very bed beside me in my room.

Yet, instinctively, I knew that this was the one hurdle I had to climb. I had to imagine the largest fear bubbling around inside me so that I could move ahead. And I had so much to do, so much I could do, to fight my disease along with the chemicals I mainlined and the radiation I exposed my chest to. I had to have a part, and I knew I would be crippled if I were afraid. My fear might stop me from really believing I could get well.

Just as Sister David Thomas, I had friends beside me, but perhaps like her, I found out that in the end, I had to face the real challenges alone and free from all the fears I had nurtured during my life.

My dying took an hour and many tears to imagine. I was in bed with my family – all of them – around me. I still had energy and life, but I knew it was ebbing from me. What did we do? We told stories. We talked about our favorite times, our happiest times, our sad times, our sweet moments of really knowing the other. I listened to them; they listened to me, and in the end, we knew that this was what we give each other. We give memories and moments, and they become part of us, of who we are and how we think. It is one way our lives go beyond the grave.

Like the poet Dylan Thomas, who urged his dying father, "Do not go gentle into that good night," I do not want to give in too easily. Yet, in the next line, Thomas tells his father to "Rage, rage against the dying of the light."

Sister David Thomas had her rage, but in the end, it didn't matter how much she screamed at her fate; it didn't matter for her nor will it matter for any of us. Perhaps the wisest of us will come to understand this.

CHAPTER 29

Guimpe Problems

I F YOU WERE EVER TO see a sister with just the guimpe on, with no veil to drape around and over it, you might think she was suffering from a throbbing toothache. The guimpe, along with the veil and the white plastic form, which sits and digs into a sister's forehead, are simply referred to as "headgear."

The plastic form is rectangular in shape and slants forward from where it rests on her brow, just above her eyes, covering the upper part of her head entirely. It curves back around and above the ears, encircling her head like a shield.

When we novices put together the veiled part of our habit, we donned the hardened gear first, followed by the guimpe to hold it securely, and finished off with the veil, which we pinned carefully to the fabric of the guimpe. Miraculously, the parts stayed together, even in the worst wind, which was a credit to the engineering skill of some woman who probably had the job of designing this apparatus as a penance; a penance she passed on to all of us.

Some of my group of newly professed sisters had very bad luck with this head attire. A few novices found their foreheads rebelling against the constant pressure, which carved a ridge into their skin and pushed down on their eyebrows. They seemed to me to take on the look of stress or worry. Headaches were a common complaint. It saddened me to see my young and healthy friends look so pinched and drawn, so that even rosy cheeks couldn't camouflage their frowning faces.

Many of us spent the greater part of meditation, prayers, meals, and duty squeezing our thumbs under the plastic for a moment's relief. Our eyes half closed, we'd sigh and rub until only distant remnants of the ache remained. Although I suffered at first from the furrowed-brow syndrome of the plastic form digging into my unlined forehead, the starched guimpe gave me more serious and longer-lasting problems.

It began innocently enough. Some red blemishes, little measles-like sores, appeared on the side of my face near my ear. Within a few months, however, I looked in the lavatory mirror at an inflamed face. Peanut-sized volcanoes, throbbing with pus and drainage, covered the side of my face and trailed down my neck. They were no longer surface sores, but deep and painful hard lumps.

I'd hold my breath as I pulled the guimpe over my face to secure it. Broadcloth is an unforgiving fabric when starched to a crispy, bleached-white roughness. Eventually, the chaffing rubbed away at the protruding skin of my infections, and bright red blood began seeping through the material. I first discovered this one evening while undressing.

The luxury of taking off my headgear and freeing my face vanished in my hands when I looked down at my discarded guimpe. It was little consolation that only my fellow sisters had seen these red stains. Off to the washroom I went to scrub the fabric until the blotches were a duller light brown, hoping my one and only guimpe of the week would dry by morning.

The next day I asked my friends to watch for stains and let me know, but that didn't stop me from slipping into washrooms whenever I could to look in the mirror—my friend and enemy at the same time. Often, I left with a wet guimpe, the blood spots reduced in mid-day to a pale rust.

This continued for weeks; the spots became routine but the pain did not. My face was a minefield and any movement resulted in explosive spasms of pain. When I turned my head, the material would catch a scab or open a red-hot blotch.

I knew my mother would have done something long ago. I wondered when Sister Charles, our novice mistress, would notice. In desperation, I'd slide into a seat near her at recreation (most unlike me) or grab the front desk in Church History class, turning my head one way and then the other, giving sister a clear view of my profile. I made an unabashed spectacle of myself but, with an increasing sense of dread, I realized she would probably never recognize my problem.

Sister Charles was truly from another world. I wondered if her feet ever touched the floor when she walked; she seemed to glide instead. She didn't have a distinct right-foot-left-foot gait, and I couldn't tell which foot was in motion at all. Her head never sat on her shoulders as my head did, either. It permanently tilted to the right—way to the right—in a relaxed way, as if she were born with a crooked neck. Her eyes were fixed in a smiling squint, upwards and sideways, like a blind person whose vision pointed inward instead of outward. She was pious and kindly, to be sure; but oblivious to people, and most certainly to mere objects, which seemed to clutter her view.

Perhaps pride stopped me from knocking on her office door sooner; I figured that if she hadn't seen my problem by now, she would never really see or understand it. Nonetheless, after several urgings from my friends, who became more and more insistent and increasingly frustrated with my lack of action, I gently rapped on her door one afternoon, listening intently for her muffled, "Come in."

I found her crumpled in her chair, her entire body tilting to the right with one leg tucked underneath her habit. She seemed very small, fragile. I knelt before her, waiting for some word of greeting or encouragement. She sat perfectly still and smiled down at me. No words. I took this as a sign that I should begin talking, which I did. I presented my case as if in court—an ecclesiastical court, I suppose. During the whole of it, she never so much as blinked, never lost her peaceful look of joy. In a tone suggesting infinite wisdom, she finally spoke as if to a child, "God does not see your blemishes. He only sees your soul."

I was prepared somewhat for this, the religious-versus-practical response, yet I could only offer rational evidence in my defense. Feeling small and stupid, I told her that pain and embarrassment occupied my mind during prayer and meditation, and I could not hear God's voice. Plus, my soiled guimpes presented a problem to others. The laundry sisters had to struggle to get them clean, and when they could not, some other sister had to wear a stained guimpe. I just didn't think I could go on like this anymore. The hard, round pimples were like awful bruises and hurt all the time. Did she think that maybe a doctor might help me? Could I get some cream to put on them? The more I talked, the more I worked myself up until my voice was a rising crescendo of desperate pleading.

"Do not worry about your guimpes," oozed out of her mouth like a kind of foggy, slow dream. I felt that my rush of words had caught her in some kind of trance because she seemed to have to snap her eyes a bit to focus on me. Then, as if she'd had time to really process my predicament and found it youthfully sweet of me to worry about the laundry sisters, she said, with an almost motherly smile, "The workers in the laundry will take care of your soiled clothes, and I don't think any of our sisters will be ashamed to wear habits with spots. We are God's servants, doing his work."

I had nothing to say. I knelt there, staring at her, waiting for more. I must have looked at her with such a plaintive expression that she went on, perhaps in an attempt to encourage me, "Your skin will clear up in time. This may be one of God's tests for you."

I knew this was my cue to leave, because her eyes looked up and away from me toward the window. Stumbling to my feet, I murmured a "thank you" and hurried to the door, grateful that she hadn't seen my eyes water.

Finding refuge in a bathroom, I cried a few tears, looked at the reddened masses now reaching my nose, and wanted to drop into some cell somewhere until God had finished testing me. It seemed that only God's magic could clear up this mess, so what choice did I have but to wait and see if indeed another representative of God noticed and took me under her wing. It was a long shot, but I had hope. I even had hope that my sores would go away as sister said they would; that one morning, I would look at myself and see smaller, less-angry red mounds.

Instead, the opposite happened. During the spring and summer, my face blossomed with the trees and flowers as if my system knew it was the growing season. I took refuge in toilet paper; packing it in under my guimpe four or five squares thick to lessen the rubbing of starched cloth on my face. It did help, but each week I found newer and nastier sores.

Fortunately, the novitiate was all but void of mirrors except for a few small ones in the bathrooms, so I did not have to see my face staring back at me, reminding me of how I looked. For this, I was grateful. My busy schedule left little time for shame, and my sister friends were protective of me. If I had to have this plague upon my house, there were many around me who helped to keep my walls from crumbling.

*Visiting with Fr. Schurman and my brother at the Motherhouse.
I have just made my profession of vows and taken the black veil.*

CHAPTER 30

Going Forth to Do His Work

W E NOVICES KNEW THAT THE real deal would come
some day. We'd be sent out like mail-order brides to the
far West, leaving to teach in a city we most likely had never seen
before, to meet a convent of sisters who were strangers to us. It
was what we were educated to do, if only for a few short years. It
wasn't a surprise. No, it was a certainty, but like many "certain-
ties" in life (like death, perhaps), we might avoid the promised
change until it hung like a billboard in front of our faces.

In April of 1965, before our profession of vows on August
6, I was immersed in the "baptism" of poverty, chastity and
obedience. As a religious order we professed to obey and keep
these three vows, at first for only a year. During my year in the
novitiate, the largest share of my education dealt with my impending profession; of taking the black veil and going forth into
the world to represent the Catholic Church and the Dominican
Order when I would be a professed sister, no longer a novice.

The majority of us would go on to teach somewhere, but a

few would be sent to hospitals to work and some would stay at the Motherhouse to study.

In her letter that April, Linda informed her parents, without many details, of our rigorous study of the vows of poverty and chastity, but she emphasized the only vow that we would actually pledge to keep during our profession ceremony…the vow of obedience.

I remember the umbrella effect of obedience, how obedience covered poverty and chastity under its girth. We could withstand, we were told, the pounding rain of temptation if we "stayed true to God in our hearts and minds." Obedience would see us through; if we were vigilant, its umbrella could not be penetrated.

Linda, having learned her lesson well, wrote, "With each vow there comes a privilege, many privileges, and a freedom." She didn't try to explain this difficult paradox—how obedience to God, as decided by our order and the Catholic Church, would set us free—and she did not describe for her parents these newfound privileges granted to us.

Her rhetoric is eerily idealistic as she continued to struggle with her explanation: "We have the freedom to fulfill a life with God. We novices need to grasp the understanding of these commitments. We have to have the strength of character to make them and keep them." Her words seem to be right out of our professed sister manual, but I know that I, too, felt the huge responsibility of becoming a "real" sister. Yet, what I think she might have been saying, and what most of us were actually thinking as we were about to be sent off to places unknown was: "This is going to be really, really tough, and I hope I don't get too scared and back out."

We were guided and directed gradually to the commitment we would make in August; though I knew that being guided and prepared might not mean being "ready." Even the eight-day retreat I was required to make before profession, according to

Canon Law, did not sufficiently cement into my willful nature just what it was I was agreeing to do by being "obedient."

The retreat coincided with Holy Week, so I received a double whammy of inner reflection and somber Liturgy...of black cloaks, which all of us wore over our creamy-colored muslin habits as a reminder of this darkest week of the church's calendar, and of a chapel bereft of adornment of any kind.

I recall such a drooping of our faces during that time, and an utter avoidance of anyone's eyes. It was easier to hide my misery and depression by closing myself off. I know that many of my friends were coping as I did—we just didn't look outward to see!

Our schedule for those eight days was grueling: silence with no outlet; hours of meditation and vigils late at night; sermons stressing the gravity of our vows and our dedication to God and our order; and, as if that were not enough, eight days' worth of the regular ceremonies we would encounter during Holy Week, plus a few new ones such as General Chapter and fasting.

But Linda, ever optimistic in the face of a great challenge, or tired of having her letters censored, or, as she has stated to me more recently, "fully indoctrinated," posed the situation this way to her parents, "Holy Week is a beautiful time to make a retreat."

Without my spring classes to keep my mind brimming with ideas and challenges, I don't know what might have become of me by mid-May. Fortunately, one of my favorite classes of my life (and I had taken many of them by this time) was in that summer of 1965 as a novice. What pleasure and mind expansion Introduction to Metaphysics gave me! Now, I admit, the topic offered a beautiful escape from reality...my reality. I could imagine for hours what it meant—really meant—to *be*. The great thing was that I didn't have to think about myself, and my existence, just existence itself. The topic had no relation to my immediate situation; therefore, attending class and thinking about the heady stuff of being was like watching a movie every day for that one hour, leaving reality at the door.

One of my friends, Jan, who left the convent as well, re-members a few more things about that Metaphysics class, which I had not remembered. (Jan was probably my true op-posite in personality. She was comfortable in herself, funny and easygoing.) First, she recalled that Metaphysics was one of the toughest classes she took and, that far from energizing her, it totally depleted her. In fact, a group of novices had no idea what the instructor was talking about! According to Jan, when we finished our duty of delivering trays in the infirmary, we met (covertly and without permission) for a tutoring class. We sat in a circle, she remembered, while I answered their questions. I picture Jan's round, open face listening intently, waiting for this mumbo-jumbo of abstract concepts to make sense. She has as-sured me that our little lessons did help; she passed the course. We repeated this evening ritual after every class. I had a rapt audience of novices hinged on my every explanation, while I was most likely grateful to them for giving me the opportunity to "carry on" about the great mysteries of being.

Somewhere in that last summer at the Motherhouse, we were given a real diversion, a time away from the rigors of our studies and preparation for profession. We were taken to Innesfail, another property owned by our order.

Again, we provided the cleaning crew free of charge, but when our jobs were finished, I truly enjoyed this retreat into nature's arms. I knew of and loved Yeats's poem, "The Lake Isle of Innisfree." Though my memories may have become exagger-ated over time, I'm certain this vacation was for me a turning *to* rather than turning *in*. The words from Yeats's poem, "And I shall have some peace there, for peace comes dropping slow…," described me as I dropped into the languor of the Innisfail days. The quiet pace of that spot in time and the waters of the lake soothed me into a sharper reality—I was going to be all right, no matter what I chose to do in August.

In addition to the blessed tranquility of Innisfail, I interacted again with the sisters who were in the class before me; the ones who helped dress me for reception and, later that evening, cut off my hair.

They came back to the Motherhouse and to Siena Heights College to take classes after their first year away from the close confines of the novitiate. Perhaps it was that some of them finally found a job they loved. Perhaps it was the confidence they gained from running a classroom with upwards to fifty students at twenty years of age. Or perhaps in their daily lives they were given the opportunity to be independent. I do not know for sure, but these same novices who seemed cookie-cutter images of each other, with their serious, downcast faces while in the novitiate, had taken on a lighter look, laughing and regaling me with stories from their first year in the trenches. The prospect of going forth was actually beginning to look good.

In Linda's last letter to her parents regarding the particulars of profession, she definitely lays it on thick. "Friday, August 6, the Feast of the Transfiguration, is a very important day in my life. This is the day of my first profession. For me it is for life."

Reading her comments today, I might be tempted to question her sincerity. I know better, however. If I could get my hands on the letter I wrote home that July, I would probably find a similar tone. We did want to feel as if we would be committed for life. Our class of one hundred women who entered the Adrian Dominican Sisters was eager to change the world, to make a difference. Like Peace Corps volunteers, we wanted a different life, and inherent in that vision of our lives was service and dedication to a cause bigger than ourselves...noble and idealistic perhaps, but real for us in the culture of the early '60s.

Our ceremony on August 6, 1965 was quite similar to reception the year before; it was all about veils. While as postulants we traded a wedding veil for a sister's white veil; as novices we traded a novice's white veil for a proper sister's black veil. We were now, in appearance at least, a real nun.

This all happened very early at an eight o'clock Mass, which our parents did not attend. Standing before our Mother General, I used the name I had been given at reception and declared this vow,

> *"I, Sister Marie Petra, make profession and promise obedience to Almighty God, to the Blessed Virgin Mary, to our Holy Father Saint Dominic, and to you, Reverend Mother Mary Jean, according to the Rule of Saint Augustine and the Constitution of the third Order of Saint Dominic of the Congregation of the Most Holy Rosary for one year."*

It's a mouthful of prepositional phrases, but I remember having the most serious intentions when I stated my vows.

I met my parents later that afternoon. I have photos of myself with my father and sister and one, too, with Father Schurman. Yes, he never missed a milestone in my journey, and as I write this, I feel sad to have lost him from my life.

About a week after this day of our profession, we novices assembled together outside on the Motherhouse lawn. I recall the sun shining all around us, the August sky brilliantly blue and exciting. Rows of chairs had been set out with a single aisle in the middle. All sixty-four of our group who had stayed through our two years of training flocked to the lawn, giddy with excitement and apprehension, hugging each other, taking hands in nervous clasps, reacting to the wonderful doom that would befall us within a mere few minutes. We would be handed a small envelope with the name and city of a convent where we would be sent to teach and live the life we had chosen.

In an attempt to contain our rather hysterical behavior, we were asked to be seated. Left to my own thoughts, I remember praying that I would get a place in Michigan. I had no sense of adventure back then. Mostly, I wanted desperately to be in a convent near my novitiate friends, Linda, Dawn, and Janet. Some of our group actually wanted to go to the far-flung corners of the United States; I, of course, did not. I'd never been west; it could have been a different country, as far as I imagined. Yet, all of us knew that our assignments could be as close as Jackson, Michigan, or as far away as either Albuquerque, New Mexico, or Buffalo, New York.

We sat this way until Mother Mary Jean herself came to our gathering. Her first words instructed us that we were to wait until the last sister had been called to accept her assignment before we opened our envelopes. What? We looked at each other stunned and irritated, our first challenge of the vow of obedience. After accepting our envelope, we had to hold it in our jittery hands, while the rest of the names were announced and other perspiring sisters popped out of their seats for their envelopes.

When Mother Mary Jean handed me that very portentous envelope, I pulled myself together enough to bow and reply, "May God Reward You, Mother." I felt such relief and anticipation at once, but I knew I would have to wait at my seat until the last name was called. Personal discipline was always the first and last lesson of any sister, whether we were aware of it or not. So I sat, sweaty hands holding my envelope, until Mother Mary Jean gave us the word.

Oddly enough, the name of the place was anti-climactic and downright funny. After looking at the city and state of our new assignments, we turned at once to the novice next to us with identical questions:

"Where's Inkster, Michigan?"

"Flossmoor, Illinois? Anyone ever heard of it?"

"Oh my gosh, I'm going to California, somewhere called Oakland."

"I'm finally going to be somewhere warm; look Winslow, Arizona. I guess that is pretty good."

Really, none of us had any idea where we were going. Finally, with more and more queries, we each held a small notion of our "place," but it was far from specific.

Nonetheless, we felt relieved, and as we talked with some of the other professed sisters, we gained new and mostly good information about our convent and school.

I was told over and over that I was one of the lucky ones. Could it be that St. Patrick's Elementary School in Joliet, Illinois, was going to be a light at the end of this novitiate tunnel?

Linda, who was going to Albuquerque, was elated. Her adventurous spirit had found a wonderful outlet in the West. Janet was headed to Dearborn, Michigan, and Dawn to Detroit, Michigan. Good friends scattered beyond my easy grasp.

Yet, surprisingly, I did not worry. I loved to write letters, and during my stay at St. Patrick's, I went through reams of paper to talk with my friends. I wrote pages and pages until folding the bulk of them and stuffing the envelope became a challenge.

Even today, with e-mail and my cell phone, I still linger over my notes to friends and family. I love the feel of paper; the special designs that will be just right for what I want to say. I love the ritual of addressing the envelope, tapping a stamp in the corner and finally licking the flap—my own mark—to send it on its way.

PART 4

Teacher

CHAPTER 31

Out In the World Again

A SHINY BLACK CAR CAME TO get me that second
week of August after profession. The other novices and I
had to be sent on our way, since a new group would be taking
our places in the novitiate, and there was no room in the inn for
sixty-four additional tenants. Classrooms all over the United
States waited for our brand-new faces and energetic bodies to
bring life and learning to them, and hospitals as well waited for
the few nurses among us who would administer to the sick.

I shared the ride with another sister from my novitiate
crowd, Sister Timothy. It made sense; she would be teaching a
few miles away from me in the town of Rockdale, Illinois. Why
drive two black cars when one could do the job? Plus, I was
saved from driving the entire five hours alone with someone
I didn't know, listening to the silence as our voices fell off, for
want of something to say.

I was lucky. Sister Timothy was without a doubt the jolliest
gal in our crowd. If her round face ever wore a frown or her
eyes ever stared dully at the world like a pair of flat black buttons, I never saw it. No one rode the waves of postulancy and

novitiate as smoothly as she.

As we neared Joliet, the sister who drove us became more animated, telling us we would be driving over one of the six bridges that crossed the Des Plaines River in the city of Joliet. I was intrigued by her account of these bridges, (built in the 1930s), and the view fanning out from our vantage point as we drove over one of them.

I did not live near water as a child, and the Des Plaines seemed to swell near Joliet like a lake. It curled and moved like a living thing, and the bridges seemed so brave and beautiful hanging in the air above those waters. Months later, when we crossed another bridge, I would move my eyes from left to right to capture the sight of each bridge suspended like a necklace on either side of us, silhouettes of structural engineering etched into the sky.

To my surprise and delight, my convent sat squarely in the middle of a neighborhood in Joliet. The houses, all distinct brick bungalows, and the lawns dotted with trees of every sort reaching out to the road gave me such a feeling of elation. Families with kids and dogs and bikes lived across from the convent.

It warmed me to be in the midst of all this regular living in an older section of town—a place of stories and history. I felt comfortable right away. I walked up the steps of the modest brick structure less fearful and more hopeful than I ever could have imagined while back in Adrian, nervously awaiting my departure.

My Mother Superior, Sister Leonard, greeted me at the door, and here was my second surprise and relief: she nearly bounced with excitement when she saw me standing on the threshold, her round face breaking into a smile that engulfed me before her arms did. She took possession of me as a mother does with a child who is entering unfamiliar territory. Holding a protective arm across my shoulder, she introduced me briefly, since we were moving all the while, to the various sections of the house, gently guiding me this way and that to the large common room where the sisters waited for me. Her handling of me was so expert that I didn't have a moment to anticipate the pressure of all those sets of eyes on me as soon as I entered the room.

And, boy, did they size me up; from the oldest sister whose mouth appeared frozen in a single line curving down at each side to the youngest sister whose eyes and face broadened in a sympathetic smile. They had been sitting in the large room when I entered, and I imagine that they stayed seated so that they did not appear to rush me. Yet, I felt like a spectacle standing there in my rumpled habit, a few small bags at my feet. Each sister said her name and a few stood out like Sister Maura, whose easy smile and welcoming words bounced into the air. I thought right then that we would be friends for sure. Sister Leonard was at my side the entire time, and when there was a lull in the air, she filled it up with, "I think Sister Marie Petra would like to see her room and relax a bit." And extending her arm toward the stairs, she led me away.

I had seen some of the professed sisters' rooms in the Motherhouse (one in which I tried on the headgear of the Mother Prioress), so I figured my room might be similar, yet perhaps a bit smaller. I followed Sister Leonard with no real expectations, but all the while I climbed, I knew that this was a big deal for me. Sister had said "her room." How could I not love a room of my own? I realized that I had not had such a spot for two years. I had unwittingly become accustomed to living in quarters with several sisters, retreating to my small alcove at night, and rarely, if ever, in the daytime. For our two years of training, we lived in a group, moved in a group, ate at the same time, studied only in common areas, and slept in dorms. Privacy was a forgotten luxury. Now, I would have a room of my own, a room with a view, and a special perk—a room at the end of the hall!

At first I was so taken with the desk and chair placed by the wall that nothing else mattered. I had not one but two windows.

One window was situated right next to the chair, so that I could look down or up at the trees while writing or studying, watch the birds, the sky, and all the special stuff you get to see when living above the earth. I could peek at the street below with its steady stream of cars, and since it was still warm outside, all of the sounds of this life floated right up to me. It was like living in a tree house.

But there was more. I had my own sink nestled into a niche in the wall. Amazing. My personal washbasin for teeth, hands, clothes. A bathroom would have made my world complete, but there was one down the hall, well, way down the hall, which I discovered rather quickly, was perhaps why I had that particular room. However, the stumbling walks to the bathroom in the middle of the night were a small price to pay for my little world set apart from the rest. I was beginning to taste the flavors of freedom, and each one was delicious.

The second window looked out on the home of a family I came to know very well, the Mulligans, whose children attended our school, all five of them. The view from that window also looked out on part of the school playground. The Mulligan home was probably three lots away from my view of it, but I came to love seeing the Mulligan children at play in their backyard and hearing the music of their voices. Their squeals and laughter from tag or "London Bridge is Falling Down" became a background to my work at my desk when the windows were opened wide to the outside.

I was twenty years old, and in all my time growing up, I had never known parents as attentive and loving as the Mulligan parents. The mother presided over the backyard with an arm to push a swing, a hand to fix a hair clip, a Band-Aid for a scraped knee, and, if needed, as a participant in a game, a referee, and, of course, a waitress carrying a tray of lemonade and cookies. Mrs. Mulligan never seemed to tire of her job of nurturing her five

children who were all very close in age. She was so much more
real than Mrs. Cleaver! Here was a mom in the trenches, not in
a pristine kitchen with her housedress perfectly ironed or her
hair swept up like a wave while she prepared a four-course meal.

Mr. Mulligan literally stepped out of the car to screams of
"Daddy, Daddy!" and into the game or activity of the moment.
He played ball with them often. Unlike many of the fathers of
my peers, Mr. Mulligan did not seem to need thirty minutes of
quiet time to settle down from work to be ready to mingle with
the family; he walked into their world seamlessly, ready for fun.

I observed a lot about parenting from my perch; and without
even knowing it, I, too, waited for Mr. Mulligan to come home
as I walked back from my classroom in the late afternoon. He
was very shy, very modest, and immensely good-looking. I
would stop and watch this family, remembering my own childhood and the sweet days of carefree monkey-in-the-middle or
freeze tag. I couldn't get enough of the life next door and down
the street and in the city: of the shops, the restaurants, and the
taste of the actual world in all its fine or tattered glory. It may
not have been the whole world, but my neighborhood in Joliet
was familiar to me. The energy bursting around me felt like a
soothing balm, full of the sounds of cars and squealing children,
of lawn mowers and bikes tooting, of wagons rumbling down
the street. And in spring and fall, the smoky tang of barbeques
and the sweet and citrusy perfume of freshly mowed grass
wafted through the air.

I had found normal again...and I knew it. Even though I
smile now at this fact—how the life of a nun might be considered "normal" by the rest of my neighbors—that feeling was
exactly what my spirit needed after novitiate. Joliet was my
Dearborn Heights, my home on Riverview. The school next to
our convent where I walked across the playground to my classes
was a little bit closer than Our Lady of Grace grade school. I

would have a real job. I would be teaching, but not just with dolls and teddy bears in front of me. Now I would have real children, each one a distinct person and each one equipped with speech and hands to write. I would love opening books with them, hearing their child voices read, watching their faces light up with understanding. Oh yes, I had waited for this chance a very long time. I could get back into a groove, orchestrated by my own hands and heart. And I thought, maybe life might be sweet again.

CHAPTER 32

Much Ado about Nothing

FOR THOSE FIRST TWO WEEKS in August of 1965, I rarely saw my private room. I had work to do and plenty of it. A second grade classroom sat waiting for me; a room empty except for desks and shelves. I was the interior decorator; the one who would bring this space to life with all kinds of itsy-bitsy stuff that I'd never dreamed could and should make a difference to anyone. All of the sisters were excited to begin, even the older ones. "Just wait," they said. "Just wait till you see what we have in the basement!"

The basement. I saw: very long tables, at least three or four of them; mounds of paper in every color and shade; scissors and paste and crayons, and big sheets of paper on rolls, so that you pulled until you had the size you needed. On the floor was a huge lug of a machine that projected an image on the wall so that I could trace a cute little picture of a bear or a child reading a book onto one of the oversized sheets from the paper roll. When I finished tracing, I could use the crayons in a myriad of colors to bring the figures to life.

Decorating a room before the school year began took at least a week. I had avoided art class in high school for the simple reason that through my grade-school years not one teacher had ever selected my artwork as an example. I learned to dread the lady with the art cart who came to our room once a week and gave us exact and copious directions for creating a masterpiece.

Fortunately for me, sisters were encouraged to help other sisters whenever needed. I never hesitated to ask one of our gifted artists to make an acorn, a haystack, a maple leaf, or any of the many autumn choices appropriate for my calendar bulletin board.

Since every sister, except maybe the upper elementary grade teachers, delightedly plunged into the business of making a calendar for that first month of school, I followed suit, figuring that it was important for the students in my class to learn the days of the week, the months, and then the corresponding numbers up to thirty-one. So, after some art angel had expertly drawn an acorn for me, I retreated to my spot at one of the tables and began tracing thirty of them on colored paper for the September calendar.

Of course, the job was finished only when I had cut out each acorn and added a few touches with crayons. This took hours. When I completed my task, I had one of perhaps five boards ready to hang. I was overwhelmed and secretly stunned. Here I was, twenty years old in the prime of my life, sitting in a basement cutting out paper images, and carefully printing letters for a group of eight year olds who may not even care.

I wonder now just why, in the beginning, this bulletin-board activity left me out of the fun loop. Did it resemble a dreaded, old-ladies' knitting circle or an old-fashioned quilting bee; the kind of sewing party that my great grandmothers loved to organize? Would all the "fun" times as a sister resemble this activity? Would my leisure hours be planned again to the minute with games and other group projects?

I worried, with a sinking in my stomach, if I could endure another year of forced fun. I had talked with some sisters who had spent their first year out in a convent teaching just as I was, and they didn't speak about things like this. Instead, they mentioned trips away from the convent, like taking a train to the city for a day. They shopped and went to movies, too. They even had lunch in a restaurant. These sisters fueled my expectations, and here I was stuck in a basement for an entire week. And every sister but me loved it!

That first year in Joliet, as I carefully tiptoed around these women I barely knew, hearing them "ooh" and "aah" over an imaginative sketch of "Mr. Period" for a punctuation bulletin board, it all appeared over the top to me. Those days of tracing curly headed girls and lion faces (for a "Something to Roar About" display of excellent work) left me longing for my metaphysics class. Oh, what had become of me?

During my bulletin-board-mania experience, I couldn't see how this mindless activity was a fitting beginning to a long and arduous year of total submersion into teaching with all of its duties: planning, presenting, correcting, recordkeeping, parent meetings, holiday programs, and the awesome responsibility of discerning what each child might need to be able to succeed.

I didn't know that the school year would whisk me away into its business and never let go. Like Huck Finn on the river, I would try to stay on my raft as it was blown about by wind and currents, and I'd be lucky to have a moment to look at the stars or dangle my feet in the water.

As our week of decorating progressed, I began to see that our paper tracing and cutting and coloring was a creative activity that launched the year for us. We spent that entire week with each other engaged in a singular purpose. Laughter and the easy flow of conversation, which hummed about our heads as our scissors clipped and our crayons colored paper, filled the dark basement and created a safe place. Shoulders leaning in together in deep discussion over this word or that one for a title, or cheers when one of us finally laid out the result of two days' work on the floor, brought us together as friends. By the end of the week, I walked to my job without my usual dread and descended the stairs leading to the lower floor, the art room and my fellow amateur marketing moguls. I had gotten to know them while we were busy creating advertisements for learning, pictures and phrases meant to tantalize our students' curiosity.

I hoped my students would like their room and find it a bright and happy place to spend their day. Yet I still wondered if any of my efforts would make a difference to the kids rushing into my classroom, When September came, I found myself standing near the classroom door greeting each shy yet eager face. I watched as their little bodies entered the room and, of all things, came to an abrupt halt at the calendar board. My new students didn't just notice the board; one of the girls raised her hand, touched the acorn for September 12, and announced, "That's my birthday!"

CHAPTER 33

Sister Marie Petra, Teacher

ONLY A LOUD WHISTLE COULD have brought the hundreds of bobbing heads and jumping feet to rest in their semi-orderly lines that first day of school in early September of 1965. My eyes widened in amazement at the quick efficiency of rows being formed far back into the concrete playground. Even more amazing, here I stood at the front of one of the rows, looking over the almost fifty heads leaning right or left to get a good look at me. Their arms were full of folders with empty sheets of writing paper and pencil holders, which in turn were full of pencils and crayons and erasers. I felt comforted by this trail of fresh and bright faces so like my own, ready for a new beginning. Yet, I was daunted by the overwhelming task of teaching the sheer number of students, stretching out so far beyond me.

As a kid, I had plenty of practice teaching my dolls and stuffed animals, lining up their listless and listing bodies on a couch or my bed. I demanded, from their poor staring faces, examples of short *a* words and other rhyming vowel combinations, which I officiously printed on an imaginary board. Eventually, my slouching forms on the couch were also treated to one of my many boxes of math flash cards. How I loved to hold a card in front of a doll, waiting for the correct answer from her while I figured it out in my head. The best part was pretending she missed it. A yardstick served as my pointer, and when one of my doll students gave the wrong answer, I tapped or at times pounded the bed or couch in front of her. It was great fun and quite therapeutic. I could be indulgent and kind to my class of subjects or a perfect monster, depending on my recent experiences with my sisters or the neighbor kids. Other than paper dolls, which all of my friends loved, I could be found frequently with my pretend class, scolding or praising their performance, until some real person asked me to be quiet.

Yet these actual bodies on that first day of school were so much more delightful than I ever could have expected—the girls with their fresh freckled faces and hair curled into ringlets held by barrettes, with blouses and skirts washed and ironed into department-store newness, and the boys with their hair spit into control and faces scrubbed pink and shiny on top of summer's bronze. Their skinny little bodies wriggled in their prison of shoes and outfits, which the past three months rarely demanded, and they assessed me with friendly, yet wary caution.

They smiled expectantly as I stalled them at the door of our classroom; some were shy and turned away from my attention, but most of the first twenty, then the second twenty, and finally the last eight or so trailing behind walked in eagerly, so crisp and full like September's bluest sky.

I loved our old and roomy classroom, even though it meant more space for bulletin boards. How bright and happy everything looked! In the '80s when I continued to teach, we would be told that too many posters and theme boards with colorful figures and sentences were distracting to our students; but in the '60s only a lazy teacher would not work her room up into a holiday frenzy. Besides, in those days we hadn't learned about attention deficit disorder, and looking back at the children of 1965, I may have had only a few mildly fidgety students out of my entire forty-eight. I can't adequately explain the difference, but I did observe a huge discrepancy as the decades moved forward.

St. Patrick's school was built in the early 1900s. Wood was the primary material for floors, walls, and desks. The windows reached from about two feet above the floor to a few feet from the ceiling. Long and lofty, they were the loveliest part of our school world. We were blessed with light. We saw not only the sky but the trees and birds as well. The floor was covered in oak boards fitted together in varying lengths, which smelled of wax and creaked when we walked. The desks were delightful—at least eight of them ran one behind the other on long metal runners. I must have had six rows of these connected desks for my large brood. When I looked up at my class, little trains of students, each in his or her own car, sat before me. I would never again see desks such as these, which sometimes reminded me of giant toboggans.

Was I ready to teach forty-eight students after only two years of actual college? Did I have any idea how I would manage so many students while teaching reading groups (three different ones), numbers, spelling, science, and, of course, religion? Luckily, our sisters had this figured out. I was assigned a mentor sister, Sister Joseph, who was a second grade teacher like myself. Sister Joseph had cut and polished many young and clueless beginners; and for the first two weeks, she had me trembling in my nun shoes whenever she discussed effective teaching methods and practices, particularly her list topper: classroom management.

Sister Joseph stood about four feet tall and two feet wide. Her eyes bulged out of their sockets at me with such penetrable directness that I fought with myself to keep looking at her while she bobbed her head around and instructed me. (Much later I discovered that she had a goiter condition, but by that time I knew and cared for her for everything I couldn't see or understand during those first two weeks.) Her face, colored in different hues of pink or red, depending on her level of excitement or calm, protruded out of her guimpe. Very soon I could read her moods by the color of her skin and the squint of her eyes, and even more readily, by the set of her thin Irish lips, which I rarely saw in any other shape except a fine, narrow line, clamped tight. Sister Joseph's mode of discourse was gruff; her manner of speaking or instructing direct and pointed. On the practical side, since my lessons with her had to be jammed into a few hours during the short week before school started, she didn't waste time with preambles to soften the message or make her demands palatable.

I had a stack of teacher manuals to study late into the night, and as one busy day followed the other, I wished for more time. Like a kitchen where the cook wants to place items in strategic spots for easy access, I was heartily encouraged by Sister Joseph to figure out which table might be the best, most efficient one upon which to arrange my manuals and daily plan book or which might be the perfect shelf for flash cards, arts supplies, construction paper, newsprint paper, and lined paper. I never dreamed there could be so much stuff to sort through for a teacher.

My young, twenty-year-old body was dragging with the heat of late August and from lifting, sliding, and carting around a mountain of materials I now had to manage. Sister Joseph, however, walked in and out of my room effortlessly, very little panting or perspiration sliding down her nose and cheeks. She never eased off from her litany of suggestions and criticisms. My runners of desks were too close together and students would be visiting; even my desk was in the wrong place—didn't I want to see their faces at all times? No teacher ever put her reading group chairs at the back of the room! And how would I keep track of all of those papers my students would be waving at me if I didn't have specific bins for finished work? If I moved the desks and chairs once, I moved them three times before the day of reckoning. Shelves were filled, and after more careful consideration, primarily by Sister Joseph, they were emptied and readjusted.

Yet, after a few days of forty-eight little bodies filling my classroom, waiting to hear from my mouth what we would do each minute of each hour for an entire school day, I wanted to hug Sister Joseph. Even with all her help, I still found myself twirling this way and that looking for some folder or stack of papers, while one child waved her hand in alarm at her desk and another pulled at my scapular for permission to use the bathroom. I blessed Sister Joseph for the pristine organization we had established, for her help in keeping me sane when the classroom buzzed in many different directions around me.

From our very first meeting Sister Joseph instructed me on her rules for order. The first and most important one was: "Don't smile for at least two months, and preferably till after Christmas. If you do, you'll lose them." I failed that test within a week—and Sister Joseph knew it. She'd pop her head into my room any time of the day without warning, and there I was "coddling" them with my smiles, with a hand on the shoulder, or, God forbid, with an unsuppressed chuckle! Not a word left her mouth, just a scowl, and I knew I was caught. I tried not to like them so much, and when a day had gone a bit over the top with student enthusiasm, I'd panic that in another week I'd have complete chaos.

Of course, when this nightmarish day happened, as it surely might, Sister Joseph would be right there beside me, squinting up at me and shaking her head. Her large protruding eyes would roll back and forth and she'd quip, "You didn't believe me."

Sister Joseph may have invented straight lines because she seemed to feel almost affronted when either my boys' line or girls' line curved through the halls like a snake. For some reason, halls were like church or funerals or the theatre, where even whispering was considered unruly behavior. I was quickly advised to stop my lines for talking or crookedness, stare at my wild miscreants and get order. Waiting for complete silence and orderly lines was clearly more important than being on time for lunch or some special class.

Fortunately, the children were trained in many classroom procedures in their first year of education before I encountered them in second grade; things like raising hands to speak and, much to my surprise, standing to recite. Every morning forty-eight delightful children stood at attention and greeted me when I entered the room with a chorus of "Good Morning, Sister Marie Petra." I was so stunned the first time this occurred that I remember stepping back, my mouth dropping open in surprise, my entire face suppressing a laugh. Often I felt taken aback by the simple trust and respect I received from my young charges.

I had liked many of my early grade school teachers, but the ones who were God's chosen few deserved even more of my respect and honor. A nun was one step down from a priest in the church. Now I was one of those sisters, and standing in front of the classroom, I realized that my students saw me in the same way. The transition to "honorable" sister seemed to occur instantly, yet I still saw myself as Patricia O'Donnell from Dearborn Heights, Michigan. When I felt like an unholy mess of a nun in the novitiate, it was my own personal and private struggle. No one was expecting sainthood from me. Now, I had these little faces looking up at me with such wonder, such regard. Wearing a habit and walking into a classroom in a Catholic school had changed my status; I was automatically put on a pedestal, and even in my black tie-up nun shoes, I felt pretty wobbly up there.

CHAPTER 34

Working with
the System

T HE DISPARITY I FELT SO strongly between the person
I really was and the person I had automatically become in
the eyes of the Catholic community, namely my second grade
students, continued to plague me. However, I did not have the
luxury of profound silence as in the novitiate, where I had many
hours in our quiet world to nurse and coddle my insecurities.
There was work to be done...and right now. My situation demanded that I plunge into my teaching responsibilities with all
my working parts.

Certainly, it helped that I had little else going on in my life
right then: no dating, which can be extremely time-consuming
and often unsettling; no worries about money or losing my job;
(well, I suppose I *could* lose my job, but that was a real long shot)
no concern for preparing my own meals either, since we sisters
had a full-time cook to take care of meals during the week. After
dinner and our evening social time, which usually lasted an hour,
I could go to my room and stay up as late as I wanted.

After I had familiarized myself with most of the second-grade curriculum, I was left with the imposing and unending weight of what elementary teachers referred to as "seatwork." Seatwork was simply a list of assignments to keep the masses busy while the teacher, in this case me, tried to give phonics or comprehension lessons to groups of children at three different reading levels.

Each reading group came up to the little wooden chairs arranged in two semi-circles and received their half hour of what resembled "individualized instruction" in the '60s. After that short and savory period of my almost undivided attention, after I finally had each little body curving into me so that I could give them a happy word or smile for effort and skill, they were sent to be on their own at their seats for an entire hour. What could possibly keep their attention while I was so very busy with my next group of warm and mostly willing subjects? Well, that turned out to be the huge challenge of a first-year elementary teacher, as well as, I might add, the forty-eight students who had to complete the piles of hand-outs each day at their seats.

Seatwork, the solution to this dilemma, appeared to be disingenuous. Wasn't all of my students' written work completed at their seat? Yes, but "seatwork" was different from math work or spelling work or any other specific kind of work. Back then we had books of phonic sheets with lessons on every short and long vowel, blend, diphthong, digraph, compound word, prefix, and suffix. These sheets helped enormously, but some of our highly-skilled students could finish off three of them in less than ten minutes.

I soon discovered the magic word was "color." Each little hand would print the correct blend to start a word, such as "plant," for instance. Those same fingers would then grasp a crayon to color the leaves green and the flower in the potted plant red or blue or yellow. Some sheets had upwards of twenty pictures!

As helpful as these phonics sheets were, however, in reinforcing previous lessons, the entire seatwork challenge both vexed and motivated me. What teacher merely wants to keep her students busy? Yet, without classroom centers (which hit the education scene in the '70s) where students could be engaged in different activities like listening to tapes, playing word games, reading or repeating words to a tape recorder, or performing some related task while their teacher was working with a smaller reading group; our only resource at the time was creating related assignments that might give our students the advantage of some personal choice in the finished product.

I worked more critically engaging assignments into my students' seatwork as often as possible. We learned to fold our unlined paper in all kinds of sections—halves, fourths, eighths, and even sixteenths. My little brood wrote a few sentences on some theme and drew pictures to accompany them; lines like, "Yesterday, I found in my pocket…" and "My bedroom reminds me of…." I enjoyed these assignments because each one was an experiment with putting words and ideas together.

The amazing thing is that back in the mid-sixties, before the onslaught of multiple television stations with an abundance of choices, before video machines in the home or even computers, my students actually took the more open-ended assignments seriously. I never tired of reading them. And the pictures—they delighted me as well as surprised me. Some of these art pieces were little gems of creativity and talent. At times I had to ask a child about a particularly detailed and imaginative picture, which didn't appear to have a connection with the story. Such wonders came out in their explanations, and the scope and range of their thoughtful development and even symbolism left me almost speechless.

I never found a truly adequate answer to the seatwork dilemma, nor did I see one in any other elementary classroom at St. Patrick's. Besides, I was not exactly a seasoned pro. I accepted the status quo because it was simply easier, and I was far too timid to consider other options. What would the older sisters think if my little ones walked from one spot to another, moving around the room like it was a playground with swings and teeter-totters?

Well, I wasn't ready to surge ahead at twenty years old or even at twenty-two. Fortunately for me, not one student groaned when I listed the seatwork assignments for the day. It seems rather astounding that out of forty-eight students, none of them scribbled their letters or words in frustration on the perfectly lined spaces of our phonic sheets. They saved me from utter despair with their easy acceptance of our classroom agenda, especially during seatwork. Day after blessed day, I watched them with a grateful heart as their heads bowed to their papers and their hands ever so carefully formed the letters, then the words, and finally the lines that became shapes and figures of detailed illustration.

Some may argue that private school children were better behaved than public school children, and therefore, more likely to accept directions and please the teacher. Yet the key ingredient in my case, while teaching at St Patrick's, was the parents. Most of the moms and dads I came to know cherished their children, yet also demanded respect from them, which radiated outward to their teachers as well as any adult who responded to them with kindness or criticism. I never felt that my little students were afraid of me, nor did they seem to be inhibited by the steady reinforcement of their parents' discipline; in fact, they appeared to be calmed and made even more carefree because of the consistency in their daily lives. My job was simply made ever so much easier because of the serious attention paid to my students at home. I have always found this to be true—no matter where I taught, Catholic or public school. Fortune smiled on me that first year of my career, and many years later, I can still feel the warm glow of living in such a community.

CHAPTER 35

Some of Them
Don't Go Away

In my three years at St. Patrick's I must have taught almost 150 students. Many of their faces are gone from me now. What remains, however, is my clear impression of mostly happy, untroubled children who devoured our buffet table of books, numbers, maps, and animal studies with little resistance. What also remains solidly etched in my memory are the faces of two boys I taught during my final year in Joliet—the year I wrestled with leaving the convent and the community of St. Patrick's forever.

I had moved "up" to the fourth grade in 1968. After two years of small eight-year-old bodies, fourth graders seemed like giants. I was quite surprised at the difference in their personalities, too. My second grade children were dutiful and eager little students, yet still rather literal in their thinking. What a transformation two years of growing had made. These fourth graders sported an honest-to-goodness sense of humor, and they loved to let anyone near them know it. The day-to-day work became so much more fun. Now I would be violating the "don't smile rule" to an even greater degree—I didn't just laugh softly as I found myself doing with second graders, I laughed heartily (and, afterwards, hoped I couldn't be heard down the hall.)

These kids got my jokes; I could tease them. I could insert a bit of irony or silliness into a lesson and their faces would crinkle in delight, and not just in delight at the joke but a pleasure in themselves for understanding the humor. They wanted to be in on everything, including the response. Within seconds of hearing and getting my humor, their eyes would bounce around like small firecrackers, searching for a suitable response to my pun or gentle taunt. They loved the retort, the banter; in fact, they reminded me of pint-sized Shakespearean actors engaged in the pure fun of repartee.

In my teaching experiences, only seventh graders were as much fun as fourth graders—and I taught every grade from one to twelve with the exception of grades six, five and eleven. I could always count on seventh graders to want to do crazy things in front of the class, especially if they could be in a group with their friends.

Now the two students I remember so well did not stand out for being humorous. Neither one was a class leader in the fine art of the quick comeback. Neither one stood out in the way that the eager, highly motivated learner does by shooting her hand up before my question left my lips or with her steady gaze of concentration while I taught, eyes never leaving my veiled head. Bobby and Keith embedded themselves into my memory by the sheer impact of their avoiding me, and mostly, by the iron jacket of sorrow each of them wore day after day, which weighed down what should have been carefree, ten-year-old hearts and lithesome bodies.

Bobby Maroney was simply a beautiful child. He had deep

blue eyes framed with extra-long, black, almost wet-looking eyelashes. His brown hair dropped to one side, grazing his eyebrows in an Elvis or James Dean sort of fashion. Every part of his face was delicately shaped; even his skin, a pure pristine white, stretched over his cheekbones in a thin, translucent layer.

Yet, the whole effect of his appearance was not in the least effeminate. If he chose to look up at me, peering out from the swath of hair covering his eyes, I would catch my breath in astonishment as if I hadn't seen him every day of that school year. His bone-china look was always surprising, and so different from the large-framed, ruddy-skinned boys who walked into my room from the outdoors, maybe after a game of catch or tag. In that first month of school, I didn't know about Bobby's disease. I had noticed that he was smaller and thinner than many of the other boys. I had seen him shake and gasp after a coughing spell so fierce that his face flushed with a rosy hue and his hands trembled with weakness. I asked only once if he was all right. His head turned slightly sideways to me from its crouch near the desk, and his eyes, blue slits of disgust, bore into me. He did not want my question, and he would not answer. What had I done? He had a cold, yes, a pretty serious one, but I certainly did not mean to single him out. Yet it appeared from his reaction that I had crossed a line.

For days he would not look at me. He'd walk ramrod straight to the reading chairs with his head pointed to the floor. His standing and sitting were jerky and quick, as if he hated the fact that he had to move at all and leave the little island of his desk. I let him have his way; no questions at the reading chairs; no stopping to look at his papers; no look or word at all. I backed off and waited, not out of fear, but out of some ancient intuition that I must.

Eventually, I inquired at the office and asked for his folder. "Oh, yes," Sister Leonard informed me. "He's struggled since he was born. Always fighting to be like other kids. Doesn't ever want to be reminded of it."

"I don't understand. Reminded of what?" I really had no clue.

"Then you will find reading his folder interesting. He has cystic fibrosis, and his disease is advancing more quickly than some. Give him lots of space. Bobby's had his share of scuffs with other kids, mainly boys. He doesn't want to be treated differently, and don't ever let him think you pity him."

"Thanks," I said. "I had no idea. I'll take this with me if it's all right, and bring it back tomorrow." I turned from the office, staring down at the folder with glassy, unseeing eyes.

Her soft voice followed me before I walked through the door. "Sister Marie Petra, remember: we can't save every one of them. Some things are out of our hands."

Of course, she was right. I tried not to watch Bobby, not to pause in my lessons when the congestion in his lungs frothed until I was certain that he could not breathe from coughing and gasping during one of his attacks. I could hear the wheeze of his breathing when I walked past him, his small head and shoulders turned toward the desk, hiding his face and paper from view. This curling-into-his-little-space is the position I remember most—Bobby simply did not open that beautiful face to us often.

There were physical signs of his illness on his body as well as the never-ending phlegm that built up inside of him. His fingers were bent and swollen; especially the tips, which fanned out wide and round at the ends like poor misshapen hammers. He had difficulty holding his pencil, yet, he forced his way from one word to the other, making his swollen fingers squeeze tightly until the tips were white from the pressure. I could read every word of his slash-like scrawl and knew how difficult it was for him when he formed circular shapes for rounded letters like *a*'s and *o*'s.

Gradually, without anyone's really noticing when, Bobby would loosen up his alert and watchful body just a bit. He would lift his hand from his elbow in a casual way to let me know that he had something to offer. I tried not to pounce on those few occasions with too much enthusiasm. I was learning. Sometimes I'd ask someone else first, and then, without looking at him directly, ask, "Bobby?" He had a way of speaking into the air right beside him, flinging off the words to his left, his eyes averted from anyone's gaze. Eventually, I discovered that he was capable of smiling as well, not often, for sure, and usually in response to some silliness going on around him or a perfectly clueless answer by another student. It was not a large grin of teeth, of course, just a slow turning up of his lips, but the look in his eyes was secret, like he had his own personal take on the situation.

We wouldn't see him sometimes for two or three days, and it never seemed easy for him to return to us. His vulnerability showed so clearly on his face, which had turned even paler, and his body, which, already very lean, was noticeably thinner. I wondered how he kept up the fight sometimes. Did he ever succumb to it or allow himself to be sick? Did his bitterness over the stigma of being sick ever soften, at least with his parents? I never knew. Within a week or so, he would work himself back into the world of school, and I was always relieved that he could muster up the courage and the energy to do so.

I do not have as many memories of Keith, the other student whose face remains clear in my mind and whose story affected me. He was a tall boy, very serious, very earnest and always well-behaved. He stood out because he seemed so much more mature than the other boys. Yet, I was happy to note that he offered a grin at times for his few pals and joined them in kickball or some other kind of game during recess. Shy and quiet, he rarely called attention to himself, so it isn't surprising that I don't have as many incidents to recall. He might have been just another very nice kid from my teaching days except for what happened late that fall of Keith's fourth grade year with me.

After school one day, Keith's only brother, who was in high school, arrived home and hung himself in his bedroom. Keith's mother, whom I knew because she often helped out at our school with different jobs, was not home at the time. We talked whenever I saw her in the office or in the halls about Keith or some school activity she was working on. I liked her and enjoyed our conversations; she had the driest sense of humor and always made me laugh. The suicide stunned not only our St. Patrick's Catholic parish, but the entire community of Joliet as well. No one had seen it coming, and the sisters who knew him had difficulty believing he took his life. We talked about his family, one of the nicest in our parish, and mourned for all of them. Keith had no sisters, so in a matter of hours he became an only child.

When I was in seventh grade a friend, Mary Lou lost her sixteen-year-old sister, Sharon. Sharon and her boyfriend were driving around in his car one night. It was late, and they were in a car crash. Mary Lou was never the same. During the funeral, a group of us who knew her well watched her scream and sob, her cries stabbing into each of us. Later, at the cemetery, she grabbed at the casket as it was lowered into the ground. We sat for hours and talked with her, listening as she told us stories about Sharon. Afterwards, she kept Sharon's picture in her room and in her wallet, and would look at it constantly.

Maybe Keith's reaction was so different from what I had experienced in Mary Lou's case because he was a boy, maybe it had to do with the age difference, and sadly, maybe it was because his brother's death wasn't an accident. Nevertheless, I was not prepared for the Keith who eventually came back to my classroom after the funeral. How could I expect him to be the same? He was still Keith, but his shy nature had become a solitary one. His eyes were flat and unexpressive, his shoulders tight, and his walk almost wooden. He moved forward like a stoic Spartan soldier. His earnest face looked at me, unchanged at times, as if he were crying out to be treated the same; but, of course, he carried on his ten-year-old back the heaviness of the tragedy.

When I felt that I could, I asked his mom if he ever talked with her about his brother's death. She said that she had tried, but he had nothing to say.

The year rolled on to June and I said my good-byes to the students. I knew I would not be back at St. Patrick's for the next school year, and it truly bothered me that I could not follow each of these boys and see if a bit of happiness lay waiting in their future. When my thoughts brought me back to them after I was out in the world attending college, I wished at times that I could disguise myself and watch from the far side of the playground as they left the building at the end of their school day. I hadn't let go. Back then and now, they remain in my thoughts, always the young boys they were when I knew them.

CHAPTER 36

New Skin

LESS THAN ONE MONTH AFTER I arrived at St. Patrick's Sister Leonard summoned me. Unlike in the postulancy and novitiate, my stomach did not flutter with anxiety, nor did my mind begin a visual search through all of my past actions to find the possible violation that precipitated my summons. I came to her office in anticipation, and I actually felt rather special that she had asked to see me individually. Wow, this was quite different.

Sister Leonard sat behind her desk, and I must confess it surprised me a bit. What kind of work did she have to do at home? I had assumed that her real work, and perhaps her only work, was to run St. Patrick's elementary school and junior high school. I never asked, but later I realized that she had to manage a home as well—the convent building where we lived. She was smiling like she usually was, in fact, even when sister wasn't smiling, her rosy, full cheeks gave her that appearance. She couldn't be intimidating if she wanted to.

I had never been in her office before and looked around. A window gave light from a spot right behind her, so that she was framed by it. She nodded for me to sit down. Then she said the magic words I had waited for all through novitiate. She came right out with it: "I am wondering if your is skin bothering you. I've watched it get worse since you've come here, and it has to hurt underneath your guimpe."

I leaned back in my chair a bit and must have stared at her in shock, but Sister Leonard sat waiting until I found my voice. "Ye-e-e-s," I drawled out in my amazement. "It's been bothering me since novitiate. I suppose you've noticed that my guimpes get bloody sometimes. I've been putting Band-Aids on the worst ones, but the blood can still seep out."

I would have continued on and on with more examples and gory details, but Sister Leonard was not my mother, and I certainly did not have to convince her.

"So you had some kind of treatment in the novitiate?" she asked. "A cream or salve to put on your face?"

"Oh, no," I said. "Sister Charles...well...sister didn't think I needed anything."

She raised her eyebrows in disbelief and stared at me for about ten seconds. I could tell from her face that she was putting it all together. She didn't mention Sister Charles again or continue with questions. Instead, she lifted her hands a little and placed them on her desk with a slight tap of her fingers and said, "Well, it is quite apparent that you need some treatment now. Right away. I would like to make an appointment for you with a dermatologist. Does that sound all right?"

"Oh, yes," I gushed without shame. "It sounds wonderful. Thank you! Thank you!"

"I'll call today and let you know when you'll be going," she said, and stood up behind her desk as if she would get this process in motion at that moment.

I said my thanks again and walked to my room feeling like a prisoner whose guilty verdict had been overturned by some benevolent judge. Relief is not a strong enough word. Dropping down to my bed, I sat for many minutes staring at the tiled floor. The shame I felt from nickel-sized sores blaring out at everyone I encountered seemed to give way like a dam, and tears spilled down my face onto my scapular. In a daze I watched the water spots make large circles on my white muslin, and eventually I felt very tired. I really wished I could roll over on the coverlet and sleep.

The dermatologist was visibly shocked when he examined my skin. He seemed irritated with the entire situation, yet he never asked me why I had not received any treatment before this visit. Sister Leonard must have given him a short history when she made my appointment. My sores were now a serious matter. A raging staph infection had taken over and I would need antibiotics.

I went to see him two times a week, but he rarely touched me. Instead, he put me under a large red lamp for about twenty minutes, which burned my skin and caused it to peel. My eyes were protected with pads from the red light that saturated my face in heat. I could pretend I was sitting in the sun for those twenty minutes. I let myself sink into the calm of the room as if I had no cares or responsibilities. Each week the mounds became smaller and less red. The doctor was worried about scarring, but at this point in my struggle, scarring was a small price to pay if my reflection in the mirror above my sink looked back at me free of sores.

I never minded the peeling or the permanent sunburned look. My students noticed the redness, though, and when they mentioned it, I told them I was getting help for the sores on my face. It was always easy to be honest with them. They would nod their heads in understanding, smiling in support. They only wanted to know one thing: "Does it hurt?"

In about three months, my new, soft-as-the-flesh-under-my-forearms skin was clear, white, and freckle-free. I had always sported a face full of those brown specks, and even if they were missing only a few months until the sun hit my cheeks and nose, it felt wonderful to have a creamy, unblemished look. Even though there were a few scars on my face near my ears, they were not deep and as far as I could tell, only noticeable if someone looked very closely.

Oh yes, I found my confidence again when talking with others, and the pain and inconvenience eventually became just a memory. I could say that I only wanted to look my best for God or some similar sentiment, but that would be dishonest. At twenty, I was a young woman who wanted to look good, and I don't remember feeling one bit ashamed about it.

CHAPTER 37

Getting to Know You

SISTER IGNATIUS ENTERED OUR COMMUNITY of St. Patrick's in that summer of 1966 and none of us was the same afterwards. It was the summer after my first year of teaching, and I was very excited to leave Joliet and return to our Motherhouse in Adrian to continue working on my bachelor's degree. The sprawling grounds would be full of the huge oaks and maples I had come to love, with flowering bushes at every turn of my head and lush green grass under my feet as I strolled to and from classes. Plus, our prayer schedule would be relaxed—nothing like the novitiate when I had last been at the Motherhouse.

In addition, I could visit with friends from my crowd whom I hadn't seen for a year, and each of us had stories to tell. We had written each other during our first year of teaching, so I was ready to hear the details, laughing and commiserating, while we shared our experiences. Yet, I hate to admit it, but school with new courses to dive into was the biggest draw.

This time I was given a choice in my classes, which made it even more exciting. Imagine, I thought, not one theological virtues course, which seemed to have the same affect on me as a nurse would in an operating room mainlining an anesthetic into my vein. And my summer would not include any moral virtues classes either, which invariably caused me to shift here and there in my seat with all the tidy saintliness. I wanted goodness to evolve in me if possible, but the endless theorizing about righteous virtues seemed only talk. I never developed a grand plan to nurture moral virtues, only a desire to be honest with myself and have the courage to change when my actions warranted it. My hopes for interesting classes in this first summer as a professed sister were high.

I had no idea that Sister Ignatius was going to be joining us at St. Patrick's for the 1966–67 school year, that is, until she announced her impending move via an invitation to "please come and meet her." Even I, naive and clueless as I still was, wondered just what was going on. What was the big hurry to gather us together *now* when we would be seeing her in a few weeks? Why didn't this sister wait until August and simply meet us when we resumed our teaching year in Joliet? Or could it be that instead of an opportunity for us to get acquainted with her, she actually wanted to check us out prior to coming to live in our convent?

About six of us from St. Patrick's were studying in Adrian that summer, and within a week, we found each other and clucked over this most unusual situation. After all, she wasn't going to be our Mother Superior; she was just another teacher. According to other nuns with whom I spoke, this big deal about meeting our new sister was unprecedented, and I was very curious.

We met in one of the college cafeterias, usually off-limits for us during the regular school year but open to us now, in order to accommodate the large crowds of sisters who came to Adrian to continue their education. Some of the older sisters from St. Patrick's grumbled as they approached the cafeteria door for our introductory meeting, and wore the slightly outraged look of "Who is this upstart anyway?" I knew immediately that it wasn't going to be a pleasant affair. Our feet moved so slowly that we could have been prisoners tied to a rope, forced to continue closer and closer to the table. Consequently, our unenthusiastic gait offered us a bit of time to study the small group already assembled, and most particularly, the new face of our hostess, and soon-to-be housemate, in Joliet.

Sister Ignatius sat at the head of a long wooden table situated near the windows and the afternoon sun. She turned her body quickly when she saw us approach, flashing a smile as bright as the blinding light of a camera. Everything about her face was intense and brilliant, and I couldn't figure out if her sparks of movement came from a nervous energy or a planned performance. I did know that taking my seat at a distance from her gave me a safe and excellent spot from which to observe her. She looked like what I always imagined Queen Elizabeth the First might look: regal, cunning, and terrifyingly beautiful.

Her eyes were a piercing ice-blue, outlined in a darker hue around the edges and framed with lashes that curled out from her lids like sun rays, reaching forever. I found it difficult to gaze at them, and even more difficult to look away. She had the classic features I had seen in the works of the master painters: a long, thin nose that pinched to a sliver at the bridge, and plump, round lips forming an almost perfect circle of fullness. Of course, her freckles were the lovely kind—golden light brown and evenly distributed about her face as if a make-up artist had placed each one with precision.

Yet, within ten minutes of guarded observation, I knew I should not trust this sister. She scared me. My reaction was from the gut, and I felt myself retreat back into my seat away from the penetrating air of danger that emanated from her. While she talked and beamed her white teeth around the table, I wondered what thoughts lurked inside her head. What driving need did this artificial invitation come from? What did she want from us, and even more unsettling, what could she want from me in the future?

Sister Joseph sat next to me, and when I saw the slump of her shoulders, her head down and veiled, I knew we had both felt a similar distrust. What brought out this distrust? I am sure my perceptions came from many things, but my very first clue had to be her manner. Her very thin body, perfectly clothed in a habit that appeared to have come from the cleaners with creases in places I had never dreamed could be possible, sat rigidly erect, her long swan's neck seeming to stretch even higher off her shoulders. From this posture, her head moved from side-to-side in such all-encompassing grandeur that one would think she was blessing us with her glances.

Of course, she had begun to speak to us during my consideration of her, and I, hesitantly, took in the first trills of her syrupy, high-pitched welcome. "I asked you to come here because I just couldn't wait to meet all of you," she said. The sound of her voice charged the air of our silence, and her eyes blinked sparks of electricity, so that in comparison we all seemed a group of stupefied lumps sitting around her.

She then instructed us concerning what to say when it was our turn (and we would have turns) beginning with the sister who happened to be at her immediate left. "Well, let's go around the table starting with you," she said, nodding to this unfortunate sister, and then continued, "Why don't you begin with your name, the grade you teach, and finally...let's see... how about a little bit about yourself, anything you think will help me remember you."

All right, was this today's lesson and were we her students? The group of us had finally awakened. By this time, I was suppressing a nervous laugh, but most of the women gathered at the table looked from side-to-side, as I eventually did, with incredulous glances that turned quickly to irritated frowns. I had no idea how my sister friends would handle this, but I figured it was going to be interesting.

The first unlucky sister stumbled through her introduction with many encouraging comments from Sister Ignatius. Sister Catherine, the young sister who had smiled at me so warmly when I was introduced to everyone on my first day at St. Patrick's, was next. I noticed she had been the only one during Sister Ignatius's introduction to sit forward in her seat and stare at her in rapt attention. Her warm voice softened the entire atmosphere as she sincerely spoke about herself, all the time holding her eyes on Sister Ignatius. She made it look easy. I wanted to sound an alarm right then to her; tell her to be careful and not so open and willing, so inviting of friendship.

Most of us zipped through our introduction, offering some superficial hobby or interest in describing ourselves. I said that I loved to read, which quite likely could have applied to most of our group sitting there. Another sister, the oldest in the house, said that she crocheted during her free time, and still another sister remarked that she liked to cook. When I finished my very short yet adequate introduction, all the time feeling like a perfect fool going through the hoops of this rigid meet-and-greet gathering, it was Sister Joseph's turn.

During the eight or so previous introductions, Sister Joseph kept her head almost to the table in a low crouch, but every so often she would turn her face toward me and roll her eyes upward with a look of pained nervousness, perhaps even anger. I wanted to protect her from this ridiculous ceremony, but what could I do? Could I stand up and say, "Sister Joseph isn't feeling well. I'm going to take her outside for some air?" Well, yes, I might have done that if I wanted to risk causing her even further anxiety, but who was I to decide if she could or could not perform the requested introduction? I sat instead with a mounting dread for her and did nothing.

When her turn came, she barely lifted her head and spoke to

the table as I watched in concern. "I'm Sister Joseph. Teach second grade." It was a low, yet distinct bark of an introduction.

Sister Ignatius waited a few seconds for her to continue and then, as if Sister Joseph was a timid new student in her class, she encouraged, "And what else can you tell us about yourself?"

A moment passed and Sister Joseph resettled herself in her seat and offered only one word: "Nothing."

The room froze as if all the air had been whooshed away with that word. Fortunately, within a few seconds the next sister sprang into action and took up the baton that saved Sister Joseph from further prodding. I did not hear the introduction because my attention was still on Sister Joseph, who lifted her head a bit from her slouch and again shot those large protruding eyes up at me, but this time a glint of spirit and resolve had taken the place of anxiety.

I had learned to value Sister Joseph's honesty and forthrightness as she guided me in that first year of teaching, and little by little, she seemed to trust me as well. We were comfortable around each other. Yet at the precise instant that she refused to say more, I wanted to hug her wide slumped shoulders. As I looked around the table, I noticed that we were a group transformed. Sister Joseph had lifted the veil and confronted the nonsense. Most of us couldn't help the hint of a smile that crossed our lips. I could feel the sisters near me sit up a little taller as if they too would not be Sister Ignatius's puppets. It felt as if a rush of air had come through the opened windows, and inside my head, silent cheers were flying with the wind out the door.

CHAPTER 38

Goodbye and Hello

I DID NOT SEE SISTER IGNATIUS again in the few short weeks that were left of our summer in Adrian; however, that does not mean I did not worry myself over her actual presence in our house. Could she really be coming to stay? I wondered if the easy flow of my days would be gone. I knew things would change, and I couldn't imagine a person like her not interrupting our easy camaraderie. She would want to control— yes, that was it. But worse than that, she would add a distinct tension, perhaps even a challenge to our way of doing things. Of course, her moves would be planned and orchestrated like the meeting in the summer.

I imagined her popping up everywhere: in the hallways, across from me at meals, as I left the shower in our communal bathroom, and worst of all, alone with me as we drove around taking care of errands or ran the large ironing mangle in the basement or cleaned the entire kitchen on a Saturday. How would I avoid her penetrating look? Her silent demand for more attention?

The new school year began in much the same way as my first

year did. We climbed down to our cave in the basement, which as if by some miracle was all ready and waiting for us, brimming over with tables of paper and crayons and scissors and glue. We plunged into the large and small tasks of the bulletin board business, grateful for the distraction.

I would wait to take a place at one of the tables until I could see her settled somewhere away from me. I knew it was shameful that I worked so hard to avoid one of my own, a fellow sister, but by now my uneasiness about her had taken over. Throughout the time that she lived with us, I never doubted my instincts warning me to be careful around her.

If she passed me in the upstairs hallway, I hurried my steps and looked frazzled as if I were late for something. I'd smile and nod, but even when she shot a question at my retreating back, I'd answer her briefly as I escaped down the stairs. I watched her at lunch—furtively, sneaking glances while my head leaned down to take a bite—and then more openly when she shared stories of her morning with her students. At first, she tried to include all of us in her sphere of attention, offering the brightest of smiles and a particularly piercing gaze for those from whom she demanded a response. If she happened to direct her conversation at me alone, I felt as if she had taken the seat beside me, grabbed my hand, and forced me to be her confidant. Finally, I learned to focus my eyes just down from her face to her upper chest.

While I was evading Sister Ignatius, I watched with increasing distress as Sister Catherine encouraged her. Since no one in the house had appeared willing to offer Sister Ignatius the kind of singular involvement she needed, it was inevitable that she would find in Sister Catherine a wonderful companion. There were small signs at first. I noticed a kind of complicit smile exchanged at meals or recreation. While Sister Ignatius had become rather quiet around us, she directed her few comments only to Sister Catherine. Then, very quickly, the two of them seemed to be together all the time. They waited for each other to walk to their classrooms, heads bent together in some deep conversation; and after school, I'd see them strolling back to the convent in similar postures.

So why would I be concerned? Could I be simply prejudiced and slanted against any friendship Sister Ignatius might have developed? Perhaps, but I'd still have to deal with this aura of exclusion that surrounded Sister Catherine and Sister Ignatius whenever they were together. I would never have interrupted their stroll to or from school because they didn't acknowledge me when I passed them.

Other sisters had certain friends in our house, but I never felt that I couldn't walk up to them and join the conversation. I didn't expect Sister Ignatius to greet me since I had spurned her attempts to engage me; but when Sister Catherine left me out of the loop, I was surprised. More and more during our times together, either at the table or during our evening recreation, the large group of us seemed to dull them. They sat with quiet faces and appeared, not exactly bored, but uninvolved.

After school one afternoon I needed to ask Sister Catherine a question, and made my way down the halls to her room. When I came to the door I saw that Sister Catherine had a visitor. Sister Ignatius was sitting on the side of the large oak desk, her head and body leaning toward Sister Catherine who sat in the chair behind her desk. They were quietly discussing something and did not notice me. After waiting by the door, I took a few steps into the room, hating to intrude, which is what I felt I was doing. Sister Ignatius moved her head when she heard my steps and stared at me. Her eyes had none of the previous sparkle and intensity I had noticed when I first met her, only a straight, cold look that seemed to say, "What are you doing here?"

Of course, I floundered around a bit, apologizing for my interruption. To my relief, Sister Catherine left her chair and came to me. I took care of my business, and while I walked back to my room, I thought, *this* is what our postulant mistresses meant by particular friendship. What they were objecting to with postulants was nothing like what I just experienced! The accusations against Linda and I while we were postulants seemed downright ridiculous now— we had never been exclusive. In fact, I remember that at the time I tried to think of instances when we sat alone or ignored the other sisters, and I could think of none.

The term, particular friendship, was odd for sure, but the feeling of discomfort others might have when around two sisters who interact exclusively with each other is very real. I understood that now, and not only did their behavior make me feel uncomfortable, it also made me feel angry. What was wrong with them? And what had happened to our quiet and kind Sister Catherine? I wanted her back, not this unresponsive robot who had replaced her.

It was one thing to find the two of them together in a classroom, but in a bedroom was another matter. We were asked to visit with other sisters in the hallways, the common room, and the dining room, any of the many rooms in the convent, except our bedrooms. When someone came to my bedroom to talk, they usually moved back from my door into the hall so that I had to join them there. All of us did this. If we did walk into someone's bedroom, we stood during the time we spent talking.

When I walked by Sister Catherine's room one evening, I was surprised to notice Sister Ignatius sitting on the bed with Sister Catherine next to her. As I passed by, their heads immediately swished toward me as one head, as if both of them had antenna wired for danger. Now even Sister Catherine sent me the flat stare. Since I couldn't drop through the planks of the hallway, I scuttled off like an errant child who has been caught spying.

I knew this was not normal behavior, even for a mixed couple. Neither my friends nor I had given each other such looks when we were with our boyfriends. We might hold hands or our guys might place a possessive arm on our shoulders, but no one would feel unwanted by such actions.

Sister Ignatius and Sister Catherine's behavior was quite different. Although I had never seen an outwardly sexual display between them, I was at a loss to understand. Did they just want to be together, and, if so, why were they so secretive and dismissive of the rest of us? If they wanted more than the platonic intimacy of a soul mate, they were doomed. They could not have that kind of a relationship in the '60s, at least, not in the convent. By now, my previous discomfort in my encounters with Sister Ignatius had changed to a growing sense of dread and alarm for Sister Catherine.

I don't remember saying a word to anyone about this, but I knew that all of us felt the same uneasiness when we were around them. Our eyes could not escape the droop of their bodies or their silence while they ate with us. They were the elephant in the room, but none of us knew what to do about it. I had great faith and trust in Sister Leonard, in her ability to handle any situation set before her. So, I figured she must have spoken with them. How, I wondered, could she be unaware of this unhealthy attachment?

I received my answer sooner than I might have imagined and with results I would never have predicted. One Saturday in December, in the early afternoon, with no forewarning from Sister Leonard, we had three visitors. I recall my total surprise as these wide, square women draped in black cloaks entered our common room. Their equally square faces were set in a flat-lined manner, not a hint of a smile or a visitor's normal greeting and cordiality. With their cloaks, they looked like three Supreme Court justices, all ready for the business of the day. As each of them was introduced, I tried not to show how strange I found this sudden visit from three superiors who were part of the ruling body of the Adrian Dominicans.

Sister Leonard did not introduce any of us, and thank goodness she didn't because I remember feeling stupefied by this visit, so unusual and alarming. Instead, she walked toward our awkward groups as we stood in embarrassed anticipation, and made a soft request. "I'm wondering if you would mind going up to your rooms for a short while. We have a few things to discuss. I'll let you know when we're finished."

Her cheeks had reddened and I noticed a slight unease in her manner. She must know why they are here I thought. I was relieved to be excused from the dull throb of danger that now seemed to pulse around me. If we were suddenly in some kind of war, these sisters might be our generals and I knew they had not come for a truce.

We took to the stairs without a word, of course, but even when we were out of range of the common room, none of us gathered to even whisper our concern. I searched Sister Joseph's face for some clue, and the look she returned seemed to carry the weight of death; she walked away stunned and shaken as if she knew what was coming.

It wasn't exactly a short visit. Three hours later we were called down to the common room. Sister Leonard didn't offer any preambles, and as soon as we were all settled on some couch or chair, she said, "Sister Catherine and Sister Ignatius have left St. Patrick's. They will be finishing the year in different schools around Chicago. Tomorrow we will have two new sisters joining us from those schools. I hope you will welcome them and do all you can to help them feel at home."

I watched her body and her round, blushed face. She looked tired, and I knew the past hours might have been some of the most difficult of her career. None of us spoke. Even now, I find it almost impossible to put into words how I felt. Other than shock, I couldn't tell how I felt. There was so much left unsaid.

My first response was to question. Were Sister Ignatius's and Sister Catherine's rooms emptied of everything, including desks, dressers, and closets? And what did the triumvirate of sister superiors say to them? Was it a discussion or a pronouncement?

Sister continued, "I know you have concerns for our sisters who have left, but I ask you out of respect to discourage any gossip or discussion of them. They will have challenges to face, and we would not want to add to them." Then, shifting in her seat and standing up, she broke our gloomy trance with the words, "Why don't we all pitch in and get some supper on the table? You have to be hungry." It was just what we needed... an activity. How intuitive of her to gather us in the kitchen, our bodies at work, as we found plates and silverware and cold cuts and other food to put on the table.

Later that night, and for months afterwards, I thought of Sister Catherine. Was she the talk of Chicago now? Did she retreat even further into herself? How did she manage this instant move into another convent and into another classroom surrounded by the questions of her sudden removal from our house?

We had never been very close, even though I had thought we would be good friends when I first saw her in the parlor on my move-in day. She seemed to keep to herself but was always kind and thoughtful to each sister in our house.

I only heard one bit of information about her after she left us. One of the sisters who replaced her said that she had been forbidden to write, speak, or see Sister Ignatius. I don't know if she ever tried. And I don't know what might have happened if she did try. Back then, I only hoped that she was able to carry on, that she would find a real friend where she was, and learn to put this behind her.

CHAPTER 39

Growing up
Catholic Again

O N SUNDAY MORNING, THE DAY after Sister Catherine and Sister Ignatius left us, the front door opened and in walked the two new sisters who would now call St. Patrick's their home. I used to wonder if great thought had been given to these choices, because I knew that if I visited every convent in the Chicago area, I wouldn't have found better replacements. They walked in with a smile, a blaze of energy, and an easy, light manner. I couldn't believe that they were just yanked out of homes and classrooms as they hugged and greeted each of us. For the year and a half that I lived with them, St. Patrick's became a happier place to be.

These two sisters were more like me, and I felt it almost immediately. When Sister Kathleen walked into our common room, I wanted to laugh. She had quite a strident gait for a woman of her size, since she was both tall and plump. Her head moved from side-to-side, surveying us as if she had just walked into a party and wanted to know where to find the fun. When she smiled at the group of us, a bit stunned from the events of the weekend, her entire face curled up.

Most sisters wore wire-rimmed glasses, but none with the same effect as Sister Kathleen. For other sisters, the small wire circles might amplify a severe angular face or intensify an unfriendly one; but Sister Kathleen's eyes, crinkling up behind those glasses could disarm anyone.

Sister Angela, who stood smiling at each of us during the introductions, had soft blonde hair and equally soft features. (By now, each sister had the choice of wearing the traditional headgear or wearing a new one, like she wore, which looked very much like our postulant veils with our hair showing around our faces.) Sister's demeanor was kind and open, and I imagined that kids in her class would go to her if they might be in trouble.

She would become my confidant and good friend in our house, along with Sister Maura and Sister Kathleen. Sister Angela had the clearest, most logical approach to any problem, yet her words were laced with understanding and empathy. She took me under her wing, as Sister Joseph did, but in her own way.

We finished out that year together, which was a little over four months, talking endlessly, sharing school and family stories, and becoming friends. I didn't really have a friend before they came. Sister Joseph was my mentor, but she wasn't a peer; and Sister Catherine, although always ready to share teaching materials or help me with special students and curriculum problems, kept to herself. (In fact, she had not encouraged anyone to become her friend until Sister Ignatius.) Now, it seemed, my situation had changed drastically: not only did I have a friend, I had three of them.

For that first year and a half at St. Patrick's, I had kept my feelings inside, only sharing my doubts and concerns with a few good friends from our crowd. I wrote to them often, and letters became a wonderful release—my only release. Now, as June approached and each of us at St Patrick's prepared to leave for Adrian or other places, I knew I would look forward to coming back. Our convent would seem more like a real home to me, and I knew that even though my doubts would still plague me, I would feel easier and less lonely. I had finally made friends.

Adrian was always a lovely place to be in the summer, but this particular summer, I felt older, less timid and a bit more confident. Plunging into my studies placed me right back in my comfort zone of books and learning. I had always had more freedom as a professed sister, but in Adrian in 1967, I actually realized it. Something was shifting in me, and I understood that when I returned to St. Patrick's to teach another year. By that time, I had been in the convent for four years. At eighteen, when I entered right after my senior year of high school, I knew only my small box of a world: Catholic and Irish. When I finished the novitiate, the lid on my box of rules and doctrines had been sealed even more securely.

What was different, then, in the fall of 1967? For the most part, it was my attitude. I had begun to lift the lid on the box filled with my long-held beliefs enough to allow myself to really look at them. These were simply baby steps, but I felt the change when I came back to my convent in Joliet. I wasn't a person split in two with the yes/no of doubt wagging me back and forth like a dog's tail. My insides weren't exactly peaceful, but neither were they churning in fear. Maybe I could look at things without guilt and shame rearing up like monsters to stifle me. I began to wonder if God's eyes might look at me without judgment and disappointment.

It was wonderful to be back with Sister Kathleen and Sister Angela and Sister Maura, but we didn't have hours each day to sit in a restaurant over lunch or walk to the park and sit on a bench all afternoon while getting to know each other. Instead, one of our classrooms was where we gathered after a school day.

Even though our conversations might include a teaching topic, invariably, we discussed ourselves: our growing up years, our high school days, and what brought us to Adrian, Michigan, and the convent.

On the weekends, we had more time, and nice days might find a few of us taking a stroll around the neighborhood. At night we found a surprise refuge on the roof of our convent. The first time one of my friends suggested that we meet on the "sunroof" later that evening, I thought it was a joke. Why would a convent have a sunroof? Just who would use it? The idea of the four of us lying on towels and tanning seemed ludicrous. Yet, we never used it during the day—it was our nighttime refuge.

Our first excursion came in August after we returned to St. Patrick's for the school year, and we continued until the weather turned cold. I would sit in my room after the sisters had all gone to bed, waiting at least an hour before quietly venturing out my door to meet my friends. We walked up an inside stairway and came out on a flat roof with concrete sides about two feet high all around it. Wearing our nightgowns, we crept low to the ground; even though it was night, we did not want to be seen. It was so exciting, not because it was forbidden, but because we did this secretly. The summer air was still warm and soft on our skin, and our nightgowns lifted like hot-air balloons with the wind so that we hiked the fabric up to our knees and scrunched it underneath us. Our white gowns shone in the moonlight, and our legs splayed out like white pillars. It was all pretty dreamy and magical. We'd sit quietly, throw our heads back, and take it all in for a few minutes.

Often our nights took on the shape of a philosophy seminar. My older and more seasoned friends became my fellow students who turned out to be my teachers. Our talks were startling with the what-ifs of our faith and church traditions. When school began these discussions became a wonderful release from the day-to-day school agenda. I relished every moment. I listened more than I offered to reveal for quite some time—mostly because I was trying to work through my initial fear of change. Heaven and hell were pretty real for me, and God's will in my life was a strong arm holding me back. I carried around a yoke of confusion and doubt that kept me quiet, but the new air of freedom and change brought about by Pope John XXIII could not be denied, and my friends couldn't contain their joy over the new openness of our church.

In my gradual loosening of the shackles of fear, one concept more than any other turned my head and my heart in a new direction: it was the idea of a loving God. That made all the difference. My fear was only that: fear—nameless and baseless. It was all right, even healthy, to verbalize the feeling that I couldn't see myself in this life forever. My friends weren't shocked. They helped me shape that feeling into real events, into concrete examples of what "couldn't see myself" meant.

Well, I knew that I wanted a more permanent home. Knowing that at any time I could be sent to another school in another state or even another country left me feeling unstable. I wanted a real family, my family, near me—that group of people who are always tied to me.

Little by little my friends gave me permission to question. Wasn't it selfish to want a real family? Didn't every sister want to have her family near? Wasn't this what we were sacrificing for, a larger good?

No, I was not selfish. When I looked around the table at dinner, trying to make the sisters fit into the new shape of my family, it was all right to know that it would not work for me.

When I felt like a fraud for my lack of piety, for the rambling nature of my prayers, and my rote responses to the Mass, the Rosary, the Stations of the Cross, and any of the other countless church rites, that as well wasn't worthy of damnation. Perhaps

I needed other ways to pray.

It was Sister Angela who sought me out away from our roof to continue what I think of now as conversations with myself. She was my capable and necessary prompter who pushed me to examine my jumbled feelings, whether of fear or guilt, and bring them out of the tangle and into real sentences, real thoughts. Her wide-open face was disarming, and very gently she would nudge me back to, "So, how do you feel today?"

Once, when the question "What do you think you want?" was lifted up onto the air between us, I gasped when the image shot upon my mind was not what I wanted for my life, but what held for me the whole of what I did not want. The image I saw was a sister in the infirmary, one for whom I brought trays of food, sitting alone in a chair by the window. There was no family around her; no sisters or brothers, no nieces or nephews; no children from her many classrooms; and no one to keep her company in her sick room. It was the image that haunted me after the novitiate—a poster, large and lifelike—that I could not shake away.

Finding my way out of my deeply established belief in the gravity of sin or the absolute teachings of the church was more difficult to maneuver, yet, I only had to listen on that rooftop to hear a different chord replacing the repetitious strain of punishment, obligation, and sacrifice that I had grown up hearing.

Sister Kathleen was the most vocal. Like many Catholics, she suffered through years of looking at the back of the priest's head during Mass, answering the Liturgy in Latin, and slipping into a confessional while a priest pronounced her forgiven and declared her penance for her sins: "Five Our Father's and five Hail Mary's" or much more if she were truly bad.

All of my friends doubted they would ever see a change in our habits, yet here we were, our hair resting on our foreheads and even our ears and necks showing! If the church was ready to pull back the doors and let outside air refresh our traditions, why would I stay frozen in place?

I would ask my pals, "When did you start to feel free enough to question all these church traditions?"

They would throw back their heads and laugh, not at me, but at my childlike naiveté.

I, too, had to smile when one of them said, "When we left the novitiate, Sister Marie Petra. That's all we had to do. Get out in the real world with real people."

"I know," I told them, "and I think I can let go of some of this heaviness I carry around—guilt and fear and things like that. But, when I go back to that missionary from grade school, and all those years that I carried around his words, and the possibility that he was speaking to me, I just don't know."

"So you believe the missionary spoke as if he were God himself?" I heard flung softly out into the darkness. "Look, he spoke from religious passion, not from a direct command of the church."

From another place on the roof I heard, "And you were a child, an impressionistic nine-year-old girl who took everything to heart. Now you're an adult. Wouldn't God want you to make an adult decision, free from all the guilt and fear of hell you carried around as a kid?"

I couldn't say what God might want, but I sure wanted to make a twenty-two-year-old decision now and leave the child behind. And if I could never really leave the child behind, I wanted to at least try to allow my older self to be open and honest, not just about religion but about what I really wanted. Why was I so sure that what I wanted was not what God wanted? How much longer did I want to feel paralyzed with guilt for even thinking of leaving my vocation and distressed at the possibility of staying another year?

After months on the roof, I could have conversations with myself without any prodding because I already knew the questions to ask. From November through January I kept my own counsel and ruminated. I wondered if perhaps I had wanted to keep the little child in me. Maybe I was frightened by freedom, when the choice was mine alone and the mistakes were as well. Maybe the convent appeared to me as another very safe and predictable cocoon, like my years growing up attending only Catholic schools, following the Catholic religion dutifully so that very little of what lay beyond our narrow world was open for me.

Up to now, I had really only thought of myself as rebellious, but now I could see that my occasional grasps at independence were mostly a child's stubbornness. And I wanted more than a half-lived life in which fear of failure or damnation (or what I now saw as the fear of choosing), stopped me from taking some real steps toward what I really wanted. This is what I had to look at.

These revelations came down upon me as a great sonic boom. I was shaken into a surprising calm, which left me still and free to think clearly without all the cloudiness of what I thought I should do, had to do. I had begun to grow up, to think for myself, and I knew this with every fiber of my being. Shakespeare said, "The readiness is all." I was ready. That's about all I knew for sure at that point, but it was all I needed.

Eventually, I began to ask questions like: What would I want to do first if I left? I began to actually consider the possibilities. I could go back to school, finish my degree and teach. Perhaps I could find an apartment? Live alone? Or not. Maybe meet someone like Mr. Mulligan or Father Schurman. Were men like the two of them out there, and should I even be thinking this way? Yes, I could admit the truth, and for no other reason than it was how I did actually feel. When I was around Father Schurman, my heart started jumping around in my chest, and Mr. Mulligan, well, he was pretty wonderful, but I wouldn't let my heart jump around because he was married.

I remember so clearly opening myself to what seemed like a flood of light, as if my heart had shutters and, once opened, desire surged out into the day. It was delicious and scary at the same time, but mostly, my body turned giddy inside, and caution was pushed far, far away.

I was a teenager on vacation away from my parents, in my friend's convertible with my hands in the air, screaming at life. The roller coaster of potentialities had me on a wild ride, and I allowed it to sweep me along, taking in the sights. This frenzy of imagination did not last, of course, but I knew it was necessary, and once I came down from my lofty journey, I realized that I had all winter to ponder the inclinations of my spirit.

CHAPTER 40

How to Say Goodbye

BY FEBRUARY OF THAT SCHOOL year in 1968, I had made my decision. In my mind I tried, sometimes successfully, placing myself in a desk at some college or in an apartment near the campus. I imagined colors draping my body, slacks instead of skirts, or if I grew brave, short dresses, which I had observed, were the style at the time and green flats on my feet, even heels. In another moment, I wondered what it might be like without the clean, pleasant smell of muslin wafting around me all the time. It was a perfume I had come to live in, a lingering smell that seemed to come from my own pores.

Of course there was much more to think about than muslin. Living in the world would heap upon me new responsibilities; my new freedom of going about as I chose would entail getting there and coming back, handling money, and taking care of possessions.

Fortunately, in the area of transportation, I had an edge, because Sister Leonard had suggested that I learn to drive when I first came to St. Patrick's. However, at that time in the cold of February, the image of me driving my own car (although rather unlikely since I had absolutely no money to buy one) to shop for food and clothes or pull into a movie theatre or restaurant seemed like an illusion of grandeur.

One thing I knew for sure was that I wanted Sister Leonard to know my decision as soon as possible. The gnawing in my stomach wouldn't let up until I told her, and though I wasn't afraid to confide in her—I respected her above any sister I knew—I simply didn't want to see a look of disappointment cross her face. I always felt comfortable with her from the moment I saw her at the front door of St. Patrick's, and through the years of living there, she had welcomed my humorous comments and attempts at wit. I knew she liked the spirit I brought to our house. Yes, deep down, I longed for her approval in this, and her insights as well.

She didn't act a bit surprised as we sat in her office and I gave her the news. Could it be that she had sensed my tentative heart all along? She asked me how I came to my decision, and wondered what I thought I might do when I left. Not one mention of "I hate to see you go" or "Will you carry on the work of God in your new life?" or any indication of disappointment.

She did tell me that she would miss me, and we talked for a while about how I would get ready to fit myself back into the world. I never thought she would question me because in the past I had always felt her trust, solid and real around me. I knew I would miss her, too, and as I rose to leave, a bit teary-eyed, she came around the desk and hugged me like my mother would have, because she knew my journey out the door wouldn't be easy.

In April of that year, Sister Leonard suggested that I spend a day in Adrian to talk with my postulant mistress and novice mistress about my decision. It would help to finalize the process in my head, and besides, it would be considerate to give them the news and say good-bye. She would go with me.

So what did I think? She asked. My fear of Sister Louis

Edmond and my memories of Sister Charles ignoring my problems brought a wide-eyed look of "Oh, no! Please not them!"
before I could stop it.

Sister Leonard looked amused and put her hand on my
shoulder. "It will be OK. You'll see," she said.

I knew this was the right thing to do, and knowing she would
be with me made it less intimidating, but for sure it made my
stomach start to flip. What if they discouraged me and told me
to go back and really think about this? What would happen to
my new resolve? Another year of indecision would be unbearable. Finally, I calmed down and reminded myself that I was
not going there to "ask" their permission, I was going to inform
them of my decision.

It appeared that Sister Charles, my novice mistress, had
stayed in her office chair all those years since I had spoken with
her in the novitiate about my skin problem. Curled up like a
child with her legs underneath her, she tilted her head down so
that her good ear faced me, her hand cupped around it like a
shell. I felt I was caught in a time warp. There was one signifi-
cant change: I did not kneel but I sat in a chair near her desk.
She asked about my work at St. Patrick's, her eyes large and
wild with fervor, and when our conversation lulled, I told her
my news of leaving the order.

Of all of the possible reactions from my mistresses I had
imagined before leaving for Adrian, I had never expected the response I was about to hear. Sister Charles had begun to wave her
hand at me toward the end of my short talk, as if to shush my
words. When she could contain herself no longer, she said, "Oh,
no, Sister Marie Petra, we haven't challenged you enough! You
should have been sent to the islands! You haven't had enough
to do. This has caused your unhappiness. We'll send you to
Santo Domingo. It's a beautiful place, and the children need us
so much. You will be happy there. I will talk with Mother Mary

Jean. Don't worry. Our sisters are working in many different places, and we'll find the right place for you."

She had leaned very close to me, her eyes fluttering in excitement and all of her body upright and alive. I could not believe what I was hearing. The islands? My heart was beating right through my skin, and I thought of saying, "thank you," and heading for the door. Did she think I was merely complaining? She watched all of my astonishment quietly and seemed to relax, a knowing smile taking shape as if she had solved this dilemma.

"You see?" she said. "We can work this out. There's no reason to be in a rush."

How strange it felt to change so quickly from amazement to irritation...and with my former novice mistress, no less. I gathered my wits enough to know I had to be very firm, yet respectful. "No, Sister Charles," I said. "I don't want to go to the islands. I came here to let you know that I was leaving. I have thought for a long time over this, and I know I am doing what is right for me."

She slumped in her chair at my words, and her disappointment was so visceral, I felt the air palpitate around me. It was awful to think I had caused her to feel this failure. I said goodbye, thanking her for taking the time to see me. If I thought it would help, I might have taken her hand and told her it was not her fault at all. But she had nothing more to say to me, her eyes staring off toward the floor. So I turned to go, walking through the door and down the hall in a stupor, saddened a bit, yet relieved to have one meeting over.

As if planned all along as a blessed contrast, my meeting with Sister Louis Edmond was a delightful and helpful surprise. For sure, at this point, I was ready for an easier conversation, but I knew not to expect that from Sister Louis Edmond. She had been the postulant mistress I had always tried to avoid. Her penetrating eyes, if directed at me, would launch me into a frenzy of paranoia.

Yet, here she was, sitting behind a desk with a genuine smile of welcome. Sister Edmond always had the most wonderful upright posture, and her body sitting so tall in her chair, so ready to see and visit with me, was encouraging. I felt my shoulders lower in relief as I sat down to talk. She listened to every word, nodding at times, and here and there, uttering a soft "yes."

When I had finished, she remarked, "Well, you seem to have examined this situation carefully. That is the first step." She looked directly at me and waited for my reply.

"I had help," I said. "Some sisters in my house have been wonderful listeners. They prodded me till I was able to give myself permission to question. Slowly, I came to realize that I couldn't make myself fit into this life. I can't believe how much lighter I feel now."

She smiled at this and continued, "You have more work to do, Sister Marie Petra. When you leave the Adrian Dominicans next August, I want you to believe thoroughly that you are doing the right thing. We want to be sure that not a hint of doubt remains in your heart when you start your new life. Do you understand?"

"Yes, of course I do," I said. "I don't want to feel doubt after I leave. I know I'd be miserable if I had second thoughts later on, regretting what I had left. What do you think I should do?"

My mind was still taking in the idea that she wanted to help me. Here I was sitting across from my former postulant mistress, the one who seemed to scrutinize my every action, who once remarked that she hoped I'd be different from the "first" Sister Petra who had left the convent, and she was treating me as an intelligent adult, not a hint of "I always wondered about you."

"When you go home," she said, "I want you to make the decision to leave everything about your present life. As you sit at the table to eat, look around at all the sisters and say, 'I choose to leave this.' Do this the entire day. At school, as you stand in front of your class, say again, 'I choose to leave this.' All day long, I want you to really look at what you are leaving: your students, your special sister friends, the quiet time alone in your room to read or study, the convenience of having meals prepared by someone else. Choose to let it go."

Her plan for me was so logical. If I had even the smallest doubt about leaving, this process would find it. "What a great idea," I told her. "I know this will help me. It would help anyone who was leaving."

"Good," she said. "But I don't want you to do this for just a week or a month. I want you to do this until June, and longer if you feel you need it. All right?"

"Yes, I will," I said. "Thank you."

She stood up then and said she wished the best for me. As I rose from my chair, she looked right at me with those coal black eyes and said, "You're going to be just fine, Sister Marie Petra."

For the rest of that school year at St. Patrick's, I followed Sister Louis Edmond's advice carefully, every day. Three and a half months of saying, "I choose to leave this." After the first month, I felt so much stronger about my decision, so ready for August to come when I would actually be living a different life, I marveled at her wisdom. Had she counseled other sisters to follow this process? I wondered about that, but knew for sure that her suggestion was absolutely wonderful for my personality.

When the warmer May nights came upon us, Sister Kathleen, Sister Angela, Sister Maura and I couldn't wait to ascend those stairs to sit under the sky. Perhaps in celebration of my new freedom and the knowledge that soon I would be leaving, my friends had a surprise for me when we again tiptoed out of our rooms and headed for the rooftop door. The lovely air of new spring hit my face and legs like a balm, and all I could get out of my mouth was "wow." The winter had been cold and long, and our wide-open "deck" seemed to be a place far away from Joliet. I couldn't take my eyes off the sky that had been hanging over me all winter, yet so far from my view in the closed convent doors and windows.

I heard a soft rustling beside me, and then, as if it was nothing out of the ordinary, one of my friends pulled out a pack of cigarettes. I recall the stalled silence as I recorded this unusual package, so like a drink set before a reformed alcoholic. My first thought was how did you get these, but when I looked up at their faces, they were grinning happily, enjoying the mischief and the incredulous look of disbelief washing over my face.

Lighting up was easy—even after my five-year hiatus without a smoke. Inhaling was another matter. I took it slowly, and I savored every swirl entering my body, as I grew lightheaded and limp.

I had slouched low so that my body could not be seen over the cement wall. Red, coal-like embers would appear in the darkness, like lights on a boat at sea. The curling smoke snaked its way along our uncovered hair, necks, and legs, and our soft words lingered in the air around us. Soon, I noticed a faint white cloud hovering over us in undulating waves, as if the priest at St. Patrick's Church had been swinging the incense burner above our heads.

For Catholic teenagers, there was no mystery in the allure and satisfaction of a cigarette. It remained the only naughty thing left for us to do. Hounded with stories of unfortunate girls who had gone wild, which to my parents involved drinking, partying, or allowing a guy to take advantage of me (this last example being one that took me a few years to figure out—I was probably eleven when the warnings began), the opportunities for fun were slashed almost to nothing. In the '60s, everybody seemed to be puffing. Therefore, most of my friends considered smoking a bit bad, but acceptable. At the age of twelve, I coughed, choked, and fell back on my friend's bed in a dizzy faint from my first cigarette.

Many mild evenings found us on our roof before that last

day of school in June. Our talk was easy. I remember those evenings as a languid sweetness, maple syrup slowly dripping into a pail. We explored the possibilities of my very soon-to-be-new life, and at times, the scenarios they set before me brought a rush of abandon like rolling down a hill as a child. Blood would pulsate through my veins, and I'd feel I could tackle anything.

The focus of our talks, however, was no longer centered primarily on me. Sitting near them, I held the calm of decision inside me, and I wasn't surprised when two of them spoke about leaving. So we talked about their possibilities and latent dreams, and even though there was not a war going on around us, I used to see us as soldiers hunkered down in a bunker when a lull in the firing had given them a reprieve. Their cigarettes, like ours, would flare red in the dark tunnel of earth. Perhaps they found themselves thinking about what it was that they really used to want—that far away fantasy, which in that moment and in that place seemed more real than anything around them.

CHAPTER 41

Getting the Red Skirt

"I'M WONDERING IF WE SHOULD think about what you are going to wear when you leave here. You'll need a new suit of clothes, you know."

I was sitting in Sister Leonard's office—again. I was beginning to feel like her special project, and I couldn't have been more surprised at her words. How do I respond to this? I wondered. Was she talking about sewing a few things? Getting some items at St. Vincent de Paul's?

In those weeks after talking with Sister Louis Edmond, I had been concentrating so pointedly on reinforcing my decision that I hadn't dwelt on clothes, except when I looked at my fellow sisters' habits and my own habit and repeated the words, "I choose to leave this." The "leaving this" part referred to the entirety of the habit, a white and black image. I did not often go beyond my statement to consider the new Patricia, sporting blouses, pants, and dresses, even though such images filled my thoughts when I first made my decision to leave. It was May now, and I would be leaving the order in August.

"I guess I do need to think about that," I said. "How do we

usually take care of this? Because my parents can send me some money and...."

Sister had raised her hand to stop me. She was clearly amused but did not want to hear more of my solutions. "No, we will take care of you here. You'll need to go shopping."

She hesitated while I sat in amazement. Shopping? In a store?

"Let's see," she continued. "You'll need shoes, of course. Dresses maybe. Some slacks and tops. You might even want a purse now." She was having fun surprising me, making suggestions.

I laughed at the thought of a purse. What would I put into it?

"So...I walk into a store with my habit on and ask to try on some clothes? This will feel very different."

"Yes, it certainly will. But I suspect you'll have some fun dressing up, don't you think?" My shopping trip seemed to excite her more than me.

"I don't know. Will someone go with me? I think I'd feel conspicuous choosing clothes all by myself.".

"Oh, yes, you should go with someone."

Thank God, I thought.

"How about your sister, Maureen? She lives close by, and she will definitely be able to give you some good advice on your selections. Maybe she would be a better choice than one of our sisters here. What do you think?"

Although she waited for my response as if the thought had just occurred to her, I knew that Sister Leonard had worked out the details before we talked, knowing that I would not understand how to proceed with something as foreign as selecting clothes off the racks in stores I had not entered in years.

I was so relieved. "I'd love to have her go with me. Shall I call her so we can find a day?"

She nodded, smiling and pleased.

Like a teenager who's been given permission to buy the prom dress she pined for, I rushed around her desk to grab her large round shoulders in a hug.

By the time I left her office, the idea of *clothes*—of colors and sizes and shapes; of legs and arms showing; of a body form, my body form, appearing again out of the folds and drape of cloth—began to settle into me. My pictures were fuzzy and not fully developed, but I remember that after our conversation I allowed myself to imagine the possibilities.

At Sunday Mass, my eyes peered far to the left of where I knelt to watch the slow trail of women moving up the aisle at communion. I knew enough not to stare and whip my entire head toward them, but, nonetheless, I stole enough glances at their dresses, skirts, or slacks to get a few ideas of what I might like.

Maureen came to pick me up on a Saturday morning when neither she nor I was working. We had the entire day together, and I had no time restrictions. I might get back by nine o'clock, if I wanted. I also had $150 in a small change purse, which I asked Maureen to keep since I didn't have pockets in my habit. This was quite a bit of money in 1968. I had never expected any money at all from my convent to send me on my way, so Sister Leonard's generosity touched me—like my own mother she was determined to take care of me. Even Maureen was surprised when I got into the car and gave her the purse.

"What is this?" she asked. "Mom gave you money?"

"No, the money is not from mom," I said. "Sister Leonard gave it to me. It's a lot, Maureen, a hundred and fifty dollars. She has been so good to me," I told her.

"Wow, that is nice," she said. "But remember, Patty, you taught school here for three years and never got any money of your own. You deserve this."

She was still rather protective of me; and, much to my surprise, she figured that after I had told the sisters I would be leaving, they would shun me and treat me like an outsider or defector who might be contagious. Yet, I had never experienced any fallout from my decision to leave the convent either from the sisters at St. Patrick's or any other sisters I met.

"So," I said, "what do you think I should get with all this money? I'm excited. I haven't really shopped for myself in years."

"I know," she replied. "There's so much out there. I think we're looking for a few things that will get you through the first week or two, right? Like a dress or two, some slacks...Patty, you're going to love dressing up again."

"I'm a little nervous though," I admitted. "I mean, how do we do this? Do we pretend the clothes are for you? Do I slip off to the dressing room and try them on?"

We collapsed in laughter at the thought of sneaking around stores, and somehow, shoving me through a door to try on a pair of slacks.

Maureen shot me a sober look then and said, "No, Patty, we're not going to pretend. Why should we? We'll both go in the dressing room, and you'll just go out where the mirror is and see what you think. No one is going to say anything."

"What?" I laughed. "You know they're going to look at me and wonder what happened. We're just going to have to keep a straight face...like nothing is wrong."

"You're going to have to take that veil off when you try these outfits on," she said. "How's the rest of your hair look?"

She knew the answer, and the picture of me with my uncovered head, hair all skewed and hanging in different lengths, got us going again. Our shopping trip was certainly going to be an adventure. By the time Maureen pulled into the parking lot at the Oakbrook Mall, we were both feeling a little feisty.

Maureen told me that Marshall Fields was the best place to go. A "fine ladies store" was what she said. It was huge...and crowded. Every few feet some woman or man nodded and greeted me with "Good morning, Sister," or just "Sister" and stepped aside for me to get through. I hadn't counted on this—people deferring to me as if I was special, making room for me because of my habit. I wasn't even going to be wearing it much longer.

My former excitement was waning for sure. This was going to be tougher than I thought. Maureen watched me and smiled, her lovely eyes smiling at those who stopped to greet me, and without a word, she moved me through the aisles, brimming with bodies coming and going around us.

We came to the women's section, and when I saw the racks and racks of dresses, the colors and fabrics making a circular rainbow, I truly doubted I would find anything when there were so many. Besides, I had no idea what size I might wear. I moved tightly along with Maureen like we were Siamese twins, and this helped. Maureen rifled through the dresses (she had decided I was a size six or eight), pausing at certain ones, waiting for me to consider them and give her a nod to go on.

At one point, we were so engrossed in our mission to find a few perfect dresses that when a voice next to us asked, "Out on a little shopping trip, Sister?" we jumped together like a pair of startled cats.

After quite a few inquiries coming from the women and men shopping near us, the type of questions that were clearly searching for more information, "Nice day to shop with a friend, sister," or, "You seem as excited as your friend about her clothes," we found it best to simply smile and acknowledge the attempt at conversation. We didn't offer explanations. The more we seemed to cause a stir, the more we smiled, all the way to the dressing rooms.

By this time I had lost my original reserve, perhaps because of the stares and looks, but I figured that whether I stood by Maureen like a dull mannequin or forged ahead to really shop, we would still be under scrutiny. I chose to step away from Maureen to check out dresses that caught my attention, even taking them off the rack to get a good look.

After what seemed like an hour of my feeling like the elephant in the room, Maureen and I had amassed a heavy pile of garments, which we carried on our arms and headed for the changing cubicles. I tried on each outfit alone, because the room was the size of a postage stamp, while Maureen waited outside. She'd hear me laughing behind the door or groaning in disgust and would demand to see an outfit, ignoring my protests that a certain dress made me look dowdy or frumpy, or a pair of slacks was simply too small or large. Most of the time, I'd give in to her appeals and crack the door about eight inches to appease her. She'd poke her head in, and we'd both double up, trying to suppress our giggles.

At times, I opened the door wide and posed for her, knowing the dress was perfect. We'd look both ways and I'd walk to the large mirror to get the full effect. Yes, there were shocked looks, double takes, and stares when other shoppers came out of the dressing rooms to check out their own outfits in the mirror, but we both seemed to get used to it. I'd scurry back to my cubicle, my head down, and we'd start all over again.

Maureen, who could be very regal when she wanted to, stood straight as a rod next to my changing room. I imagine that she warded off any comments by gazing piercingly into the distance, her five-foot-nine frame towering over most of the women.

I remember only three of the outfits from that shopping trip: a deep red dress of linen/cotton fabric with a mandarin collar and peephole at the neck; a light blue cotton-check dress with a gathered skirt and white collar; and finally, a pair of white slacks with a red-and-white striped boatneck top. We even found a purse—Maureen, like Sister Leonard, must have told me I would need one—and shoes, although I can't remember any of them.

We stopped at Maureen's apartment for dinner, where my brother Jim and his girlfriend as well as Maureen's husband, John, were waiting. They all wanted to see my new civilian clothes, so I pulled each piece out of the bag and held it up to a chorus of "oohs" and "aahs." Jim's girlfriend and my brother-in-law wanted more than just a blouse hanging from my hand, they wanted me to "dress up" right there in Maureen's place.

Well, I couldn't do that. Women were one thing but, silly as it might seem now, showing off my purchases for the men left me feeling squeamish. I still had a few months to go before I would be free of my vows. Prancing around for men, I guess, even if those men were only my brother and brother-in-law, seemed wrong. I would only show the gals.

I have a picture today of me wearing the white slacks and striped boatneck top because John, after asking Maureen if I was finally dressed in one of the outfits, flung open the door of the bedroom and took a photo of me standing helpless and surprised, my hair an amazing array of unusual lengths. It surprises me even today that minus the hair, I did look pretty good.

If I had walked out the door of Maureen's place and sat outside, greeting her neighbors and standing to shake their hands, they would never know that I had just slipped out of the habit that was now lying on Maureen's bedroom floor.

We had some dinner and Maureen brought me back to the convent. It was late; most of the sisters would be in their rooms, and I could sneak in with bags of all sizes hanging from my arms like a last-minute Christmas shopper. I loved my purchases and knew I needed some items to wear, but the sheer number of bags, of lovely things that hung from my arms, sobered my mood when I thought of laying my bounty before my sisters. What would they think of all these silly fashions?

As I balanced my load, trying to silence the crinkles and crunches of bags as I walked through the hallways to the common room, I wondered how I would ever handle the steps to my room without causing a stir. Before I ever reached the stairs, however, I was stopped in my tracks, my head turning from one side of the living room to the other where every sister in my house sat smiling and waiting for me. It is a picture I will never forget.

Eventually, some sisters helped me settle the bundles on the floor since I had not moved an inch. The entire day had been a walk through unknown territory, so full of surprising moments and mixed feelings, but this response was really a marvel to me.

"Oh, my, look at her packages," I heard from one corner.

From another spot I heard, "You must be so tired."

Then, a whole choir of them asked, "Can we see everything?"

Oh, no. Are they serious? Could they really be interested in looking at this stuff? It felt like a party with much laughter and elevated voices—and all of this at nine o'clock, which was pretty much our bedtime.

What could I do but kneel on the floor and begin to pull out a piece of clothing from one of the bags nearest me? Before I had cleared the item from the bag, Sister Leonard, or perhaps one of the older sisters, said, "No, we want a style show. We want to see the clothes on you."

I watched in confusion as a few sisters who were closest to me picked up my huge haul from the floor and took it upstairs to my bedroom.

I peered out at them and asked, "Are you sure? It's pretty late."

Lifting one dress after another over my head and stepping into numerous pairs of slacks at Marshall Field's had left me very tired. I really wanted to go to bed and look at my new clothes the next day with a fresh and rested body.

It was not too late they objected. "We have waited all night to see you come down the stairs in your new clothes," one of them pleaded.

It was strange to feel so befuddled at the scene, like I could not catch up with them. As I looked in wonder at these new, uninhibited sisters who had replaced my former housemates, I was urged heartily to hurry up and start dressing.

Up the stairs I went. The bags covered the floor of my small room. I flung my habit on the bed and dug in. I lifted up the first outfit, pulled it on, and headed for the living room.

Our stairs had a landing where the direction of the steps took a U-turn. As I rounded that corner where the sisters first had a view of me, I heard a long drawn out "oh," the kind you might hear at a beauty pageant when the contestants come out in their evening gowns. But they didn't just want to look. I was summoned with "Come here, Sister Marie Petra, let me feel that lovely fabric," and a pair of old, gnarly hands rubbed the skirt.

I found myself walking around to each sister and coming away with comments like "Such an elegant red color!" and "Doesn't she look stately, like Jackie Kennedy?"

They fancied the dresses over the pants and tops, yet they touched each outfit and urged me to turn around like a real model so they could see it from every vantage point. They thought the blue dress was the most feminine. The red linen dress, however, was their absolute favorite, as it was mine.

Oh, how this amazed me. Their sheer delight over my worldly clothes gave me a lift that I can almost feel today. I knew after this "fashion show" that I would be all right. How this seemingly frivolous event might be capable of shoring up my confidence is quite a mystery. Perhaps the love and support of each one of my housemates was all I needed to send me on my way. They were my sisters, my friends, whether in the convent or out in the world...it did not matter.

Maureen with the white Karmann Ghia,
our "getaway" car.

CHAPTER 42

Taking Me Back

M Y ASSIGNMENT FOR MY LAST summer as a sister really saved me. The convent where I was sent stood in a small neighborhood in Harvey, Illinois, and the place held me like a walnut in a shell. I was anonymous, all but invisible, unknown to the folks there and very free to relish my going forth as just another "sister." I think of my last eight weeks there as a reprieve, a gift of time.

Since I had taken vows for a year the previous August in '67', I needed to wait until the exact day in '68' to leave. Then I would be free of my obligations as a Dominican sister.

A few months earlier, after my talk with Sister Louis Edmond, I had sent off numerous letters to my sister friends explaining my decision to leave. I knew I would not see them in Adrian this summer, and without a letter, I could not say good-bye. Many responses were supportive, but a few cautioned me to act slowly and suggested why I might be feeling restless. Are you absolutely sure, they asked? Will you regret this later? Their words stunned me into a frozen state, and my heart spun in place until I could calm myself. Why hadn't I expected this response, I wondered?

What do I say to them? I exhausted myself trying to reassure my friends that I was happy and comfortable with my break from the convent, that I had consulted our mistresses and my superior in Joliet, and that they had helped me through the process.

If my energy had been drained by letters coming from miles away to my convent in Joliet, and now to the convent in Harvey, letters which I might handle alone at my own pace, how could I have dealt with face-to-face encounters in Adrian if I had been sent there for the summer semester? How would I have ever coped with the questions and probing, kindly meant and intentioned, which might descend upon me at any time, either while walking to class, leaving the cafeteria, or while studying in the library?

The onslaught would never have ended—each day one new face might have looked at me in sadness and worry. My story of leaving would have been the albatross around my neck, and who knows what I might have done to get rid of it. Yes, I was saved by this decision to tuck me away from the world; I came to this conclusion while I lived in Harvey that summer.

I taught remedial reading and math every morning of the week, and afterward I was blissfully cut loose from my responsibilities to do as I wished. I didn't know anyone, so left to my own devices, I walked the quiet streets of Harvey. I walked past homes nestled near each other with happy flowers waving in the breeze and trees spreading their arms for shade. Sometimes it felt like I was walking into a story from my childhood; the look and feel of the neighborhood felt so much like my home in Dearborn, Michigan. At times, my concentration would be so deep that a voice from my blurry surroundings would surface, as if from a dream. "Good afternoon, sister," would come from some spot ahead of me. My body would whip around, startled by the greeting, and the poor man watering his grass would be quick to apologize, "So sorry to startle you."

On warm, sunny days a book was my companion. I remember

a favorite chair in the shade where I devoured one title after another. Many times, though, I wanted notepaper and pen—letters to my friends and family were my primary means of conversation. My requests for stamps must have put a dent in the finances for our bursar because I know that each day I licked at least one envelope for the post office.

The sisters at this little convent were kind and friendly, but many of them were older and simply wanted to sit with their knitting or some similar activity. They weren't rushing to get outside like I was. My surroundings these final few months of my life as a nun were safe and predictable, so important for me, and solitude was a welcome robe to wrap myself in. Besides, I loved this "vacation" from classes, the endless crowds of people, and the frenzy of the summer schedule of Adrian.

Consequently, by the end of July I had trouble sitting still. One more week and I would be Patricia, Patty or Pat O'Donnell again. I felt eager, nervous, and a bit worried as if these three distinct emotions were melded into a single schizophrenic feeling. My housemates had to repeat themselves to get my attention as I fidgeted, forgot, and fumbled my way around them. Inside my mind I couldn't help putting myself in the future, as a student at Oakland University in Rochester, Michigan. The what-ifs involving me, a twenty-three-year-old living in a dorm and attending classes with students four years younger, consumed me. How would this work out, and wouldn't a tiny apartment off campus be so much easier? Well, yes, but how would I get to school without a car?

My application was filed quite late, and actually, I was fortunate to be accepted at the last minute. My parents and my brother Jim had made the arrangements while I finished out my vows in another state. A dorm was the only option open for me.

When my sister, Maureen, arrived at the convent on my final day as a nun in August, I restrained myself from grabbing her in a dance right there in the entryway. She was twenty-four, just one year older than I, and every inch of her looked like a woman of the world—a business world in her case. She had always looked lovely in high school, but now, with a job to add to her purchasing power, she literally lit up the space with color and charm. Her thin models' legs seemed to stretch forever from the hem of her skirt, and her dress graced a body made for clothes.

I thought maybe I could get my hair to look like hers, coming forward in long swirls to my chin. She had come directly from work, and I knew she hadn't had a chance to relax. Well, I thought, she'll have lots of time for that tonight since she would be spending the night with me. She carried a bright pink overnight bag, very stylish and chic, that she had just purchased. I, on the other hand, had an old suitcase from home that my mother sent to me.

The entire time I greeted her, we were standing in a hallway with doors on either side. I remember thinking how excited she seemed to be about taking me away, yet cautious, not sure how it would all work out. I led Maureen to our quarters, a place with parlors and rooms for overnight guests. A separate door led into the sisters' residence just beyond us, and that door was closed. When she had settled her bag and we finished looking around the little apartment, we sat down. After catching up on her news and then some family news, we had my news, which we both already knew. I was leaving the very next day. Now what?

Our state of malaise was interrupted by a knock at the door. Standing with a tray of food was one of the younger sisters I had enjoyed getting to know that summer. Maureen stood up, of course, and we talked for a while. Later Maureen would tell me how relieved she was when the sister hugged me outside our door before she left. Until our shopping trip in the spring, I had never realized how much she worried about me, and the reaction some might have to my leaving. She nibbled at the food and I talked about which outfit I should wear.

"The slacks, Patty," she said. "Save the dresses for later. Besides, we're just going to my place. Nothing special." I agreed and set my "going away" outfit aside.

By the time Maureen had finished her dinner it was probably seven o'clock. I placed her tray just inside the inner door to the convent as the young sister had suggested I do. When I came back to our sitting room, I realized it was going to be a long night and I felt claustrophobic.

We discussed my very near future—what I would be doing for the rest of that week. I would spend the next day and night with my sister. Then, the following morning, my sister or her husband would drive me to the airport, and I would catch a flight to Detroit where my brother would be waiting for me. The two of us would then continue to Oakland University where I would register for classes. Wow...into the ring that fast. Yet, the rest of my time before school started was pretty much unplanned, an oversized blank canvas hanging in my mind.

We chatted, sat quietly, adjusted ourselves in our chairs, looked at the walls, and finally Maureen couldn't take it any longer.

"So, we're leaving as soon as we get up, right?" she said. In other words, when can I get out of this place?

"Well, no, not exactly," I said. "We're supposed to go to Mass and have breakfast here tomorrow."

It seemed perfectly normal to me then, but her eyebrows shot up in disbelief. Oh no, I thought.

"Who says you have to do this?" Maureen said. "Patty, I don't want to go to Mass tomorrow. And why would we stay for breakfast? Your vows are over tomorrow. That's what you said."

"Gosh, Maureen, I just thought it would be all right," I said. "I think they were trying to be nice."

"Well then, they'll understand if we just want to go," she reasoned. "Patty, this place gives me the creeps. It will be all right.

You'll see. They won't care. Let's just get out of here as soon as we wake up."

And then, as if it had just occurred to her, she said, "And what will you wear to Mass, your habit or your other clothes? You're not a nun tomorrow. Won't it feel funny to be with them in your slacks?"

I could see her point. Why would we need to finish this off with Mass and breakfast, delaying my exit? Besides, she was nice enough to come and get me. Why would she want to stay around here one more minute? She had a husband at home, and we would be better off when we got there.

"OK. We'll go in the morning," I said. "I see what you mean about Mass and all. I do want to get out of here, too. I guess I'm still thinking like a nun. I want to do this right. I've come this far."

Relief flooded her face, and I knew we had made the right decision. But there was still nothing to do but go to sleep, and both of us sat perched on our chairs like pigeons in a cage. By now, I was not tired, and Maureen was certainly not ready for bed. She would have the day off tomorrow to spend with me, so she was actually on a mini-vacation. I could see that another thought had occurred to her as she shuffled around.

She looked at me, a quizzical look forming around her eyes. "Patty, when are your vows really over?"

At first, I didn't have a clue what she was getting at. "Tomorrow, like I said. It was a year today that I made my vows."

As if I had no brain at all, I encouraged her, "Why?"

She broke into the biggest smile and challenged, "Well, doesn't tomorrow begin after midnight today?"

I was trapped for sure. She was positively elated with herself as she waited for me to get it.

"Yes...but..."

"Look," she continued, "we shouldn't even have to sleep

here. Why wait till five or six in the morning? Your vows are finished at 12:01!"

"I don't know...sneaking out in the dark after midnight," I said cautiously. "I'll feel weird. What if they hear us?"

I knew I sounded like a ten year old, but my resolve to do everything right so that I wouldn't have regrets was haunting me.

"Patty, they won't hear us," she said. "I promise. We'll be so quiet. Think about it. We can be at my house in an hour, sleep in nice beds, and wake up when we want tomorrow. It really doesn't make any difference, does it, whether we leave right after midnight or at six in the morning? You're free right after midnight, Patty. You have finished your vows like you said you would. Please. You shouldn't feel bad about this."

She made so much sense. I had no argument; in fact, even my body loosened up at the thought of leaving early. Had I even wanted to stay for Mass and breakfast? No, I just figured I was following what others had done before me. Here we were, the two of us, just like when we were kids, scheming our way out of something.

"Well, I guess we have a few things to pack, and I have to change my clothes. Oh, my god, Maureen, it's going to feel so good to be out of here in a few hours."

Sometime around midnight after we had packed our things and tidied up the place, we headed for the door. When we looked back to see that we had gotten everything, Maureen noticed my habit hanging on a hanger in the very order that it would have appeared on a sister's body and said, "Patty, what about your habit? Aren't you going to take it?"

"What?" I said. "What would I do with it? Of course not."

"Well, it does belong to you," she said.

"Maureen, I'm not going to wear it, but someone else will. You've got to be kidding. I'm leaving it."

"What about your veil?" she said, like this might be something

I *would* really want.

Our conversation struck me as so absurd. I stifled a laugh and whispered, "No! I don't want any of it. Let's get out of here."

We tiptoed towards the door not daring to look at each other. I held my breath, really, until we were down the walk. Of course the moon was out and it was blessedly warm. The air rustled my hair...all of it. My new flats couldn't be heard on the sidewalk with their soft leather soles. Since I was watching my bags and my footsteps so as not to fall, I hadn't seen her car until we were almost next to it.

I swung around to her, "Maureen, you didn't tell me you drove the Karmann Ghia! And the top is down!" I remember that the pearl white color glowed in the moonlight.

She grinned because I was so completely surprised, but shushed me so we could get our stuff in the car's very small trunk. Within minutes we were on the road traveling to her house. When she turned onto a major crossroad, we picked up speed and I swear it was like flying right up in the air above me. We were laughing and hooting, our hair streaming across our faces. I'll never forget that moment of total exhilaration, the sky above us and the streetlights shining up the trees. We were on a magic carpet ride in her pearl-white Karmann Ghia, and she was taking me to another land.

We saw a gas station up ahead, and I asked, "Could we stop for a pack of cigarettes?"

"I have some. You can have one of mine," she said.

"Thanks, but I really want to get one of my own. My first purchase as an ex-nun." We laughed.

"Wow," she said. "Just don't smoke the whole pack tonight."

"I won't." She pulled into the parking lot, and I stepped out of her small car and approached the station as if I had been doing it all summer.

We lit up and practically choked, laughing as we inhaled. It was wonderful—me in a white convertible, the moon over my head, a cigarette in my hand, the smoke trailing off behind us. That's the lasting image I have of us. I guess the rest just went up in smoke.

The Last Word

The first event happened 3 days after I left the convent.

I FLEW TO DETROIT WHERE MY brother Jim picked me up at the airport and drove me to Oakland University to register for classes. We were walking up to the campus buildings when I heard whistles and shouts from some workers near us. I looked at my brother and said, "What are *they* yelling about?"

He laughed. "You, Patty. They're whistling at you."

"Me?" I hesitated a bit and dropped my head like a bolt to my chest. What I saw stopped me in my tracks. I did not have my habit on, in fact, I could see all the way down past the blue fabric of the dress to my legs and the little flats on my feet. It was quite a shock. I had chosen a feminine, yet not too showy outfit to wear that morning, but in those early days back out in the world, my perception of myself was lagging behind in the convent where I had been for five years. It was a "twilight" moment, and I wondered how long it might take for me to see myself as Patricia O'Donnell, college student.

That same day as Jim and I went from one building to another, signing up for classes, I left my purse at just about every place we went. Jim would look at me as if to say, not again, and head back to the room where we hoped my bag would be. Every time he took off to hunt for it, he found it lying on some chair or safe with an office person at her desk. I had so little in this purse that it seemed a silly accessory. That would change as time went on – to the point of buying a much larger bag for all the "necessary" items that I thought I needed.

The second event happened while I was living in Jerome, MI. I was about 37 and lived with my two children while I filed for divorce from my first husband.

I was teaching at Siena Heights University campus at a grade school there, yes, the same place where I lived in training as a sister. I had lost my job at the school near my home because of budget cuts. It was a difficult time, but the kids and I held together. One day as I walked across the campus, I came upon Sister Mary Paul, my high school principal at Rosary. She lived at the Motherhouse then and asked me if I would like to have lunch with her. What could I say, "No, I can't imagine sitting across from you for an entire lunch?" I joined her, and we went down to the completely remodeled refectory where I used to eat, now a brightly lit café with small tables and colorful walls and décor.

I was nervous, but not anything like I used to be in her presence. If someone had told me back in high school that one day I would sit across from her and pour my heart out upon the table between us, I would have laughed and dismissed it as ridiculous. Yet that is just what I did. She listened to my story: of my marriage, my two wonderful children, and my impending divorce.

She listened as if she had listened to similar stories many times, and when I finished, she said, "You did the right thing, Pat. Don't look back. Take good care of yourself. You're a strong woman, and I see your life moving forward." She even put her hand on mine while I talked. I felt such concern from her and understood that I had just begun to know her.

Sister Mary Paul had changed in the years since I knew her at

Rosary High. She always possessed a great deal of courage, and now sister had funneled that quality into becoming a different person. It still inspires to me today to think of her, and what I can do to become more than I thought I might be.

P ATRICIA O'DONNELL-GIBSON taught English and literature for thirty years. *The Red Skirt, Memoirs of an Ex Nun* is her first book. Retired now, she lives in Michigan on Paw Paw Lake with her husband and two cats. Their combined family is quite large; between them they have seven children and thirteen grandchildren.

STUDY GUIDE AVAILABLE AT

www.TheRedSkirt.com